Thomas Jefferson on American Indians

M. Andrew Holowchak

Series in American History

Copyright © 2025 Vernon Press, an imprint of Vernon Art and Science Inc, on behalf of the author.

All rights reserved. No part of this publication may be reproduced, stored in a retrieval system, or transmitted in any form or by any means, electronic, mechanical, photocopying, recording, or otherwise, without the prior permission of Vernon Art and Science Inc.

www.vernonpress.com

In the Americas:
Vernon Press
1000 N West Street, Suite 1200
Wilmington, Delaware, 19801
United States

In the rest of the world:
Vernon Press
C/Sancti Espiritu 17,
Malaga, 29006
Spain

Series in American History

Library of Congress Control Number: 2024936953

ISBN: 979-8-8819-0139-4

Also available: 978-1-64889-105-2 [Hardback]; 979-8-8819-0052-6 [PDF, E-Book]

Product and company names mentioned in this work are the trademarks of their respective owners. While every care has been taken in preparing this work, neither the authors nor Vernon Art and Science Inc. may be held responsible for any loss or damage caused or alleged to be caused directly or indirectly by the information contained in it.

Cover design by Vernon Press. Image "Gall, 'Pizi', Hunkpapa Sioux Chief (c. 1838-1894)" by Insomnia Cured Here https://www.flickr.com/photos/tom-margie/26261356432, CC BY-SA 2.0 DEED, https://creativecommons.org/licenses/by-sa/2.0/

Every effort has been made to trace all copyright holders, but if any have been inadvertently overlooked the publisher will be pleased to include any necessary credits in any subsequent reprint or edition.

To a cherished friend & contumacious Irishwoman, Bridget.

Table of Contents

	List of Figures	vii
	List of Tables	ix
	Preface	xi
	PART I. The Nature & Culture of Indians	1
Chapter 1	The Enlightenment & the Science of Race	3
Chapter 2	Jefferson's Bout with Buffon & Raynal	11
Chapter 3	Cataloging the Tribes of Indians	25
Chapter 4	The "Laws" of Indians	41
Chapter 5	The Languages & Origins of Indians	53
Chapter 6	The Morality and Aesthetic Sensitivity of Indians	75
Chapter 7	A Dig into an Indian Burial Mound	93
	PART II. Thomas Jefferson's Indian Policy	107
Chapter 8	British & Early American Indian Policy	109
Chapter 9	Philosophical Interlude	131
Chapter 10	Thomas Jefferson's Indian Policy in Gist	145
Chapter 11	Jefferson's Indian Policy in Praxis	161
Chapter 12	Indians in Jefferson's "Empire for liberty"	179
Chapter 13	American Indian Policy after Jefferson	199

Appendix 209

Index 213

List of Figures

Figure 1-1:	Sixteenth-Century Portuguese Trade Routes	5
Figure 1-2:	Carl Linnaeus	6
Figure 2-1:	Comte de Buffon	12
Figure 2-2:	Powhatan Warriors	17
Figure 2-3:	Iroquois Women Working	18
Figure 2-4:	Abbé Raynal	21
Figure 2-5:	David Rittenhouse	23
Figure 3-1:	Native American Tribes in Virginia	26
Figure 3-2:	Mattaponi and Pamunkey Rivers	30
Figure 3-3:	Hutchins' Villages of Illinois County	34
Figure 4-1:	Postcard of Captain John Smith	43
Figure 4-2:	Palisaded Powhatan Village	44
Figure 4-3:	Indians Sharing Peace Pipe	48
Figure 4-4:	Hawkins' Georgian Plantation	50
Figure 5-1:	Page of Jefferson's Indian Vocabularies	60
Figure 5-2:	William Dunbar	62
Figure 5-3:	Benjamin Barton Smith	63
Figure 5-4:	John Sibley	69
Figure 5-5:	Siberians Migrating into the Americas	71
Figure 5-6:	Edward Rutledge	72
Figure 6-1:	Indian Hunting a Buffalo	78
Figure 6-2:	Indians Torturing at the Stake	83
Figure 6-3:	Mingo, Chief Logan	85
Figure 6-4:	Senecan, Chief Red Jacket	87
Figure 6-5:	Postcard 1 of Entrance to Monticello	88
Figure 6-6:	Postcard 2 of Entrance to Monticello	89
Figure 7-1:	Henry Marie Brackenridge	98
Figure 7-2:	Hopewell Mound Group by Chillicothe	102
Figure 7-3:	Parsons' Drawing of Ohioan Archeological Site	103
Figure 7-4:	Layout of Marietta's Site, Squier and Davis, 1838	104
Figure 7-5:	Mounds at Poplar Forest	105
Figure 8-1:	British, French, and Spanish Land Claims in Early North America	111
Figure 8-2:	Boundaries with Proclamation of 1763	112

Figure 8-3:	Gen. Harmar's Defeat	117
Figure 8-4:	Henry Knox, Secretary of State	120
Figure 8-5:	William Augustus Bowles	124
Figure 8-6:	Spain-Occupied Florida, West and East c. 1800	126
Figure 9-1:	John Locke	132
Figure 9-2:	Governor John Sevier	133
Figure 9-3:	Justice John Marshall	137
Figure 9-4:	General Andrew Jackson	140
Figure 9-5:	Trail of Tears	142
Figure 10-1:	Trade between Whites and Reds	148
Figure 10-2:	Indian Males' Hunting Lifestyle	152
Figure 10-3:	Shawnee, Chief Tecumseh	157
Figure 10-4:	Battle of Fallen Timbers	158
Figure 11-1:	Pontiac Speaking to Natives	165
Figure 11-2:	Map of North America, DeLisle, 1718	172
Figure 11-3:	Governor William Henry Harrison	174
Figure 12-1:	U.S. Map, c. 1810	184
Figure 12-2:	Indian Women Farming	190
Figure 12-3:	Galileo Galilei	195
Figure 12-4:	American Philosophical Society	196
Figure 13-1:	James Monroe	200
Figure 13-2:	Major Ridge	201
Figure 13-3:	Shawnee, the Prophet Tenskwatawa	204

List of Tables

Table 3-1:	Manahoacs	27
Table 3-2:	Monacans	27
Table 3-3:	Powhatans (From North to South)	28
Table 3-4:	Northwest of the United States	35
Table 3-5:	Within the United States	36
Table 3-6:	Croghan	39
Table 3-7:	Bouquet	39
Table 3-8:	Dodge	39
Table 5-1:	Earth	55
Table 5-2:	Chthonic (Earthy) Animals	55
Table 5-3:	Animals	55
Table 5-4:	Foodstuffs	56
Table 5-5:	Comestibles (Trees, Water, Animals, &C.)	56
Table 5-6:	Air	56
Table 5-7:	Birds	57
Table 5-8:	Waters	57
Table 5-9:	Humans & Relations Among Them	57
Table 5-10:	Bodily Parts	58
Table 5-11:	Human Attributes	58
Table 5-12:	Human Attributes	58
Table 5-13:	Indian Terms	59
Table 5-14:	Numbers	59

Preface

Jefferson, in a letter to John Adams (11 June 1812), writes mawkishly of childhood memories of the great Cherokee warrior and orator Outassete[1]—"the warrior and orator of the Cherokees [who] was always the guest of my father, on his journies to & from Williamsburg." Jefferson relates that on one occasion, as a young boy, he saw Outassete's farewell oration to his people before the warrior embarked on a trip to England. The moon, to which the warrior seemed to speak, was "full of splendor." Jefferson adds, "His sounding voice, distinct articulation, animated actions, and the solemn silence of his people at their several fires, filled me with awe and veneration, altho' I did not understand a word he uttered." Jefferson then stops unexpectedly and begins to write of the Cherokees' current status, which, according to his own wishes for them, is, in his eyes, considerably improving.

The passage shows Jefferson, as a youth, had a considerable amount of reverence for American Indians. There is little doubt that this early incident profoundly determined his attitude as an adult concerning Native Americans. The passage also suggests, by the way Jefferson immediately turns from the pleasant reverie to more practical concerns, some amount of pain mixed with pleasure: ambivalence.

Jefferson consistently clung to the notion of Native-American equality with Non-Native Americans in their capacities for moral and aesthetic sensibility, imagination, and intelligence. Needing their lands for westerly expansion and given their avowed equality, he, while president, sanctioned a plan of integration and miscegenation with white Americans, though he was silent about the latter to American Natives, in exchange for their "surplus" lands. That was a plan that, to some extent, had been in praxis decades before his presidency—at least, inasmuch as frontiersmen had for decades been interacting with Natives and, at times, intermixing. It was the plan adopted by the nation's first president, George Washington and a plan that would be continued for three presidencies after Jefferson.

---

[1] See Edwin Morris Betts and James Adam Bear, Jr. (eds.), *The Family Letters of Thomas Jefferson* (Columbia, MO: University of Missouri Press, 1966).

That plan was, of course, oversimple. While leaders of some American Indian "nations" were sympathetic to adopting the ways of the Whites, many more were not, and of those who willingly agreed to integrate, or at least take up husbandry, many did so because the alternative they recognized was extinction. The conversion, thus, was anything but willful.

As we shall soon see, Jefferson's feelings toward Native Americans were generally amicable, often warm. As president, for instance, he advised Chief Little Turtle of the benefits of inoculation for prevention of smallpox had him and some 10 of his warriors inoculated, and he gave the great chief some vaccine to take with him to his tribe.

At other times, Jefferson was snappy. As president, he often acted with hostility toward American Indians and, on at least one singular occasion, he even pined for their extirpation.

What was the reason for Jefferson's changed, execratory attitude toward the American Indians, given his express recognition of their equality? Was that execration aimed merely at some nations or was it generalizable to all Natives?

We do know that Jefferson's overall attitude toward American Natives was ever curious. That comes out remarkably in a letter to Captain Meriwether Lewis in readiness for what is today dubbed the Lewis and Clark Expedition. Jefferson sends Lewis a lengthy letter (20 June 1803) of instruction for his trip "to explore the Missouri river, & such principal stream of it, as, by it's course & communication with the waters of the Pacific Ocean may offer the most direct & practical water communication across this continent, for the purposes of communication." What catches the cautious reader's eye is that a large portion of that communication is devoted to instructions concerning American Indians that Lewis will certainly meet along his journey. The biddable Lewis, for the avowed purpose of future commerce, is to catalog

> the extent & limits of their possessions; their relations with other tribes or nations; their language, traditions, monuments; their ordinary occupations in agriculture, fishing, hunting, war, arts, & the implements for these; their food, clothing, & domestic accomodations; the diseases prevalent among them, & the remedies they use; moral & physical circumstances which distinguish them from the tribes we know; peculiarities in their laws, customs & dispositions; and articles of commerce they may need, or furnish, & to what extent.

Lewis is also enjoined to glean what he can of Indians' morality and religion, for those aiming to civilize and instruct them can best do them by adapting "their measures to the existing notions & practices of those on whom they are to operate." He is empowered to invite "influential chiefs" to visit him in Washington at "public expense."

Much has been written in biographies on Jefferson about his views of Native Americans. Yet that "much" has taken the form of scattered comments on Jefferson and American Indians, not articulation of a thesis. There have, however, been two books fully devoted to that subject—Anthony F.C. Wallace's *Jefferson and the Indians* (1999) and Bernard Sheehan's *Seeds of Extinction: Jeffersonian Philanthropy and the American Indian* (1973), before that. This book has been crafted, in large part, to add and, in some respect, to be a corrective to those books.

Sheehan offers a depiction of Jefferson's American Indian policy as a sort of philanthropic extension of George Washington's policy. Jefferson's contribution is the addition of goodwill toward the Natives, though the overall policy is still the elimination of their culture. The text is often chewy because Sheehan takes what appears to be a Progressivist slant. He aims to explain Jefferson's Indian policy by reference to extant "isms" of the time, e.g., noble savagism, paradisaic pastoralism, and environmentalism. "Noble savagism was a universal statement of perfection" and "the idiom of paradise predicted instant apocalypse," while "environmentalism lacked the decisive moral clarity that the mythic vision of paradise and the noble savage supplied."[2] Jefferson's failed Indian policy is explicable by the failure of the mythical "isms" of the day to deal with then-current nodi.

Yet Sheehan's historiography, if I am correct in dubbing it Progressivist in the manner of the historical subjective-relativist Carl Becker[3] ("every man his own historian"), leaves us understanding little. It imposes a quasi-explanation for Jefferson's failed policy through Sheehan's conception of the mythic explanatory concepts that predominated in Jefferson's time, and that is the problem of historical subjectivism for all Progressive historians. For instance, Sheehan introduces "environmentalism" as "the interaction [of humans] that took place in the physical setting," and we are led to believe that this common-sense notion,

---

[2] Bernard Sheehan, *The Seeds of Extinction: Jefferson Philanthropy and the American Indian* (New York: W.W. Norton & Company, 1973), 115–116.

[3] Carl Becker, "Everyman His Own Historian," in *The American Historical Review*, Vol. XXXVII, No. 2, 1932, 221–36.

which is an accepted part of all sociological explanation, is somehow endemic to, and just another of the myths of, Jefferson's day.[4] Sheehan, unfortunately, spends too much ink on the interplay of the mythical isms he introduces, and while he does address fully many of the problems the U.S. government faced concerning Native Americans as it dealt with the westerly expansion of the frontier, he covers very few of the particulars of Jefferson's Indian policy. At the book's end, readers are left wondering whether this is really a book on the early U.S. government's American Indian policy with some discussion of Jefferson along the way.

Wallace's book, in contrast, is unabashedly vitriolic—especially its introduction. He paints Jefferson as a psychopathological narcissist whose policy, cloaked in moralistic language that suggests genuine concern for Indians, is essentially and merely Jefferson-serving. For Wallace, self-concern, cloaked in other-concern, is Jefferson's *modus vivendi*.

Yet Wallace nowhere explains in the body of his book how Jefferson's narcissism informs his American Indian policy, which Wallace admits is in gist Washington's. Wallace owes readers numerous illustrations of how Jefferson's narcissism influenced his Indian policy such that we see plainly the corruption of the policy begun and adopted by Washington and his Secretary of Defense, Henry Knox. Wallace, however, gives none, and so his psycho-pathological-narcissist thesis is unavailing. Since much has been made of Wallace's book, I offer a critique of Wallace's thesis, which I call the Subtle Muscularity Thesis, in the appendix.

What is my take?

When I wrote my first book on Jefferson—*Dutiful Correspondent: Philosophical Essays on Thomas Jefferson*—I included an essay on Jefferson and Native Americans. In that essay—the gist of the argument I still maintain as true—I noted that Jefferson's views on Indians were characterized by ambivalence. Jefferson both loved and hated Native Americans at times because he loved Native Americans. That was not posited as a thesis, for it should be obvious to anyone who examines Jefferson's presidential writings on Native Americans, but as an observation. Jefferson was, through his father Peter, frequently exposed early on and directly to mysterious but congenial American Indigenes, and he came to respect profoundly their courage, physical endurance, artistry, integrity, and most importantly, their large love of liberty, even if they were "uncivilized." Though uncivilized, they showed marked signs to Jefferson of being readily civilizable. The embrace of liberty was, for Jefferson, key. Thus, Jefferson, *qua*

---

[4] Bernard Sheehan, *The Seeds of Extinction*, 21.

politician and philosopher, hoped that they would mix their blood with Whites—that is, miscegenate—and become part of what he saw was a great American "empire for liberty." That was Jefferson's great political experiment, the subject of the second part of this book—especially in the final chapter.

Readers will find my historiographical approach to be unique: analytical. Being both by disposition and by choice more philosopher and analytician than historian, my interest in Jefferson typically concerns his mind—*viz.*, what he thought about man and the world in which he inhabited, or in other words, Jefferson as philosopher and natural scientist. I am seldom hunting for new data that might force historians to rethink the conventional wisdom on some event or personage. I instead customarily examine "old" data, as it were. I aim to scrutinize very carefully primary sources and, even more carefully the secondary sources that profess to shed light on the primary sources. My aim is to offer a different take, based on a thorough analysis of materials, on historians' readings, especially Sheehan's and Wallace's. Consequently, my chief motivation for this book is to expiscate precisely what Jefferson thought about the nature and culture of Native Americans. My aim is to answer questions such as these: Did Jefferson consider American Indians to be naturally inferior in body or mind to other races? Was the "incivility" of Indians for Jefferson the result of an American climate inferior to that of Europe? Did Jefferson think that Indians had any artefacts or monuments indicative of some degree of civilized living? Were Natives, for Jefferson, the equals of other races in moral and aesthetic sensitivity? Why did Jefferson uptake the study of different Native American vocabularies and collect their artefacts? Why did Jefferson, in general, ignore certain significant aspects of Indians' culture, like their spirituality? To what extent did Jefferson's Indian views qua philosopher or natural scientist shape his policies as president toward Native Americans?

And so this book's focus is expiscation and critical analysis of Jefferson's ambivalent views on Aboriginal Americans and his policies toward them as a politician. It is not, however, a sustained and full discussion of the various Native-American tribes of his day, for that is neither required to justify my *modus operandi* nor am I qualified—few are—to proffer such a discussion. Moreover, I discuss the views and policies of other leading politicians of Jefferson's time—Knox, Washington, Adams, and Jackson—but only as they enable us to situate and assess Jefferson's views and presidential policies.

Jefferson's attitude toward Native Americans was different from other presidents before and after him: It was shaped by profound ambivalence and profound respect for their love of liberty through extensive study of them inasmuch as his time allowed. His ambivalence was the result of their love of liberty—their general unwillingness to give up their way of life, miscegenate with Americans and become civilized.

Jefferson was fascinated by Indians, and so they were for him a lifelong object of study in the manner of a natural philosopher. He found them to be the *in potentia* equals of civilized persons in imagination, intelligence, and morality—an illustration of Jefferson's profound respect for Native Americans and covered fully in the first part of this book.

Things *in actu* changed, however, when Jefferson became president, and he had the opportunity to actualize, at least partly, his republican principles. With an investment in North America as a potential "empire for liberty," which might in time stretch across the continent, he hoped that Indians, through miscegenation and integration with Whites, would be part of that empire. Miscegenation and integration, however, entailed the death of "uncivil" Native American customs, habits, and even spirituality, which could not be separated from customs and habits. Yet experience showed amalgamation to be a will-o'-the-whisp, for even those Native Americans who consented to a large measure of integration refused to be completely integrated—*viz.*, "civilized" wholly in the manner of Americans. Indians were not being asked to mix culturally with Americans but to abandon their ethnicity, and that was, graspably, just too much to ask.

This book has two parts.

Part I, "The Nature & Culture of American Indians," concerns the natural philosopher's admiration of Indians through extensive study of many of their nations. I begin with some discussion of the "science" of race in Jefferson's day (chapter 1). I then turn to his critique of the writings of Comte de Buffon and Abbé Raynal on the New World in the next chapter. In chapter 3, I limn Jefferson's catalogs of the tribes of American Indians in the seventeenth and eighteenth centuries. The fourth chapter is a discussion of Jefferson on the "lawlessness" of Native Americans. Chapter 5 concerns the languages and origins of American Indians—Jefferson's interest in the first is chiefly to decide the second. Chapter 6 looks at Jefferson's assessment of the moral and aesthetic capabilities of American Natives. Finally, chapter 7 examines the significance of Jefferson's dig into one of the American Indian barrows near Monticello.

Part II concerns Jefferson's American Natives' policy, mostly during his years as president. In chapter 8, I discuss the early American Indian policy from the time of British occupation of Colonial America to Jefferson's day. Chapter 9 is a philosophical interlude. By looking at thinkers like John Locke and Emmerich de Vatel, I examine the thorny philosophical issue of American Indians' claims to ownership of the lands they occupied. In chapters 10 and 11, I flesh out and critically analyze Jefferson's on-the-quiet plan for miscegenation and his obsession with the acquisition of American Natives' lands. In the last chapter, I explain why the liberty-loving Native Americans never really fit into Jefferson's plan for an "empire for liberty"—a United States that would stretch across much or all North American, perhaps even South Americam and was robustly Jeffersonian republican.

I end with an afterword, which discusses America's Indian policy after Jefferson till the presidency of Andrew Jackson, which marks a decisive turning point in American policy, and an appendix, which is a review of Wallace's book.

Throughout the book, I use "American Indians," "American Aborigines," "Native Americans," "Indians," "Aborigenes," and "Natives"—the last three were typically used in Jefferson's day and should not be taken as pejorative or as depriving American Indians of personhood—as equivalent terms to refer to Native Americans in the aggregate. That does not imply that each of the various tribes or nations of Indians—and the number of tribes throughout North America was very large—had numerous cultural commonalities with all others. It is merely a convenience that enables me—as it did, for instance, Jefferson, Washington before him, and Jackson after him—to write about the Aboriginal people he encountered in the aggregate, which was typically done in Jefferson's day. As we shall see, that is in large part the reason why the Early American Indian policy failed. Political policies tended to deal with Indians in the aggregate, while the *ethnoi* of the numerous tribes were many and varied.

As has been my habit in prior books, none of the letters from or to Jefferson or other Founders are fully cited. His letters are freely available on *Founders Online*. I offer full citations for all other of his writings.

PART I
The Nature & Culture of Indians

Chapter 1

The Enlightenment & the Science of Race

"The natives of North America ... are of a red or copper color"

On a trip from the Rocky Mountain west to the eastern sea-coast, a "philosophic observer," says Jefferson to William Ludlow (6 Sept. 1824), would see a temporal survey of "the progress of man from the infancy of creation to the present day." In the West, he would find only lawless savages, the indigenes of the North American continent, and as he traveled easterly, he would come to see frontiersmen, farmers, and finally, on the eastern seacoast, seaport citizens. The survey is, in a sense, temporal because, for Jefferson, there is a natural movement over time for humans from the states of what he considered to be vulgar barbarism to refined civilization—what has come to be called stadialism, that is, the notion that societies, like individual humans, pass through stages of maturation. Yet in various parts of the globe—e.g., Africa and the Americas—that movement has been stultified, as duly noted by early European explorers.

This chapter is a discussion of Jefferson's purchase of stadialism—a form of Enlightenment progressivism. It is a purchase that informs his political policies concerning Native Americans (see Part II), and it is perhaps the driving force of his ambivalence, which shapes his Indian policy as president toward Indians. Thus, I begin this book with Jefferson's stadialism and return to it in the final chapter.

Stadialism was popular in the late eighteenth century and early nineteenth century—though it goes back to Books VIII and IX of Plato's *Republic*—and can be found in the writings of Scottish and French thinkers, coetaneous with Jefferson. For Jefferson, who much read Scottish philosophers, the improvement was typified by the ever more efficient use of human intellection and continued refinement of the human moral-sense faculty. Such improvement, for Jefferson, could readily be quantified by humans' usage of land. Indians, who tended to scavenge and hunt for food, required much land for subsistence, and thus, they underused their lands. Husbandmen put land to full use. Yet land could be overused. Urbanites, such as citizens of large cities like London or Paris, exploited their lands, for with too many persons crowded into insufficient space, they resorted to gambling, whoring, drinking, and crime while they stripped the land of its natural resources.

Along with discussion of the stages of human development, there was, beginning in Jefferson's day, also scientific discussion of the races of men, and of how those races were shaped, improved or impaired, by land and climate as well as the habits they formed on a land and in a climate. Native Americans, like African Blacks, were considered by all to be savages—for Stadialists, members of the first and most primitive group of humans on the Stadialist scale. Was their savagery due to natural defectiveness, or were they merely in need of exposure to civilized living and moderate climates?

Jefferson—who always approached nature as a natural scientist, as he ever observed, measured, recorded, and even critiqued things—attempts to answer that question in the third part of Query VI of his *Notes on the State of Virginia*, where he tackles the productions of Virginia: its minerals, vegetables, and animals. Yet a few comments are needed prior to Jefferson's analysis.

"Race" and "racism" are hot potatoes today. It is customary for today's historians, for instance, to vilify or sanctify persons of the founding of America according to the categories of being an owner of slaves or of not. Owners of slaves are frequently villainized, even if they, like Thomas Jefferson, have done much in their time to improve the human condition. Moreover, it is ever presumed that the issue concerns Whites enslaving Blacks. There is no discussion of white slaves, Blacks who owned slaves, and black Africans' involvement in the trade of slaves. Vis-à-vis Jefferson, there is seldom a vibrant discussion of all that he did throughout his life to end trafficking of slaves. When there is discussion, it occurs only or mostly in a manner to expose his hypocrisy.[5]

Yet "race" is a relatively recent term, though it had its provenance in Greco-Roman antiquity: Plato, Aristotle, and especially the Hippocratic physicians. All noted that differences in living conditions led to physical and psychical differences. The best human condition was to be had through moderate living on a human-friendly land with a moderate climate. Greece for Aristotle, was just such a land, situated from the chilly North and from the scolding South.

Yet the ancient world of Aristotle was not as large as Jefferson's world. Adventurers and businessmen of Jefferson's day sailed to Africa, the Americas,

---

[5] See M. Andrew Holowchak, *Rethinking Thomas Jefferson's Views on Slavery and Race* (Newcastle upon Tyne: Cambridge Scholars, 2021).

India, China, and the Philippines (e.g., Figure 1-1) to discover new routes of trade and for the adventure of discovery. They thus saw peoples of various levels of refinement and of stark physical differences: color of skin, texture of hair, and bodily differences such as facial differences and amount of bodily hair. And so, natural scientists, who were studying the various species of biota and seeking to classify them, also took up the study of the various types of humans. Thus, the science of "race" had begun.

Figure 1-1: Sixteenth-Century Portuguese Trade Routes

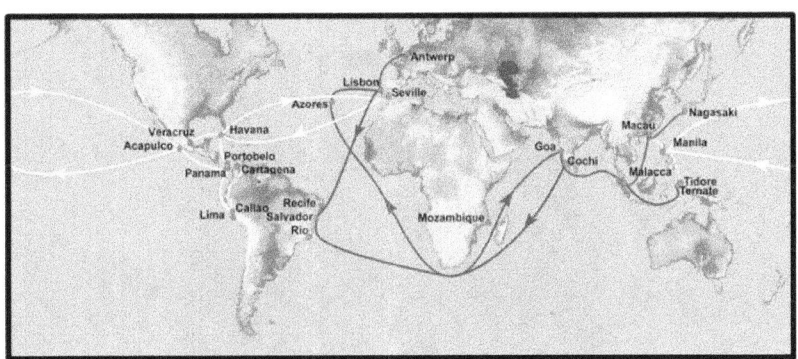

There was no consensus on the exact number of races of humans in Jefferson's day, as there is no exact number today. Scientists now consider the concept to be relatively meaningless—it answers to no fixed biological criteria—though it is commonly and usefully employed. The naturalists of Jefferson's day, however, presumed that the observable differences between peoples of different regions were explicable by underlying physical variations, typically the result of exposure to unique environments over time. I include discussion of a few.

In *Systema Naturae* (1735, Tenth Edition), the preeminent Swedish botanist and taxonomist Carl Linnaeus (1707–1778, Figure 1-2) breaks down primates into four species: *Homo, Simia, Lemur,* and *Vespertilio. Simia* included primates such as monkeys, orangutans, and apes, while *Homo* included only humans. Linnaeus divided *Homo* into *Homo diurnus* (Day Man) and *Homo nocturnus* (Night Man). The former, he divides into four subspecies—five or six if one counts monsters or human defects and wild men as a subspecies. The criteria for differentiation were geographic location and color of skin. Under *Homo diurnus,* he lists *Homo Rusus (Red, Americanus); Homo Albus (White, Europeus); Homo Luridus (Yellow, Asiaticus); and Homo Niger (Black, Afer).* The categorization links coloration of skin to continental separation. (1) Native Americans (Reds), he adds, are bilious (angry), but upright and honest; (2) Europeans (Whites) are sanguine (blooded) and muscular and fleshy; (3) Asians (Yellows) are black-biled (depressive), inflexible, and severe; and (4) Africans (Blacks) are phlegmatic (stolid) and relaxed.[6] The categorization squares neatly with the physical dispositions, listed by the second-century physician Galen and certain Hippocratic physicians centuries before him, in which humans were said to comprise four humors: bile, blood, black bile, and phlegm.

Figure 1-2: Carl Linnaeus

When he turns to discussion of Native Americans, Linnaeus writes:

> Of copper coloured complexion, choleric constitution, and remarkably erect. Their hair is black, lank, and course; their nostrils are wide; their features harsh, and the chin is scantily supplied with beard. Are obstinate in their tempers, free, and satisfied with their condition; and are regulated in all their proceedings by traditional customs. —Paint their skin with red streaks.

---

[6] Carl Linnaeus, *Systema Naturae*, ed. 10 (Stockholm: 1758), 44–45.

"Most of the American nations ... eradicate their beards, and the hair from every part of the body except the scalp." Of the Pantagonians of lower South America, Linnaeus states, "[They are] of vast size, and indolent in their manners.⁷

A second celebrated naturalist, and poet, playwright, and novelist (e.g., *The Vicar of Wakefield*) was Oliver Goldsmith (1728–1774). In his *An History of the Earth, and Animated Nature* (1774), Goldsmith limns "six distinct varieties in the human": (1) those short, dull, and dark-grey persons "found round the polar regions"; (2) the olive-colored, black-haired, short-legged but large-thighed, and very robust and strong "Tartar race"; (3) the slender, black-haired, Roman-nosed "southern Asiatics," whose color varies from olive to near black; (4) the gloomy, indolent, stupid, mischievous, soft- and woolly-haired "negroes of Africa"; and (5) the beautiful, large-limned, and largely intelligent "Europeans."⁸

Of (6) Native Americans, Goldsmith writes:

> The inhabitants of America [are] as different from all the rest in colour, as they are distinct in habitation. The natives of America (except in the northern extremity, where they resemble the Laplanders) are of a red or copper colour; and although, in the old world, different climates produce a variety of complexions and customs, the natives of the new continent seem to resemble each other in almost every respect. They are all nearly of one colour; all have black thick strait hair, and thin black beards; which, however, they take care to pluck out by the roots. They have, in general, flat noses, with high cheek bones, and small eyes; and these deformities of nature they endeavour to encrease by art: they flatten the nose, and often the whole head of their children, while the bones are yet susceptible of every impression. They paint the body and face of various colours, and consider the hair upon any part of it, except the head, as a deformity which they are careful to eradicate. Their limbs are generally slighter made than those of the Europeans; and I am assured, they are far from being so strong. All these savages seem to be cowardly; they seldom are known to face their enemies in the field, but fall upon them at an advantage; and the greatness of their fears serves

---

⁷ Carl Linnaeus, *Systema Naturae*, 45–46. It was thought that the Pantagonians were giants. They were not giants, as was reported by the first discoverers, but were of larger size on average than Europeans.

⁸ Oliver Goldsmith, *An History of the Earth: And Animated Nature* (London: 1774), Chapter XI.

to encrease the rigours of their cruelty. The wants which they often sustain, makes them surprizingly patient in adversity; distress, by being grown familiar, becomes less terrible; so that their patience is less the result of fortitude than of custom. They have all a serious air, although they seldom think; and, however cruel to their enemies, are kind and just to each other. In short, the customs of savage nations in every country are almost the same; a wild, independent, and precarious life, produces a peculiar train of virtues and vices: and patience and hospitality, indolence and rapacity, content and sincerity, are found not less among the natives of America, than all the barbarous nations of the globe.[9]

There are for Goldsmith, as with Linnaeus, no natural differences between humans. "Upon the whole ... all those changes which the African, the Asiatic, or the American undergoes, are but accidental deformities, which a kinder climate, better nourishment, or more civilized manners, would, in a course of centuries, very probably remove."[10] The notion of racial differences being natural would lead, beginning in Jefferson's final years, to robust discussion of monogenesis versus polygenesis—the last, the notion of separate creations for certain of the different races to account for superior and inferior races.

French political philosopher Constantin François de Chassebœuf, *viz.*, Comte de Volney (1757–1820), in *Les Ruins* writes of Chinese as governed by "insolent despotism," Tartars as ignorant and ferocious, Arabs as mired in tribal anarchy and familial jealousies, and Africans as seemingly "irrevocably doomed to servitude." Of Native Americans, he says: "The Indian, borne down by prejudices, and enchained in the sacred fetters of his castes, vegetate in an incurable apathy."[11]

I end with Georges Louis Leclerc, best known as Comte de Buffon (1709–1788, see Figure 2-1). Buffon declines to taxonomize sharply humans, as did Linnaeus, or even crudely, as did Volney. He argues that different "races" of humans are explicable by environment. In "On the Degeneration of Animals" (1766) and "On the Epochs of Nature" (1778), he maintains that food and land have a marked influence on man's "internal form." Exposure to certain types of

---

[9] Oliver Goldsmith, *An History of the Earth*, 229–30.
[10] Oliver Goldsmith, *An History of the Earth*, Chapter XI.
[11] Constantin Francois de Volney, *The Ruins*, trans. Thomas Jefferson (Fairford, England: The Echo Library, 2010), 68.

food and land over time leads to "the general and constant characters in which we recognize the different races and even nations which compose the human genus."[12] The implication is that certain climates and foods, poorly suited for human thriving, promote human degeneration, which he thinks will occur in time to all animals transplanted to America. He is overall convinced that civilized living will not only prevent human degeneration, but also work toward improvement of internal form through better nutrition and some degree of taming climate.[13]

The naturalists, all European, of Jefferson's time inclined to the notion that noticeable variations among humans in different regions are circumstantial—that different circumstances over time lead to alterations of the human organism. Want of nutritious food and inhospitable climate lead to human decrepitude. A climate frigid immobilizes humans and retards human thriving. A climate too hot overwhelms humans and retards human thriving. In both instances, there is little stimulus for humans to civilize. The intimation in all such cases is that barbarism is remediable. The retardation is reversible if the savages are exposed to a congenial climate and to an advanced culture.

Buffon's greatest work was his *Histoire naturelle, générale et particulière*, begun in 1749 and incomplete at his death in 1788. The work is massive—36 volumes with an additional volume crafted from his notes after his demise—and Buffon will endeavor to list and describe all the mineral, vegetable, and animals of the world.

Jefferson will take issue with some of Buffon's claims concerning degeneration of animals as they have application for the animals, Native Americans included, of North America. It is an unthinkably extraordinary challenge for Jefferson, for he considers Buffon, as we shall see, to be the world's foremost naturalist. That I take up in chapter 2.

I close by noting that Jefferson appropriated the claims of the leading naturalists of his day on race and numerous other issues. That appropriation, as I show in the next chapter, was not always uncritical. Being exposed to and having studied Indians throughout much of his life, he tended to disagree with the conclusions of those naturalists concerning Indians.

---

[12] Georges-Louis Leclerc Buffon, "De la dégénération des animaux", *Histoire naturelle, générale et particulière*, vol. 14 (Paris: Imprimerie Royale, 1766), 313–16.

[13] Georges-Louis Leclerc Buffon, "Des époques de la nature", *Histoire naturelle, générale et particulière: supplément*, vol. 5 (Paris: Imprimerie royale, 1778), 1–254.

Chapter 2

Jefferson's Bout with Buffon & Raynal

"Our only appeal on such questions is to experience"

Query VI of *Notes on the State of Virginia* is titled "Productions Mineral, Vegetable and Animal," and the title itself is certainly derived from Buffon's celebrated *Histoire naturelle, générale et particulière*. Jefferson begins with Virginia's "subterraneous riches": its gold, leads, copper, iron, pit coal, marble, limestone, slate, schist, stone, earths, niter, and salt. He then turns to Virginia's medicinal springs and other watery oddments; the native vegetables—medicinal, esculent, ornamental, and useful; the farmed plants; and last, the animals of Virginia.[1]

The natives of Virginia Jefferson covers under the umbrella of animals—humans for him being merely a species of "animal." His motivations for empirical study of the Native Virginians are many. First, many of the customs of natives are less than civilized, and so he wishes to grasp why that is the case. Are they of a like nature to Africans, who, though exposed to civilized culture, seem to absorb little of it—which is suggestive of being naturally deficient? Second, Jefferson had a singular interest, from his days as a boy, in Virginian natives. Native Americans were curiosities. Though culturally retrogressive—e.g., they exposed their women to intense physical labor[2]—they possessed a freedom that exceeded that of any civilized society. Last, the preeminent naturalist, Comte de Buffon (Figure 2-1)—"the most learned … of all others in the science of animal history"—has asserted that "la nature vivante est beaucoup moins

---

[1] For an expiscation of and critical analysis of Jefferson's great book, see M. Andrew Holowchak, *Thomas Jefferson's* Notes on the State of Virginia: *A Prolegomena* (Wilmington, DE: Vernon Press, 2023).

[2] In his "Memorandums on a Tour from Paris to Amsterdam, Strasburg, and back to Paris," Jefferson writes: "Every Indian man is a solider or warrior, and the whole body of warriors constitute a standing army, always employed in war or hunting. To support that army, there remain no laborers but the women." Thomas Jefferson, *Thomas Jefferson: Writings*, ed. Merrill D. Peterson (New York: Library of America, 1984), 651.

agissante, beaucoup moins forte"[3] in the Americas.[4] By implication, people endemic to the Americas will be noticeably inferior to the people of Europe. That is just what Buffon in his study of Native Americans claims to have shown.

This chapter concerns Jefferson's "bout" with the foremost naturalist of his day—Comte de Buffon. Buffon claims that Natives are naturally inferior to other humans due to the avowed wetness and coldness of North America, not due to any systemic study of North America. Jefferson takes Buffon to task. He accuses the great naturalist of shoddy empiricism—leaping to conclusions with insufficient and skewed data—and shows that there are good reasons to believe that Indians are the intellectual, imaginative, and moral equals of all other humans.

Figure 2-1: Comte de Buffon

---

[3] "Living nature is much less active, much less strong."
[4] Thomas Jefferson, *Notes on the State of Virginia*, ed. William Peden (Chapel Hill: University of North Carolina Press, 1954), 47.

Jefferson begins by asserting that his own experiences, abundant though not superabundant, with Virginian Natives are at odds with Buffon's conclusions. Moreover, why should nature show hemispheric partiality? "As if both sides were not warmed by the same genial sun; as if a soil of the same chemical composition, was less capable of elaboration into animal nutriment; as if the fruits and grains from that soil and sun yielded a less rich chyle, gave less extension to the solids and fluids of the body, or produced sooner in the cartilages, membranes and fibers, that rigidity which restrains all further extension and terminates animal growth." Jefferson sums, "The truth is, that a Pigmy and a Patagonian, Mouse and a Mammoth, derive their dimensions from the same nutritive juices."[5]

Jefferson's mention of the mammoth is not accidental. Jefferson has broached his discussion of the animals of Virginia with critical discussion of the bones of a massive animal, found at the saltlicks on the Ohio River—what is today Big Bone Lick State Historical Site in Kentucky, just east of the Ohio River, and to the southwest of Cincinnati. He begins with what is now known as the bones of the mammoth, the "Big Buffalo," because it creates an enormous problem for Buffon's thesis that nature is weaker and less active in the Americas. Those bones reveal what was at the time the world's largest known land animal and such an enormous animal should not have been possible in North America.

Buffon's argument is more nuanced. Jefferson gives it in four principles.

> 1. That the animals common both to the old and new world, are smaller in the latter. 2. That those peculiar to the new are on a smaller scale. 3. That those which have been domesticated in both, have degenerated in America: and 4. That on the whole it exhibits fewer species. And the reason he thinks is, that the heats of America are less; that more waters are spread over its surface by nature, and fewer of these drained off by the hand of man.

Jefferson sums for Buffon: "Heat is friendly, and moisture adverse to the production and development of large quadrupeds."[6]

How has Buffon come to conclude that the Americas are colder and wetter than the Americas?

---

[5] Thomas Jefferson, *Notes on Virginia*, 47.
[6] Thomas Jefferson, *Notes on Virginia*, 47.

"We are not furnished with observations sufficient" to decide such issues,[7] though Jefferson has been, since 1776, taking meteorological readings of temperatures wherever he has been, and his motivation is, at least in part, to address Buffon on the coolth of the Americas.

Jefferson begins by supposition. He takes as hypothesis "that moisture is unfriendly to animal growth."[8] That claim is certainly not obviously *a priori* true, since is it impossible to access metempirically nature. "Our only appeal on such questions is to experience," and he maintains that experience is against Buffon's supposition. In warm and moist climates, experience shows that vegetables thrive. Vegetables are the food, mediately or immediately, of all animals. Where food is plentiful, animals thrive and improve in bulk insofar as "the laws of their [structural] nature will admit."[9] So, it seems, warmth and wetness are ideal for animals' thriving. In that regard, Buffon should acknowledge that the Americas are superior to Europe apropos of wetness, while Europe is superior to the American apropos of warmth. He has not.

Moreover, one of the largest known animals, the "Big Buffalo," has been found in a climate that is said by Buffon to be cold and wet.[10] That should not be possible according to Buffon.

Jefferson then appeals to three comparative tables, given to cast sufficient doubt on Buffon's assertions concerning animals' inferiority in the Americas. He compares animals found in both countries; animals endemic only to one; and animals domesticated in both. Jefferson's aim is not to refute Buffon—there are insufficient data for that—but "to justify a suspension of opinion until we are better informed."[11] The data gleaned and limned do warrant suspension of opinion on the matter.

Jefferson then questions, given the data of his tables, Buffon's data. "It does not appear that Messrs. de Buffon and D'Aubenton have measured, weighed, or seen those of America." The data come from "travellers," but "was natural history the object of their travels?" Did such travelers measure and weigh the animals they observed? Answers to such questions "would probably lighten their authority, so as to render it insufficient for the foundation of an hypothesis." Buffon himself

---

[7] Thomas Jefferson, *Notes on Virginia*, 48.
[8] Thomas Jefferson, *Notes on Virginia*, 48.
[9] Thomas Jefferson, *Notes on Virginia*, 48.
[10] Thomas Jefferson, *Notes on Virginia*, 48.
[11] Thomas Jefferson, *Notes on Virginia*, 49.

has altered his data and conclusions in subsequent editions of his works, and "further information will, doubtless, produce further corrections." Yet Jefferson is not condemning Buffon. Additional data in honest empirical work will certainly force reevaluation of it. Yet Buffon is still "the best informed of any Naturalist who has ever written."[12]

Jefferson has thus far given sound arguments against that notion that coolth and wetness are agents prohibitive of growth and thriving of living things. He next turns to North American Indians and Buffon's arguments of their physical defectiveness.[13]

Jefferson begins his analysis of Virginian natives with a lengthy quote from Buffon. I give it *in toto*:

> Although the savage of the new world is nearly the same stature as the man of our world, one must not to make an exception to the general fact that all living nature has become smaller on that continent. The savage is weak and has small organs of generation, He has neither hair nor beard. He has no ardor for his female. Although faster than the European because he is more accustomed to running, he is, however, less strong in body. He is also less sensitive, and more timid and more cowardly. He has no vivacity, no activity of mind; that of the body is less an exercise, a voluntary movement, than it is an action caused by need. Sate him of hunger and thirst and there will be no inclination for any movement; he will remain stupidly resting on his legs or lying down for days at a time. The reasons for the savages' isolated manner of living, and for their remoteness from society need not be pursued.
>
> The most prized spark of the fire of nature has not been allotted to them. They lack ardor for their female, and also love for their fellow men. Indifferent to the most vital and most tender of feelings, their other similar sentiments are cold and languid. They express little love for their fathers and their children. The most intimate tie of all, the familial tie, is with them of no large significance. Society from one family to another has none

---

[12] Thomas Jefferson, *Notes on Virginia*, 54.
[13] Sayre makes the empty claim, "The fact that Query VI discusses Natives and African Americans as animals only seems to confirm suspicions of Jefferson's racism." The claim is fatuous. Jefferson categorizes all humans as animals. Gordon M. Sayre, "Jefferson and Native Americans: Policy and Archive," *The Cambridge Companion to Thomas Jefferson*, ed. Frank Shuffleton (Cambridge: Cambridge University Press, 2009), 67.

> at all: hence no community, no republic, no social state. Physical love is their morality. Their hearts are cold, their society is frigid, their rule is harsh. They look upon their wives only as servants for work or beasts of burden, whom they charge, unceremoniously, with the burden of hunting, and on whom they force without mercy, without gratitude, tasks which are often above their abilities. They have few children, and they attend little to them.
>
> Everything is affected by their principle defect of character. Savages are indifferent to the other sex because they lack sexual potency, and this indifference to the other sex is the fundamental defect of their nature, which prevents them from flourishing, and which destroys the seeds of life, and at the same time, prevents the roots of society. Man is no exception here. Nature, by refusing him sexual potency, has mistreated and debased him more than any other animal.[14]

Prior to critical analysis of Buffon's numerous assertions on the barbarity, savagery, and truculence of American aborigines, Jefferson begins with a disclaimer. He cannot profess to speak on behalf of the Indian of South America, of which he has no direct knowledge, so he restricts his comments, based partly on his own knowledge, but mostly on the reports of others, better informed, to the North American Indian. "I can speak of him somewhat from my own knowledge, but more from the information of others better acquainted with him, and on whose truth and judgment I can rely." Given his objections to the "travellers" who gave Buffon his data on American quadrupeds, one can be sure that Jefferson is careful that his sources are reliable, or relatively so.[15]

In a letter to Marquis de Chastellux (7 June 1785), Jefferson is less vague concerning his data. "I have seen some thousands myself, and conversed much with them, and have found in them a masculine, sound understanding." He also talks of "much information from men who had lived among them." Those are the frontiersmen and Indian agents whom we shall see in the second part of this book.

In keeping with the tenor of his *Notes on Virginia*, the examination is completely empirical. Jefferson begins by addressing Buffon's "principle defect"

---

[14] My translation from French. Thomas Jefferson, *Notes on the State of Virginia* (Richmond: J.W. Randolph, 1853), 62–63.

[15] It is strange that Jefferson offers no caution that his universalizations are merely roughly applicable, given the large number of North American tribes and their ethnic diversity.

of the Indian male. "He is neither more defective in ardor, nor more impotent with his female, than the white reduced to the same diet and exercise."[16] The intimation here, which will be characteristic of Jefferson's defense of Native Americans, is that they are shaped by their customs and habits, not by lack of ardency, as Buffon says. Why Buffon feels the need to reduce all American Indians' behaviors to one root cause is unclear.

Jefferson has much to same about Natives' courage. They are brave when circumstances demand bravery. Whether it is by nature or by education, they are inclined to use strategy to defeat enemies and preserve themselves, though they are educated "to honor force more than finesse." When overwhelmed by enemies, warriors prefer death to surrender—even to Whites, who tend to treat their, prisoners, well. When tortured, they endure "with a firmness unknown almost to religious enthusiasm with us." In more complex dangerous situations, they are more deliberate.[17]

Figure 2-2: Powhatan Warriors

Jefferson also challenges the notion that "family" is a relatively vacuous term for Indians. Males' affections begin with their most intimate connections and then widen "from circle to circle, as they recede from the center." Thus, they are "affectionate to [their] children, careful of them, and indulgent in the extreme."

---

[16] Thomas Jefferson, *Notes on Virginia*, 59.
[17] Thomas Jefferson, *Notes on Virginia*, 59–60.

Moreover, they are not emotionless. Even the most valiant warriors weep over the loss of their children, though they try to hide their sorrow. Oliver Spencer, who spent some eight months as a young teen in Indian captivity, says that Cooh-coo-cheech, the prognosticator who was tasked with looking after the boy after he was taken into captivity in Southern Ohio, was reduced to tears when she had to part with the boy. She had begun to think of the boy "as her child."[18] Moreover, Indians are true friends, as fidelity among them is strong "to the uttermost extreme."[19]

Vis-à-vis natives' sluggishness of mind, Jefferson counter-remonstrates thus: "His vivacity and activity of mind is equal to ours in the same situation; hence his eagerness for hunting, and for games of chance."[20] Jefferson says nothing about Natives' capacity for genius—capacity for the highest activities of human intellection. Buffon's comments clearly forbid that, but Jefferson presumably aims to show given a change of circumstances, there would be noteworthy results. The spark exists. So too does the natural capacity.

Figure 2-3: Iroquois Women Working

---

[18] Oliver M. Spencer, *Indian Captivity: A True Narrative of the Capture of Rev. O. M. Spencer by the Indians, in the Neighbourhood of Cincinnati* (New York: Carlton & Porter, 1835), 119.
[19] Thomas Jefferson, *Notes on Virginia*, 60.
[20] Thomas Jefferson, *Notes on Virginia*, 60

The Indian man, Jefferson says in agreement with Buffon, is not as strong as the white male. "An Indian man is small in the hand and wrist," for instance, but that is "for the same reason for which a sailor is large and strong in the arms and shoulders, and a porter in the legs and thighs": use and disuse.[21]

The Indian female, says Jefferson, is stronger than the white female (Figure 2-3). The reason is again nurtural. Their women, drudges, do the work that men in white culture do. That is due to their current state of barbarism. In all barbaric societies, force has the place of law, and the stronger sex makes the weaker sex drudge. "It is civilization alone which replaces women in the enjoyment of their natural equality. That first teaches us to subdue the selfish passions, and to respect those rights in others which we value in ourselves."[22]

Buffon is right to note that Indians do have fewer children than Whites. That however is not due to lack of ardor in males. The causes, several, are not natural, but again circumstantial. First, women often accompany their men during warring or hunting, and it is inconvenient to do so while pregnant. So, they practice abortion through use of some unknown vegetable. Second, with such difficult exposures, Indian women experience want of food which makes carrying children tenuous. Moreover, during the wintery months, Natives exist by foraging in the forests—that is, they suffer some degree of famine. "With all animals, if the female be badly fed, or not fed at all, her young perish; and if both male and female be reduced to like want, generation becomes less active, less productive." Third, there is the hazard of wild animals that tends to "the purpose of restraining their numbers within certain bounds."[23]

As additional evidence that Indian women are not naturally less fecund than white women, Jefferson notes that "the same Indian women, when married to white traders, who feed them and their children plentifully and regularly, who exempt them from excessive drudgery, who keep them stationary and unexposed to accident, produce and raise as many children as the white women." When natives were enslaved by Spaniards when the continent was first discovered, they raised as many children as did Whites or Blacks.[24]

What of the glabrousness of American Indians?

---

[21] Thomas Jefferson, *Notes on Virginia*, 60.
[22] Thomas Jefferson, *Notes on Virginia*, 60.
[23] Thomas Jefferson, *Notes on Virginia*, 60–61.
[24] Thomas Jefferson, *Notes on Virginia*, 61.

There is no reason, says Jefferson, to believe that Whites are more hirsute than American natives. "With [Natives] it is disgraceful to be hairy on the body. They say it likens them to hogs. They therefore pluck the hair as fast as it appears." Nonetheless, white traders, who marry Indian women and bid them not to pluck out their bodily hairs, note that there are as hirsute of white women, or so thinks Jefferson. Even if they are more glabrous than Whites, there is little to be drawn from that. "Negroes have notoriously less hair than the whites; yet they are more ardent" with their females.[25]

Jefferson's counter-remonstrance strongly intimates that there are no salient physical differences—none, at least, that indicate natural differences between Indians and Whites. He has shown, most significantly, that Indians are equipotent apropos of their sexual impulses, and that was the basis for Buffon's auxiliary claims about derivative physical defects.

There is a lack of data to decide Native Americans' genius. "To judge of the truth of this, to form a just estimate of their genius and mental powers, more facts are wanting, and great allowance to be made for those circumstances of their situation which call for a display of particular talents only. This done, we shall probably find that they are formed in mind as well as in body, on the same module with the 'Homo sapiens Europaeus.'"[26]

Jefferson articulates the same sentiment in Query XIV, where Jefferson returns briefly to American Indians, when he undertakes an investigation of black slaves. The comparison, though brief, is telling and has never been given full consideration. While Blacks have been exposed sufficiently to American culture and they have benefitted little from it, Indians have not had sufficient exposure to American culture. Many Blacks have been exposed to the conversations of their masters and brought up in the handicraft arts, and some have been liberally educated. All have lived and worked in this country, "where the arts and sciences are cultivated to a considerable degree," yet in the main they have not availed themselves of American society and show little promise of improvement through assimilation—that is, civilizing.

In his 1785 letter to Marquis de Chastellux, Jefferson is less hesitant in his conclusions. "I am safe in affirming, that the proofs of genius given by the Indians of North America, place them on a level with whites in the same

---

[25] Thomas Jefferson, *Notes on Virginia*, 61. It is true that Blacks and Indians are less hirsute than Whites.
[26] Thomas Jefferson, *Notes on Virginia*, 62.

uncultivated state." He adds, "I believe the Indian, then, to be, in body and mind, equal to the white man."

While Buffon's claim that the climate of the Americas is unsuited for biotic thriving, an implication of Buffon's claim is that animals transported to the New World will suffer, if not immediately then mediately, from the inhospitable climate. Yet that is a conclusion that Buffon never explicitly draws—"he goes within one step of it" says Jefferson—but another Frenchman, Guillaume-Thomas "Abbé" Raynal (1713–1796, Figure 2-4), "alone has taken that step."[27] Evidence of that claim will too provide succor, though of the indirect sort, for the inferiority of Native Americans so it is important to offer some discussion of the avowed degradation of Whites, transported to America.[28]

Figure 2-4: Abbé Raynal

---

[27] TJ to Marquis de Chastellux, 7 June 1785.
[28] Writes George Washington to Marquis de Lafayette (2 May 1788): "Although we are yet in our cradle, as a nation, I think the efforts of the human mind with us are sufficient to refute (by incontestable facts) the doctrines of those who have asserted that every thing degenerates in America. Perhaps we shall be found, at this moment, not inferior to the rest of the world in the performances of our poets and painters; notwithstanding many of the incitements are wanting which operate powerfully among older nations." *The Papers of George Washington*, Confederation Series, vol. 6, *1 Jan. 1788–23 Sept. 1788*, ed. W. W. Abbot (Charlottesville: University Press of Virginia, 1997), 297–99.

Raynal's *Histoire philosophique et politique et politique des établissements et du commerce des Européens dans les des deux Indes* (1770) is a six-volume work that covers Europe's colonies in India and the Americas. Though much uneven stylistically—Raynal drew from numerous sources without striving to smooth out what he collected and there were several other contributors to the work (e.g., Denis Diderot and Alexandre Deleyre)—it was a highly popular work on anti-colonialism and it would go through over 50 editions.[29]

What interests Jefferson is a specific statement, which Jefferson quotes, from Raynal. In what follows, I give the full passage which contains the statement, which I place in italics in the following passage. "Tandis que la tyrannie & la persécution, désoloient & dessechoient la population en Europe, l'Amérique Angloise se peuploit de trois sortes d'habitans. Les hommes libres forment la premiere classe. C'est la plus nombreuse; mais jusqu'à présent, elle a dégénéré d'une maniere visible. Tous les créoles, quoiqu'habitués au climat dès le berceau, n'y sont pas aussi robustes au travail, aussi forts à la guerre que les Européens; soit que l'éducation ne les y ait pas préparés, ou que la nature les ait amollis. Sous ce ciel étranger, l'esprit s'est énervé comme le corps. Vif & pénétrant de bonne heure, il conçoit promptement; mais ne résiste pas, ne s'accoutume pas aux longues méditations. *On doit etre etonné que l'Amérique n'ait pas encore produit un bon poëte, un habile mathématicien, un homme de génie dans un seul art, ou une seule science.* Ils ont presque tous de la facilité pour tout; aucun ne marque un talent décidé pour rien. Précoces & mûrs avant nous, ils sont bien en arriere, quand nous touchons au terme."[30]

---

[29] For an English translation, see Abbé Raynal, *A History of the Two Indies,* ed. Peter Jimack (Burlington, VT: Ashgate, 2006).

[30] "While tyranny and persecution desolated and dried out the population of Europe, Anglo America was populated by three kinds of inhabitants. Free men form the first class. It is the most numerous; but so far, it has degenerated visibly. Not all Créoles, although accustomed to the climate from the cradle, are as robust at work or as strong as the Europeans at war; either their education has not prepared them for it, or nature has softened them. Under this foreign sky, the mind, like the body, has become unnerved. Lively and penetrating early, he conceives things quickly; but cannot persist, and does not have long meditations. One must be astonished that America has not yet produced one good poet, one skilled mathematician, one man of genius in a single art, or a single science. They have, roughly speaking, an easy time with everything, yet they excel at nothing. When compared to us, they are precocious and sharp at the start, but they are much behind us when they reach their end." Guillaume-Thomas Raynal, *Histoire des deux Indes,* Vol.

Jefferson is nowise astonished. He has already answered that objection in his comment on the extreme slowness of Roman science to take root in the Germanic tribes, north of the Alps. It took much time for the Greeks to produce Homer; for the Romans, Virgil; for the French, Racine and Voltaire; and for the English, Shakespeare and Milton. Should the same time pass in North America without there being its share of illuminati, then that will be a strong reason to inquire into causes of retardation.

Figure 2-5: David Rittenhouse

Dismayed Jefferson is not concerning lack of genius in America. There have been singular North Americans in its very short history. In war, America has produced George Washington, "whose memory will be adored while liberty shall have votaries, whose name will triumph over time, and will in future ages assume its just station among the most celebrated worthies of the world, when that wretched philosophy shall be forgotten, which would have arranged him among the degeneracies of Nature." In physics, America has produced Benjamin Franklin, "than whom no one of the present age has made more

---

VI, (Amsterdam, 1770), 376. Thomas Jefferson, *Notes on the State of Virginia* (Richmond: J.W. Randolph, 1853), 70

important discoveries, nor has enriched philosophy with more or more ingenious solutions of the phenomena of Nature." In astronomy, American has produced David Rittenhouse (Figure 2-5), "second to no astronomer living [but who] in genius he must be the first, because he is self-taught." Rittenhouse's orrery exhibits "as great a proof of mechanical genius as the world has ever produced," because "he has by imitation approached nearer its Maker than any man who has lived from the creation to this day."[31]

Pace Raynal, "America, though but a child of yesterday, has already given hopeful proofs of genius, as well of the nobler kinds, which arouse the best feelings of man, which call him into action, which substantiate his freedom, and conduct him to happiness, as of the subordinate, which serves to amuse him only." Such proofs exist in the science of government as well as in the arts of oratory, painting, and sculpture. We might add, given Jefferson felicitous prose, that another proof exists in the artful pen of Thomas Jefferson. And so, Raynal's "reproach" is unjust and unkind.[32]

By reference to numbers, America does contribute its full share, thinks Jefferson. There are three million inhabitants in the United States; 10 million in England; and 20 million in France. Thus, for every genius in war, physics, and astronomy America has produced, England should produce three and France, six.[33]

Jefferson's aim, overall, is to cast doubt on the notion that humans, transplanted in America, will immediately or mediately degenerate. That will be evidence of there being no climatic inferiority in North America and, indirectly, evidence that Native Americans are equal in physical vigor and genius to Whites.

---

[31] Thomas Jefferson, *Notes on Virginia*, 64.
[32] Thomas Jefferson, *Notes on Virginia*, 65.
[33] Thomas Jefferson, *Notes on Virginia*, 65.

Chapter 3

Cataloging the Tribes of Indians

"The intervention of interpreters"

Query XI of *Notes on the State of Virginia* is Thomas Jefferson's fullest discussion of American Indians. The query, titled "Aborigines," is wholly devoted to Native Americans. In it, Jefferson aims to answer a question of a French delegate, François Barbé-Marbois, in Philadelphia concerning "a description of the Indians established in that state." The delegate has readied 22 questions to be given to a representative of each American state to glean information about the young country and its member states. Jefferson agrees to reply on behalf of Virginia.[1]

This chapter, like many of the chapters in Part I, is principally explicatory. I aim merely to show Jefferson's large interest in the Natives of his young state by his catalog of the various tribes in it.

Given Jefferson's full examination of the nature of Indians in Query VI—titled "Productions, Mineral, Vegetable and Animal"—one must believe that Jefferson, ever a perfectionist, agonized much about whether to place discussion of the nature of Indians in Query VI or in Query XI, titled "Aborigenes." For the sake of symmetry, one also wonders why, given the prodigious size of Query VI—it is three and one-quarter times the size of Query XI—Jefferson did not delay discussion of Indians' nature till Query XI. The answer, I suspect, is simple. The first seven queries of *Notes on Virginia* are naturalistic (they concern nature or *phusis*); the last 16 concern *nomoi:* legal, cultural, and conventional matters.

When the first ship arrived and settled at what would become Jamestown, there were, Jefferson notes, some 40 tribes of Indians, with Powhatans, Manahoacs, and Monacans being the most numerous and "most powerful." The coastal tribes before the rivers' falls aligned themselves with the Powhatans.

---

[1] For Jefferson's account of how he came to write *Notes on Virginia*, see Thomas Jefferson, Autobiography, in *Thomas Jefferson: Writings*, ed. Merrill D. Peterson (New York: Library of America, 1984), 55.

Those tribes beyond the rivers' falls and before the Allegheny Mountains were aligned to the Manahoacs and the Monacans (Figure 3-1). The Manahoacs inhabited the land where the Potomac and Rappahannock Rivers begin. The Monacans inhabited the land around the upper part of the James River. The Manahoacs, Monacans, and the tribes friendly to them were in constant war with the Powhatans, and the languages of each were sufficiently different from the others that communication between the three was possible only through interpreters. Jefferson hypothesizes that each of the three is of unique stock and that the tribes between them are of dialects that deviate from the three stocks.[2]

The Powhatans, says Jefferson in accordance with the census of 1669, had some 30 tribes, 8,000 people, and 2,400 warriors. They occupied some 8,000 square miles. Over three of every 10 tribal members were warriors, and there was one Powhatan for every square mile.[3]

Figure 3-1: Native American Tribes in Virginia

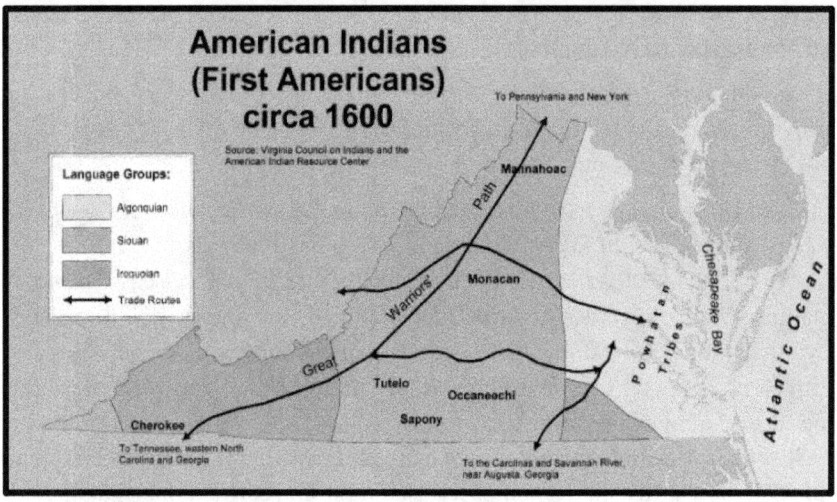

Of the Monacans, Jefferson states that they likely came from the Massawomecs (Five Nations, including Mohawks, Senecas, Oneidas, Cayugas, and Onondagas) and had dialects so distinct, from geographical separation, that "the intervention of interpreters" were often used in communications, though they sometimes

---

[2] Thomas Jefferson, *Notes on the State of Virginia*, ed. William Peden (Chapel Hill: University of North Carolina Press, 1954), 92.
[3] Thomas Jefferson, *Notes on Virginia*, 93.

Cataloging the Tribes of Indians 27

also spoke the Tuscaroran language. In 1712, the Five Nations accepted the Tuscaroras into their confederacy—thereby creating the Six Nations. In time, they also incorporated the Meherrins and Tuteloes. Given that and their western location relative to the Atlantic Ocean, it is probable that Monacans offered refuge to many tribes faced with westerly migration or extinction.[4]

Jefferson then proffers a table about what was known, or at least cataloged, about the natives, when European settlers first moved into Virginia in 1607, and then again, when the Virginian assembly made some effort to "enumerate them" in 1669. That enumeration, he goes on to add, is very likely "conjectural," as a fuller analysis of the records would "furnish many more particulars."[5] His qualification has proven to be correct.

Jefferson then gives tables that catalog the Mannahoacs, Manacans, and Powhatans. The numbers of the warriors in the last column show the "melancholy sequel of their history."

Table 3-1: Manahoacs

	Tribes	Country	Chief Town	Warriors 1607/1669
Between Patowman & Rappahanoc	Whonkenties Tegninaties Ontponies Tauxitanians Hassinungaes	Fauquier Culpeper Orange Fauquier Culpeper		
Between Rappahanoc & York	Stegarakies Shackakonics Mannahoac	Orange Spotsylvania Stafford/Spotsylvania		

Table 3-2: Monacans

	Tribes	Country	Chief Town	Warriors 1607/1669
Between York & James	Monacans Monasiccapanoes	James River above the falls Louisa / Fluvanna	Fork of James River	/30
Between James & Carolina	Monahassanoes Massinacacs Mohemenchoes	Bedford / Buckingham Cumberland Powhatan		

---

[4] Thomas Jefferson, *Notes on Virginia*, 97.
[5] Thomas Jefferson, *Notes on Virginia*, 93–96.

Table 3-3: Powhatans (From North to South)

	Tribes	Country	Chief Town	Warriors 1607/1669
Between Patowmac & Rappahanoc	Tauxenents	Fairfax	By G. Washington's	40
	Patówomekes	Stafford / King George	Patowmac Creek	200
	Cuttatowomans	King George	By Lamb Creek	20/60
	Pissasecs	King George / Richmond	Above Leeds Town	--
	Onaumaniènts	Westmoreland	Nomony River	100
	Rappahànocs	Richmond County	Rappahanoc River	100/30
	Moràughtacunds	Lancaster / Richmond	Moratico River	80/40
	Secocaonies	Northumberland	Coan River	30
	Wighcocòmicoes	Northumberland	Wicocomico River	130/70
	Cuttatowomans	Lancaster	Corotoman	30
Between Rappahanoc & York	Nantaughtacunds	Essex. Caroline	Port Tobacco Creek	150/60
	Màttapomènts	Mattaponey River	**********	30/20
	Pamùnkies	King William	Romuncock	300/50
	Wèrowocòmicos	About Rosewell	About Rosewell	40
	Payènkatanks	Turk's Ferry / Grimesby	Turk's Ferry / Grimesby	55
Between Rappahanoc & York	Appamàttocs	Chesterfield	Bermuda Hundred	60/50
	Quiocohànocs	Surry	About Upper Chipoak	25/3
	Wàrrasqeaks	Isle of Wight	Warrasqueac	/140
	Nansamònds	Nansamond	Mouth of West. Branch	200/45
	Chèsapeaks	Princess Anne	About Lynhaven River	100
Eastern Shore	Accohanocs	Accom. / Northampton	Accohanoc River	40
	Accomacks	Northampton	About Cheriton	80

Ultramontane, to the west of the three main tribes, and extending all the way to the Great Lakes, there are the Massawomecs, "a most powerful confederacy, who harrassed unremittingly the Powhatans and Manahoacs," and are likely scions of the tribes of the Six Nations. Little, Jefferson acknowledges, is known of their several tribes, though he does discuss the Chickahominies, Mattaponis, and Pamunkeys.[6]

Around 1661, the Chickahominies resettled at Mattaponi River. Their chief, along with a chief from the Pamunkeys and Mattaponies, attended the Treaty of Albany (1685), which, for all intents and purposes, was "the last chapter in their history." After 1705, they were wholly integrated with the Pamunkeys and Mattaponis.[7]

We know today that the Chickahominies were accommodating to the first English settlers in Virginia, and they helped the early settlers through the savage winters. Yet, over time, those settlers forced the Chickahominies from their lands and led them to relations with the Powhatans. The Chickahominies refused anything but light political subordination under the great Chief Powhatan—that is, they paid a tribute but refused to be governed by one of Chief Powhatan's worowances (under-chiefs). They today have no reservation.[8]

The Mattaponis too, says Jefferson, have suffered. Living between the middle stretches of the Mattaponi and Pamunkey Rivers, their numbers have been significantly reduced from the some 140 early tribal members in 1607. Of them, Jefferson states that only three or four men remain, and there is likely more negro blood in them than Mattaponi blood. Having sold off their land to Whites, they subsist on some 50 acres of land on the Mattaponi River—a confluence, from south to north, of Ma, Ta, Po, and Ni Rivers (Figure 3-2). The Mattaponi River, south of the Potomac River, joins the Pamunkey River to the southeast and thereby create York River which empties into the bay at Yorktown. Their language is expired. From time to time, they join the Pamunkeys, who are some 10 miles from them.[9]

---

[6] Thomas Jefferson, *Notes on Virginia*, 96.

[7] Thomas Jefferson, *Notes on Virginia*, 96.

[8] Helen Rountree, *Pocahontas's People: The Powhatan Indians of Virginia through Four Centuries* (Norman: University of Oklahoma Press, 1990), 187–92; James Mooney, "The Powhatan Confederacy Past and Present," *American Anthropology*, Vol. 9, No. 1, 1907: 136; and Keith Egloff and Deborah Woodward, *First People: The Early Indians of Virginia* (Charlottesville: The University Press of Virginia, 1992), 33–39.

[9] Thomas Jefferson, *Notes on Virginia*, 96.

Figure 3-2: Mattaponi and Pamunkey Rivers

Originally cordial to English settlers, the Mattaponis joined Powhatan chief, Openchancanough, in the Second and Third Powhatan Wars (1622–1632 and 1644–1646), which decimated the Virginian Natives. The Mattaponis suffered in 1676 when Nathaniel Bacon's rebels attacked them and killed Yau-na-hah, their chief. Removed to their reservation, in 1683, Iroquoians attacked many Virginian tribes. That led to disbursal of many Mattaponis, many of whom fled to the Pamunkeys and Chickahominies. James Mooney, in 1907, gives no more than 40 Mattaponis on the settlement, but that number is now roughly 75. Though a relatively self-subsisting group, there is today much interaction with the Pamunkeys.[10]

Jefferson states that the Pamunkeys, too, are nearly extinct, as there are only some 10 or 12 men, though they have not suffered from admixture with non-natives. They live on some 300 acres of fecund land on the Pamunkey River, to the south of the Mattaponi River. The older member of the group try to preserve

---

[10] Helen C. Rountree, *The Powhatan Indians of Virginia: Their Traditional Culture* (University of Oklahoma Press: Norman, 1989), 114–25, and "Mattaponi Tribe, *Encyclopedia Virginia*, https://encyclopediavirginia.org/entries/mattaponi-tribe/, accessed 13 June 2023.

their language, which makes for "the last vestiges on earth, as far as we know, of the Powhatan language."[11]

Like the Mattaponi Indians, the Pamunkeys fought in the Powhatan Wars. The treaty that formally ended the war in 1646 afforded the Pamunkeys the land in King William County. That land, engulfed by a curve of the Pamunkey River, is 20 miles east of Richmond. They too were decimated by Bacon's rebels and the Iroquoian invasion thereafter. The deed of land allows for the "oystering, fishing, gathering tuckahoe, curtenemmons, wild oats, rushes, and puckwone." There are as of 2012 some 80 Pamunkeys, who divide their time between fishing, hunting, and farming on the 1,200 allotted acres, with 500 being wetlands—that is, 15 acres per Pamunkey. The tribe is self-governed. Along with their chief, seven members of council are appointed. Their original language and tribal customs are lost.[12]

Finally, the Nottoways, says Jefferson, comprise merely a few females. They are seated on meandering Nottoway River, in Southampton County, and the lands too around that river are largely fecund. They had entered, early on, into agreements which concerned guarantees that certain lands be preserved for them. Those laws appointed trustees "to watch over their interests, and guard them from insult and injury."[13]

Yet the census of 1669, Jefferson asseverates, shows one extraordinary result of European settling: in the short span of 62 years, the aborigines had been reduced to one-third of their former number. "Spiritous liquors, the small pox, war, and an abridgment of territory, to a people who lived principally on the spontaneous productions of Nature, had committed terrible havoc among them, which generation, under the obstacles opposed to it among them, was not likely to make good." Despite the ills introduced to the American natives by Whites, Jefferson asserts that it is not the case, as is customarily assumed, that their lands were stolen by conquest. The lands in upper Virginia have been acquired by purchases "in the most unexceptionable form," and many of the lands in the lower country have been acquired similarly.[14] We shall have reasons much later to question Jefferson's conclusions.

---

[11] Thomas Jefferson, *Notes on Virginia*, 96.
[12] Helen C. Rountree, *The Powhatan Indians of Virginia: Their Traditional Culture* (University of Oklahoma Press: Norman, 1989), and "Pamunkey Tribe," *Encyclopedia Virginia*, https://encyclopediavirginia.org/entries/pamunkey-tribe, accessed 13 June 2023.
[13] Thomas Jefferson, *Notes on Virginia*, 97.
[14] Thomas Jefferson, *Notes on Virginia*, 93–96.

After limning what Jefferson knows of the tribes of Native Americans in the eighteenth century in Query XI, Jefferson turns to his critical examination of the barrows or burial mounds of Indians and their provenance—both fully covered in later chapters, in which I focus on the culture of American Indians. Before ending the query, he offers a list of current knowledge of aboriginal tribes.

Jefferson begins, "I will now proceed to state the nations and numbers of the Aborigines which still exist in a respectable and independent form." As their boundaries are not well-defined or well-known, he pledges to give "a Catalogue all those within, and circumjacent to, the United States, whose names and numbers have come to my notice."[15] Going beyond what he knows of the tribes of Virginia is significant. It shows a keen interest in all American aborigines. He has been making all Native Americans, inasmuch as his time allows, an object of study.

Jefferson draws from four lists. The first, in 1759, is by George Croghan, deputy agent for Indian affairs under Sir William Johnson; the second, by a noteworthy French trader and linked with Colonel Henri Louis Bouquet during the latter's expedition to Ohio in 1764; the third, by Captain Thomas Hutchins who made a study of the various tribes to ascertain their number in 1768; and the fourth, by Indian trader John Dodge in 1779.[16] I confine myself here mostly to replication of Jefferson's lists, but I begin with some account of the men behind the lists.

George Croghan (1718–1782) was an Irish trader of furs in the Ohio Country. He removed from Ireland to the Colonies in 1741, and established himself as one of the most prominent British traders with Natives in a territory where there were mostly French traders. Success in trading was due to an appetence for learning much about the languages and customs of the Ohioan Natives. In 1756, as Deputy Indian Agent, he assisted William Johnson of New York. Johnson was head of all Natives' affairs to the north of Ohio River. Croghan would glean hundreds of thousands of acres for the British government through grants and purchases, mostly in New York and Pennsylvania. He was very likely falsely accused of traitorous activities in 1777. Though acquitted, he was never allowed to return to the frontier. He passed, ignominiously, in 1782.[17]

---

[15] Thomas Jefferson, *Notes on Virginia*, 102.

[16] Thomas Jefferson, *Notes on Virginia*, 102.

[17] Alfred A. Cave, "George Croghan and the Emergence of British Influence on the Ohio Frontier," *Builders of Ohio: A Biographical History*, ed. Warren R. Van Tine and Michael Dale Pierce (Athens, OH: Ohio University Press, 2002), and Nicholas B. Wainwright, *George Croghan: Wilderness Diplomat* (Chapel Hill: University of North Carolina Press, 1959).

Henri Louis Bouquet (1719–1765) rose to prominence as a lieutenant colonel in the 60th Regiment of Foot of the British Army during the French and Indian War (1754–1763). When Indian warriors, under Ottawan Chief Pontiac, successfully attacked the westernmost forts of the British—Fort Pitt, Fort Detroit, Fort Sandusky, Fort Pesque Isle, and Fort Michilimackinac—Bouquet banded together a makeshift army of some 500 mostly Highlander soldiers to offer some relief the beleaguered forts. *En route* from Philadelphia, he and his men were assaulted by Delaware, Mingo, Shawnee, and Wyandot Indians, but defeated those Indians and relieved Fort Pitt. Bouquet is remembered by a base biological tactic during the battle for Fort Pitt. He distributed two smallpox-infested blankets and a kerchief to the Delawares. By 1764, Bouquet became the commander of Fort Pitt. In fall 1764, he led some 1,500 soldiers into the heart of the Ohio country, by Coshocton today. He died in 1765, after being elevated to brigadier general and put in command of all British soldiers in the Southern Colonies.[18]

Thomas Hutchins (1730–1789) was a geographer, surveyor, cartographer and engineer. He became a lieutenant in the French and Indian War and established himself as a soldier in General Bouquet's ragtag troop of 500 Highlanders. With the success of Bouquet's mission, Hutchins drew up a plan for new forts that Bouquet actuated. By 1766, Hutchins was officially an engineer in the British Army and joined Croghan, Deputy Indian Agent, in traveling down Ohio River to survey the lands gained by the Treaty of Paris (1763), which ended the war. Much traveled to the frontiers of the North and South, he was elected member of the American Philosophical Society in 1772. Despite his work for the British government over the decades, Hutchins sympathized with the Colonies' cause in the American Revolution and served in some capacity in the war from 1780 till its end. On July 11, 1781, Hutchins formally became Geographer of the United States. Figure 3-3 is an example of one of his maps. While on an assignment for the U.S. government in 1789, Hutchins died.[19]

---

[18] Bouquet to Jeffery Amherst, 13 July 1763. Collin G. Calloway, *The Scratch of a Pen: 1763 and the Transformation of North America* (Cambridge: Oxford University Press, 2007, 73.
[19] Fredrick Hicks, "Biographical Sketch of Thomas Hutchins," ed. Fredrick Hicks *A Topographical Description of Virginia, Pennsylvania, Maryland and North Carolina, Reprinted from the Original Edition of 1778* (Cleveland: The Burrow Brothers Company, 1904), 7–51.

Figure 3-3: Hutchins' Villages of Illinois County

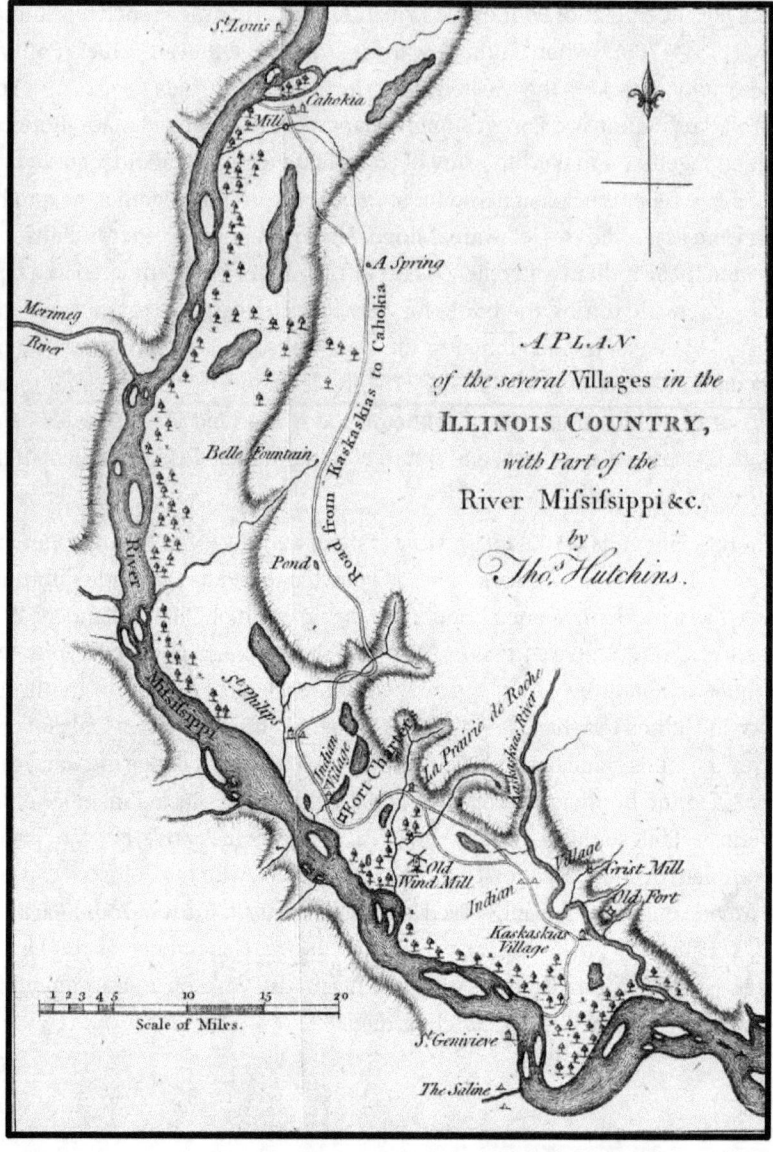

John Dodge (1751–1800) was born in Connecticut to a Baptist minister of the same name. He moved to Detroit, where he bought land in 1776. He was said to be a trader from Detroit but the records, conflicted, state that he was confined to a British jail for "having been in arms with the rebels." In May

1778, he was sent to Quebec for confinement. Months later, Dodge escaped and met with General Washington in Philadelphia in 1778 to talk about "some matters relating to Canada worthy their hearing." A 1779 letter to the Continental Congress is revelatory: "I have Ben one of the grateest Suferers that is now in the united States of Ameraca Both in Person and Property. I have Sufferd Every thing But Death Robd Plundered of Every far thing that I was master of But loock upon it as an honour that I have Suffard in so just a Cause as we are now Engagd in and very happy that I have made my Escape from the Enemi after Being Prisener two years and nine months I think it my Duty as I am now in the Service of the united States to Enform your honnours of the Proceedings and Carriings on in the Department whare I am." Dodge would be appointed Indian Agent in 1780 and would be located in Kaskaskia, now Illinois. Letters find him much travelled: at Sandusky, Fort Pitt, Detroit, Michilimackinac, Quebec, Boston, New York, Philadelphia, Vincennes, Kaskaskia, St. Genevieve, and New Orleans. He died in 1800.[20]

I turn now to Jefferson's lists of Indian nations northwest of the United States and within the United States. Jefferson gives data by Croghan, Bouquet, and Hutchins for tribes northwest of the United States and adds data by Dodge for tribes within the United States.

Table 3-4: Northwest of the United States

Tribes	Croghan	Bouquet	Hutchins	Location
Oswegatchies	-----	-----	100	Swagatchy, on St. Lawrence R
Connasedogoes	-----	-----	300	By Montreal
Cohunnewagoes	-----	200		Same, above
Orodocs	-----	-----	100	By Trois R's
Abenakies	-----	350	150	Same, above
Little Algonkins	-----	-----	100	Same, above
Michmacs	-----	700	-----	St. Lawrence R.
Amelistes	-----	550	-----	Same, above
Chalas	-----	130	-----	Same, above
Nipissins	-----	400	-----	Head of Ottawa R.

---

[20] Clarence Monroe Burton, "Introduction," *Narrative of Mr. John Dodge during His Captivity at Detroit* (Cedar Rapids, IA: Torch Press, 1909), https://www.gutenberg.org/files/33344/33344-h/33344-h.htm, accessed 14 June 2023.

Tribes				Locations
Algoquins	-----	300	-----	Same, above
Round Heals	-----	2500	-----	R. aux Tetes Boules, east of L. Superior
Messasagues	-----	2000	-----	L. Huron & L. Superior
Christinaus/Kris	-----	3000	-----	L. Chistinaux
Assinaboes	-----	1500	-----	L. Assinaboes
Blancs (Barbus)	-----	1500		
Sioux, Meadow		2500		
Sioux, Woods	10,000	1800	10,000	Head & W. of Mississippi R.
Sioux		-----		
Ajoues	-----	1100	-----	N. of Padoucas R.
White Panis	-----	2000	-----	S. of Missouri R.
Freckled Panis	-----	1700	-----	Same, above
Padoucas	-----	500	-----	Same, above
Grandes Eaux	-----	1000	-----	
Canses	-----	1600	-----	S. of Missouri R.
Osages	-----	600	-----	Same, above
Missouris	400	3000	-----	On Missouri R.
Arkanzas	-----	2000	-----	On Arkansas R.
Caouitas	-----	700	-----	E. of Alibamous R.

Table 3-5: Within the United States

Tribes	Croghan	Boliquet	Hutchins	Dodge	Locations
Mohocks	-----		160	100	Mohocks R.
Onèidas	-----		300		East of Oneida L. & head branches
Tuscaròras	-----		200	400	Between Oneidas & Onondagoes R's
Onondàgoes	-----	1550	260	230	Near Onondago L.
Cayùgas	-----		200	220	North branch of Cayuga L.
Sènecas	-----		1000	650	Waters of Susquehanna, Ontario, & heads of Ohio

Cataloging the Tribes of Indians 37

Aughquàgahs	-----	-----	150	-----	East Susquehanna, on Aughquagah
Nánticocs	-----	-----	100	-----	East Susquehanna at Utsanango, Chaghtnet & Owegy
Mohìccons	-----	-----	100	-----	Same, above
Conòies	-----	-----	30	-----	Same, above
Sapòonies	-----	-----	30	-----	N. branch of Susquehanna R. at Diahago
Mùnsies	-----	-----	150	150	Same, above
Delawares (Linnelinopies)	-----	-----	150	⎫	Same, above
Delawares (Linnelinopies)	600	600	600	⎬ 500	At branches of Beaver Cr., Cayahoga R. & Muskingham R.
Shàwanees	400	500	300	300	Sioto R. & branches of Muskingham R.
Mìngoes	-----	-----	-----	60	On branch of Sioto R.
Mohìccons	-----	-----	⎫	60	
Cohunnewagos	-----	-----	⎬ 300	-----	Near Sandusky R.
Wyandots	⎫	300	⎭	⎫	Near Detroit & Ft. St. Joseph
	⎬ 300			⎬ 180	
Wyandots	⎭		250	⎭	Same, above
Twightwees	300	-----	250	-----	Miami R. near Ft. Miami
Miamis	-----	350	-----	300	Same, above
Ouiàtonons	200	400	300	300	Wabash R. near Ft. Ouiatonon
Piàkishas	300	250	300	400	Same, above
Shakies	-----	⎫	200	-----	Same, above
Kaskasias	-----	⎬ 600	300	-----	Near Kaskasia
Illinois	400	⎭	300	-----	Near Cahokia, Quebec
Proirias	-----	800	-----	-----	On Illinois R.

Tribe					Location
Pouteòtamies	⎤	350	300	450	Near Ft. Detroit & Ft. St. Joseph
Ottawas	⎥		550	300	Same, above
Chippawas	⎥		⎤ 200		On Samguinam Bay of L. Huron
Ottawas	⎥	5900	⎦		Same, above
Chippawas	⎬ 2000		400	⎤ 5450	Near Michillimakinac
Ottawas	⎥		250	⎥	Same, above
Chippawas	⎥		400	⎥	Near Ft. St. Mary on L. Superior
Chippawas	⎥		-----	⎥	Villages on L. Sup.
Chippawas	⎦	-----	⎤		By Puans Bay, L. Sup.
Shakies	200	400	⎬ 550	-----	Same, above
Mynonàmies	-----		⎦	-----	Same, above
Ouisconsings	-----	500	-----	-----	Ouisconsing R.
Kickapous	600	300		⎤ 250	On L. Michigan & between L. Michigan and Mississippi R. (from Kickapous to Musquakies)
Otogamies, Foxes	-----	-----	⎤	⎥ -----	
Mascoutens	-----	500	⎬ 4000	⎥ -----	
Miscothins	-----	-----	⎥	⎥ -----	
Outimacs	-----	-----	⎦	⎥ -----	
Musquakies	200	250		⎦ 250	
E. Sioux	-----	-----	----- **BEGIN GALPHIN**	500	E. heads of Mississippi R. & isles of L. Sup.
Cherokees	1500	2500	3000	-----	W. North Carolina
Chickasaws	-----	750	500	-----	W. Georgia
Catawbas	-----	150	-----	-----	On Catawbas R. in South Carolina
Chacktaws	2000	4500	6000	-----	W. Georgia
Upper Creeks	-----	-----	⎤ 3000	-----	W. Georgia
Lower Creeks	-----	1180	⎦	-----	W. Georgia
Natchez	-----	150	-----	-----	-----
Alibamous	-----	600	-----	-----	Alibama R. in W. Georgia

Cataloging the Tribes of Indians

Table 3-6: Croghan

Lezar	400	-----	-----	Mouth of Ohio R. to mouth of Wabash R.
Webings	200	-----	-----	Mississippi R. below Shakies
Ousasoys Grand Tuc.	4000	-----	-----	White Cr. of Mississippi R.
Linways	1000	-----	-----	On the Missisipi

Table 3-7: Bouquet

Les Puans	-----	700	-----	By Puans Bay
Folle Avoine	-----	350	-----	Same, above
Ouanakina	-----	300	-----	
Chiakanessou	-----	350	-----	Conjectured to be tribes of the Greeks
Machcous	-----	800	-----	
Souikilas	-----	200	-----	

Table 3-8: Dodge

Mineamis	-----	-----	2000	NW of L. Michigan, to heads of Mississippi R. & up to L. Superior
Piankishas	-----	-----		
Mascoutins	-----	-----	800	By Wabash R. & toward Illinois R.
Vermillions	-----	-----		

Concerning his data on the tribes of Indians within the United States, Jefferson lists additional data from Croghan, Bouquet, and Dodge (italicized data, above). Those data he keeps separate from other data prior to it inasmuch as they "might be different appellations for some of the same tribes already enumerated."[21]

---

[21] Thomas Jefferson, *Notes on Virginia*, 107.

Chapter 4

The "Laws" of Indians

"Great societies cannot exist without government"

One of the peculiarities of Indian culture is their being "separated into so many little societies." Jefferson writes in Query XI of *Notes on the State of Virginia*, "This practice results from the circumstance of their having never submitted themselves to any laws, any coercive power, any shadow of government."[1]

The etiological intimation of the sentence is that choosing to have no government and no laws necessarily restricts their size. It might be, of course, that Indians choose small societies and that obviates government and laws—that is, their manner of living makes impossible large societies.

Like many of the chapters in the first half of this book, this chapter too is expiscatory. I continue to flesh out Jefferson's thoughts on Native Americans through study of many of their nations. The focus here is how Natives, with no written languages and thus no formal laws, preserve order and social harmony.

Living in small societies without laws, "their only controls are their manners, and that moral sense of right and wrong" that is a part of the nature of every man. Thus, they maintain social order by coercion: by contempt or expulsion from society. Though far from perfect as a means of preserving order, "crimes are very rare among them."[2]

The lawlessness of Native Americans, for Jefferson, is not necessarily anathema. To the question of whether no law is preferable to too much law, as is the case with civilized Europeans, Jefferson asserts that anyone experienced of both will choose the former. "The sheep are happier of themselves than under the care of the wolves." Jefferson sums, "It will be said

---

[1] Thomas Jefferson, *Notes on the State of Virginia*, ed. William Peden (Chapel Hill: University of North Carolina Press, 1954), 92–93.
[2] Thomas Jefferson, *Notes on Virginia*, 93.

that great societies cannot exist without government: the savages, therefore, break them into small ones."³

It is a sentiment iterated in other letters of Jefferson's Parisian years. To James Madison on January 30, 1787, Jefferson distinguishes three societies: those without government (Indians), those in which "the will of every one has a just influence (United States and to a lesser extent, England), and those of force (all other monarchies and republics). He adds that societies without government might be the best, but they are "inconsistent with any degree of population." Two weeks earlier (16 Jan. 1787), Jefferson tells Edward Carrington that the Indians "enjoy in their general mass an infinitely greater degree of happiness" when compared to Europeans. In place of law, there are public praise and shame, which work as effectively as law. The letters indicate an early, nascent form of republicanism at play among the Indian nations.⁴

Despite lack of government, Jefferson notes that crimes are rare. Minor offenses are punished by contempt; major offenses, by exclusion. He reflects on their dearth of law, "Whether no law, as among the savage Americans, or too much law, as among the civilized Europeans, submits man to the greatest evil, one who has seen both conditions of existence would pronounce it to be the last: and that the sheep are happier of themselves, than under care of the wolves." The sentence is parturient. Both manners of living are extremes, but from the perspective of the happiness of the *hoi polloi*, a small society without government is greatly preferred to a large society with coercive government.

The scenario, given Jefferson's limited access to the tribes of Native Americans throughout what is today the United States, was more involved. Let us consider, for illustration, the political structure of the early Powhatan community, numbering some 15,000 at the time of young Captain John Smith's (1580–1631, Figure 4-1) arrival in 1607 at what would become Jamestown.

---

³ Thomas Jefferson, *Notes on Virginia*, 93.

⁴ Hellenbrand argues that defects of Indians' government for Jefferson reduce to the fact that "Indian government was a product of instinct, not reason." He fails to grasp that every just government is founded for Jefferson on instinct, as the principles of Jeffersonian republicanism are grounded on the fundamental axioms of morality—a point that I make all too frequently in publications. Harrold Hellenbrand, "Not 'To Destroy But to Fulfil' Jefferson, Indians, and Republican Dispensation," *Eighteenth-Century* Studies, Vol. 18, No. 4, 1985: 529.

Figure 4-1: Postcard of Captain John Smith

Virginia's Indians numbered some 50,000 at the time of Smith's arrival. The first settlers that the adventurers met were Powhatans who spoke a language now called Eastern Algonquian.[5]

The Powhatans, matrilinear, were under the leadership of their chief, Wahunsenacawh (1545–1618), who had inherited six tribes in the sixteenth century through his mother. The names of the original tribes were Powhatan, Arrohateck, Appamattuck, Pamunkey, Mattaponi, and Chiskiack. By 1607, there were 30 tribes, each with its own weroance (chief). Weroances secured their leadership by accumulated wealth through accumulated tribute, which included amassing skins, pearls, copper, shells, and corn from members of another tribe in exchange for favors. Thereby, their political stability was achieved through strengthened economic ties.

The lands occupied by the Powhatans included the Tidewater region, from the Potomac River to the James River, and parts of the eastern shore. This area measured, as we have seen in the prior chapter, roughly 8,000 square miles.

---

[5] In what follows, I trace out the account given in my (with brother David) book, *A "Biography" of Lynchburg: City with a Soul* (Newcastle upon Tyne: Cambridge Scholars, 2021), 2–12. In that account, we draw mostly from Helen C. Rountree's books, *Pocahontas's People: the Powhatan Indians of Virginia through Four Centuries* (Norman: University of Oklahoma Press, 1996), esp. 3–15, and *The Powhatan Indians of Virginia: Their Traditional Culture* (Norman, OK: University of Oklahoma Press, 1990).

Powhatan natives lived in small, often elevated villages near rivers (e.g., Figure 4-2), which were used for both food and transportation. The elevation of their villages was needed to keep away from the periodic freshets of the rivers and as a defensive posture in the event of war with another tribe.

Powhatans were not merely foragers and hunters, but they also farmed. The crops they produced were corn, squash, pumpkins, beans, and tobacco. They also ate fish, oysters, and tuckahoe, an edible plant in the marshy areas, as well as nuts, grains, vegetables, mushrooms, roots, blueberries, strawberries, plums, and raspberries. Men provided game such as deer and smaller game like squirrel, opossum, rabbit, wild turkey, and duck.

Figure 4-2: Palisaded Powhatan Village

For transportation, since they lived by rivers, Powhatans used birch bark or hollowed-out tree trunks as canoes. For clothing, men wore deerskin breechcloth that was passed between the legs and attached to a belt. Leggings and moccasins were worn when hunting in the forest. Women wore deerskin aprons but also wore leggings and moccasins when in the fields or when gathering food in the forest. Fur cloaks were worn in the winter months. Clothes were generally decorated with painted designs and had fringes and beads attached. The chiefs had cloaks made of the feathers of birds. These cloaks were tied on the left side and reached below the knees. Both men and women had tattoos on their bodies and painted their faces with red paint mixed with nut oil.

Education for the young consisted of introduction to tribal responsibilities. Between the ages of 10 to 15, Powhatan boys learned all they needed to know and were then pronounced men and were initiated as such in a process called *huskanaw*, which involved a ritual death and rebirth. Praise and shame informed the educative process.

Young natives were taught obedience and to have respect for their elders. Education for children was indoctrination for their future social roles. They were especially taught respect and self-control. By puberty, youths were roughly treated as adults, and young girls were readied for marriage.

Marriage for Powhatans was chiefly for child-bearing purposes. To secure that end, parents played a significant role in the process, though marriages were not arranged. A young man would have to show the parents of the prospective bride that he could protect and provide for his future wife. Thus, he would "woo" her parents through an abundancy of gifts of food. A girl would have to show the prospect of bearing healthy children. There would then begin a process of negotiation, prior to marriage.

Once there was an agreement between the parents of the young man and of the girl, a marriage-payment was given to the parents of the bride as recompense for their loss of domestic labor of the girl. The marriage-payment was, in effect, a formal statement of the woman's value.

As soon as the groom-to-be got together a house and the necessary household items, the bride was brought to the new house. There the wedding ceremony took place, as a string of beads measured by the man's arm length was broken over the couple's hands, joined together by the bride's father or guardian. The marriage was now complete. Marriages were expected to last, but divorces did sometimes occur.

Powhatans were not monogamous. Tribal chiefs, especially Wahunsenacawh or Chief Powhatan, were to have as many wives as they could afford. The number of wives was a symbol of wealth. William Strachey (1575–1621), of Virginia Company of London, reported in his *History of Travaile into Virginia Britannia* that Chief Powhatan had over 100 wives. Each too paid a marriage-payment, but there were no negotiations, as marriage to a chief was construed as a signal honor and great status for the bride and her parents. Once a wife had a child by a chief, she was sent back to her own village and having done her duty, she was formally considered divorced. The child would remain with her, until the child was old enough to live with the chief's other children.

Wahunsenacawh, the wealthiest and most powerful of all the chiefs, was born about 1547. He did not rule absolutely, though he was an astute, strict, and energetic ruler, who was sometimes noted for cruelty. Captain John Smith, in *A True Relation of such Occurrences and Accidents of Note as Happened in Virginia* (1608), described thus the Powhatan Chief:

> Their Emperor proudly [lay] upon a bedstead a foot high upon ten or twelve mats, richly hung with many chains of great pearls about his neck, and covered with a great covering of *Rahaughcums* [raccoon skins]. At his head sat a woman, at his feet another, on each side, sitting upon a mat upon the ground, were ranged his chief men on each side [of] the fire, ten in a rank, and behind them as many young women, each a great chain of white beads over their shoulders, their heads painted in red, and [he] with such a grave a majestical countenance as drove me into admiration to see such state in a naked savage.

Chief Powhatan decided all matters of his people, though he was advised by a council. For instance, when the chief and his council decided on a course of war, their decision required the approval of Chief Powhatan's priests. Those priests had a significant status, as they were thought to communicate with the transmundane spirits and could divine their wishes. Thus, their advice was crucial.

Thus, as we have seen, though there were no formal laws among Powhatans, there was aplenty political structure, driven by praise and shame. That was an observation of Jefferson's friend, Charles Thomson, who graciously provided Jefferson with extensive notes, most on the Natives in or around Virginia, on the latter's book, *Notes on the State of Virginia.*[6] It was also characteristic of numerous other Indian nations.[7]

Among other Indian tribes, there was policing, though no formal laws to guide it. W.C. MacLeod mentions an "internal police system" to enforce orders and inflict punishment for disobedience used by Ojibwe (southeast Canada), Cree (mostly north and west of Lake Superior), Osage (south of Missouri River), Pawnee (Nebraska and Northwest Oklahoma), Menominee (Wisconsin and Upper Michigan), Oglala (South Dakota), Blackfoot (Montana), and tribes of the Southeastern woodlands, among others. Policing was the duty of a fraternity of warriors, given assignation through ceremony by tribal chiefs. Policing would then be their sole function. Policing entailed supervising hunting parties, ensuring attendance at religious festivals, overseeing public works, duty as sentinels, guarding property, arbitration in disputes, and curbing violence within their tribe. Violence was curbed willy-nilly by bringing forth the "sacred pipe" for offended persons to smoke. Pipes also functioned ceremoniously to seal a treaty for peace, to conclude a significant commercial transaction (e.g., Figure 4-3), to signal the start of war, to mark a singular social decision, to secure favorable weather for a journey, to bring rain in times of drought, and in general to eschew evil and bring good. It was also ceremoniously used to pleasure the spirits by allowing the agreeable smoke to rise to the heavens.[8] Punition consisted mainly of flogging or ruination of the guilty person's property. Resistance to punition was a warrant for death. Murder, whether willful or accidental, was anathema in all tribes and punished by the most severe and dreaded penalty: ostracism. The existence of policing Natives involved a degree of structure to some tribes, which Jefferson seems to disallow. There were no police in northwestern Atlantic tribes.[9]

---

[6] Charles Thomson, "Notes on *Notes on Virginia*" (Appendix I), in Thomas Jefferson, *Notes on the State of Virginia*, ed. Frank Shuffleton (New York: Penguin, 1999), 210–11.

[7] Robert J. Miller, "American Indian Influence on the United States Constitution and Its Framers," *American Indian Law Review,* Vol. 18, No. 1, 1993: 144–45.

[8] Editors, "Calumet or 'Peace-pipe' of the Indians," *The Quebec History Encyclopedia,* http://faculty.marianopolis.edu/c.belanger/quebechistory/encyclopedia/calumetpipe.htm, accessed 7 May 2023.

[9] W.C. MacLeod, "Police and Punishment among Native Americans of the Plains," *Journal of Criminal Law and Criminology,* Vol. 28, 1937: 181–201.

Figure 4-3: Indians Sharing Peace Pipe

Though there were no formal laws, written and on paper, for Indians, there were customary ways of dealing with problems. Many Indians, especially those of the Eastern Woodlands, used wampums, which were literally strings of (generally) white-seashell beads.[10] Coastal Natives collected seashells and used them as items for trade with inlanders. Shells, too, were threaded on a string and used ornamentally and also made into belts, which signified singular events, such as proposals for marriage, alliances between tribes, captives taken from a battle, and treaties with Whites. Many tribes had a keeper of wampums, who guarded the belts and was expert in reading them.[11] Wampums, thus could be used to help settle disputes in the manner today that barristers use precedents.

Like many other tribes, the Senecans of Western New York believed in witchcraft. On one occasion, when a member of their tribe unexpectedly declined and died, and the medicine men of the tribe could not explain the

---

[10] From the Narragansett tongue, a species of Algonquins.
[11] Anthony F.C. Wallace, *The Death and Rebirth of the Seneca* (New York: Vintage Books, 1969), chap. 8.

decline and death, a woman who attended the dying man was accused of witchcraft. It was decreed, after a trial by the Senecans, in pursuance of custom, that she was a witch and should be executed. "She had been regularly tried and condemned by their laws, and her death was in conformity with usages that had been in existence among them from time immemorial." Whites who witnessed the trial ridiculed the Natives for believing in superstition. The great Senecan orator and chief, Red Jacket, replied: "Do you denounce us as fools and bigots because we still believe that which you yourselves believed two centuries ago? You black coats [missionaries] thundered this doctrine from the pulpit, your judges pronounced it from the bench, and sanctioned it with the formalities of law."[12]

Interactions with local and federal governments over time led to the introduction of laws into Aboriginal nations. For example, though there were no formal laws within tribes, there were formal laws through legal agreements between tribes and the U.S. government as early as 1778. Such agreements, beginning in the 1830s, were sovereign-to-sovereign, which means that each side was considered as its own government and each had equal bargaining power, though the U.S. government when agreements were not had, had the final authority, so it was ultimately sovereign.[13] That was captured by the U.S. government's designation of tribes as domestic and dependent. It was also evident that no tribe was able to attain equal bargaining power until it was formally recognized by the U.S. government. Recognition of tribal sovereignty could also be terminated by the federal government. As it was with the federal government, it was the same with tribes and individual states. I cover this fully in chapter 8.[14]

I end with a significant attempt to "civilize" the Natives by North Carolinian Colonel Benjamin Hawkins (1754–1816), who was the most significant Indian agent in the South and who began corresponding with Jefferson as early as 1783 on Indian vocabularies and other aspects of Indian culture. In 1785, Hawkins was appointed by the U.S. Congress as an agent to bargain with the Creeks over land. He thereafter was involved in several important treaties. In 1796, George Washington appointed him General Superintendent of Indian Affairs. He was

---

[12] J. Niles Hubbard, *Red Jacket and His People, 1750–1830* (New York: Burt Franklin, 1886), 289–90.

[13] The sovereign-to-sovereign bargaining arrangement has led to remarkable incoherencies in Indian laws with the federal and local governments. See Philip P. Frickey, "(Native) American Exceptionalism in Federal Public Law," *Harvard Law Review*, Vol. 119, 2005: 431–490.

[14] Helen C. Rountree, *The Powhatan Indians of Virginia*, 114–25.

to interact with all tribes south of Ohio River, with a focus on the Creeks, who were the most ferocious and belligerent.[15]

Hawkins' first task was to win their trust. He defended Native Creeks against encroachments of cupid and unscrupulous frontiersmen, but he demanded that Creeks honor their pledges. He worked unrelentingly, but his work was demanding and often had little effect. He wrote to Governor James Jackson of Georgia, "I find it an arduous undertaking with a few assistants to make the impressions I wish on the minds of my red charges who are scattered over a wild country of at least 300 miles square." Many Creeks considered him to be an intruder, a destroyer of Creek culture, and for a time, his safety was an issue. Yet his integrity won over most Creeks, and he was never harmed.[16] This is illustrative of the impossibility of the task of being an Indian agent whose sympathies were with the Indians and yet who answered to the U.S. government. Hawkins would retain that post till his death in 1816.

Figure 4-4: Hawkins' Georgian Plantation

Hawkins did what he could throughout his life to civilize the belligerent Creeks. When he moved from North Carolina to Georgia, he began by teaching

---

[15] Merritt B. Pound, *Benjamin Hawkins: Indian Agent* (Athens: University of Georgia Press, 1958), 130 and 161.
[16] Merritt B. Pound, *Benjamin Hawkins*, 156.

them ranching (e.g., cattle and pigs), farming (e.g., wheat, cotton, and corn), the cottage industries (e.g., making cloth) (Figure 4-4), and acquainting them to U.S. laws. Creeks, along with his slaves, cleared many hundreds of acres for his plantation. They planted cash crops, and he soon acquired over 1000 head of cattle and other animals for his plantation.[17]

Yet Hawkins found social organization on kinship, not law, to be an albatross to civilizing Creeks. It was one thing to behave as a civilized person. That, however, did not give them the foundation for civilized living. To become fully civilized, they needed to be Christianized and politicized in the intricacies of American law. Concerning the last, there needed to be political structure with laws. The Creek nation was too large and the various towns of the nation were relatively independent. That made inculpation a chaotic, if not impossible, task. He says in 1799: "The Creeks never had, till this year, a national Government and law. Everything of a general tendency was left to the care and management of the public agents, who heretofore used temporary expedients only; and amongst the most powerful and persuasive was the pressure of fear from without, and presents." Thus, he assembled the Creeks' chiefs to "carry the laws of the nation into effect" through selection of a Creek warrior as agent for each town to oversee enforcement of laws. The Creeks' chiefs agreed.[18]

By the time of Jefferson's presidency, the plan had been remarkably successful. Jefferson says in his First Annual Message (8 Dec. 1801):

> Among our Indian neighbors also a spirit of peace and friendship generally prevails, and I am happy to inform you that the continued efforts to introduce among them the implements and the practice of husbandry and the household arts have not been without success; that they are becoming more and more sensible of the superiority of this dependence for clothing and subsistence over the precarious resources of hunting and fishing, and already we are able to announce that instead of that constant diminution of their numbers produced by their wars and their wants, some of them begin to experience an increase of population.[19]

---

[17] Merritt B. Pound, *Benjamin Hawkins*, 130.
[18] Merritt B. Pound, *Benjamin Hawkins*, 161–62.
[19] Thomas Jefferson, First Annual Message, *Thomas Jefferson: Writings,* ed. Merrill D. Peterson (New York: Library of America, 1984), 501.

The civilizing program, having met with some success, was ultimately quashed by a split within the Creeks, some filiopietistic, some progressive. Angered by the constant demands to sell their land to Whites, certain Creeks, called Red Sticks, rebelled. The result was the Red Stick War of 1813–1814. The rebels attacked Fort Mims (today, in Alabama) and thereafter, a force comprising Cherokees, other Creeks, and Whites led by General Andrew Jackson annihilated the Red Sticks and razed most of the towns in the territory of the Creeks. Hawkins was devastated. It was, Hawkins thought, the undoing of his lifelong work.[20]

I have much more to say about the process of "civilizing" Indians throughout the second part of this book.

---

[20] James W. Holland, "Andrew Jackson and the Creek War: Victory at the Horseshoe Bend," *Alabama Review*, Vol. 21, No. 4, 1968: 243–275.

Chapter 5

The Languages & Origins of Indians

"I have it much at hear"

We saw that Jefferson's instructions to Captain Meriwether Lewis in the preface included much about the Natives that Lewis would meet on his journey westward. Those instructions included acquaintance with their nations, numbers, and, of course, languages.

Thomas Jefferson was an unquestioned linguaphile. He was capable in several modern languages—his native English, of course, as well as French, Italian, and some Spanish that he learned, says he, while reading *Don Quixote* in Spanish as he crossed the Atlantic[1]—and he knew Latin well, Ancient Greek, and perhaps even Old English, and loved few things more than reading the ancient authors in their ancient languages. "He derived more pleasure from his acquaintance with Greek and Latin than from any other resource of literature," says granddaughter Sarah Randolph.[2]

Languages for Jefferson were alive and ever changing, as the circumstances of human experience were ever changing. "Nothing is more evident than that as we advance in the knowledge of new things, and of new combinations of old ones," he writes to Joseph Milligan (6 Apr. 1816), "we must have new words to express them." With the numerous discoveries of the sciences, for instance, there was a need for new words, neoterism. Jefferson states to John Adams (Aug. 1820) that progress in science demands new concepts— neologies like "oxigen, cotyledons, zoophytes, magnetism, electricity, hyaline, and thousands of others expressing ideas not then existing." To grammarian John Waldo (16 Aug. 1813), Jefferson says that usage is "the arbiter of language," and it gives "law to grammar," not "grammar to usage." Languages are so central in day-to-day human affairs that Jefferson thought

---

[1] TJ to Joseph Delaplaine, 12 Apr. 1817. The account is specious, as Jefferson was introduced to Spanish at William and Mary College.
[2] Sarah N. Randolph, *The Domestic Life of Thomas Jefferson* (Cambridge: University Press, 1939), 292.

that they should be the object of study after primary education in grammar schools. In the grammar schools, the subjects are to be Ancient Greek, Latin, French, Spanish, Italian, and German, and English grammar, *inter alia*.[3] Study of languages provides mental exercise, suited to a mind not fully matured, in readiness for the subjects of serious study at a university, for those of inclination and ability.

Jefferson, too, was fascinated by the various languages and dialects of American Indians, given his exposure to them as a boy at Shadwell, when he noticed some were extraordinary orators. A significant part of his attention to the study of Indian nations was devoted to the study of their various "tongues." That was undertaken both to disclose relationships among the nations and to answer what was to him an intriguing question: Were Native Americans the scions of Eastern Asians, or Eastern Asians, of Native Americans?

Consequently, Jefferson, in time took to collecting words from varied Indian tribes. In 1787, he receives Indian "vocabularies" from federal agent to Southern Indians, Benjamin Hawkins (Aug. 4), and replies appreciatively: "I must add my thanks too for the vocabularies. This is an object I mean to pursue, as I am persuaded that the only method of investigating the filiation of the Indian nations is by that of their languages." The notion here is that the study of Natives' languages is the best way to disclose familial relationships between tribes. The chief reason for the collection, aside from his amaranthine intellectual inquisitiveness, is to decide the question of their provenance and their relationship to those persons of Eastern Asia. "I endeavor to collect all the vocabularies I can of the American Indians, as of those of Asia, persuaded that if they ever had a common parentage it will appear in their languages."[4] Jefferson is still in France at the time and there is little he can do on his own to collect Indian words.

In May 1791, Jefferson and James Madison begin a tour of the northern states Connecticut, New York, and Vermont. On June 14, they visit the Unquachog Indians at Poosepatuck on Long Island, New York. While Madison's notes on the trip make no mention of the visit,[5] Jefferson writes in his 1791 Memorandum

---

[3] Thomas Jefferson, *Notes on the State of Virginia*, ed. William Peden (Chapel Hill: University of North Carolina Press, 1954), 147.
[4] TJ to James Madison, 12 Jan. 1789.
[5] James Madison, "Notes on the Lake Country Tour, 31 May–7 June 1791," *Founders Online,* National Archives, https://founders.archives.gov/documents/Madison/01-14-02-0023, accessed 16 June 2023.

The Languages & Origins of Indians

Book: "Genl. [William] Floyd's. breakfd. & dind. Visited the Unquanchog Indians. Lodged at Terry's."[6]

Jefferson catalogs numerous words of that tribe. He prefaces his vocabulary: "Unquachogs. About 20. souls. They constitute the Pusspátock settlement in the town of Brookhaven S. side of Long island. The language they speak is a dialect differing a little from the Indians settled near Southampton called Shinicocks and also from those of Montock called Montocks. The three tribes can barely understand each other."[7] The collection is under 200 words. I give it below.

Table 5-1: Earth

Clay	Squoint	Clay	Puckwé/squoint
Sand	Yaac	Dirt	Puckwé
Water	Núp	The whole world	Wáame-pámakíu

Table 5-2: Chthonic (Earthy) Animals

Snake	Skwk	Bug	Seukr
Worm	Húquer	Worm	Húquer
Fly	Mucháwas	Musketo	Murráquitch

Table 5-3: Animals

Cow	owsen	Turkey	Nahiam
Horse	Hosses	Chicken	Kekeeps
Sheep	Sheeps	Hog	Hog
Dog	Arsúm	Fox	Squírrútes
Squirrel	Moccás	Mouse	Poquáttas
Rabbit	Móhtux	Rat	-----
Deer	Hátk		

---

[6] Jefferson and Madison stayed at Floyd's house on the Forge River in Brookhaven Township. Thomas Jefferson, "Memorandum Books, 1791," *Founders Online*, National Archives, https://founders.archives.gov/documents/Jefferson/02-02-02-0001, accessed 16 June 2023.

[7] "Jefferson's Vocabulary of the Unquachog Indians," *The Papers of Thomas Jefferson*, vol. 20, *1 April–4 August 1791*, ed. Julian P. Boyd (Princeton: Princeton University Press, 1982): 467–470. I have arranged differently Jefferson's material for ease of apprehension.

Table 5-4: Foodstuffs

Potato	Panac	Squas	Áscoot
Wheat	Maróomar	Bread	Ap
Rye	Rye	Oats	Oats
Tobacco	Tobac	Hominy	Samp
Meat	Weeows		

Table 5-5: Comestibles (Trees, Water, Animals, &C.)

Tree	Péewye	Pine	Cw
Oak	Húchemus	Hickory	Wusquát
Appletree	Appeesanck	Peach tree	Péachesanck
cherry tree	Chérrysanck	Grape	Cátamenón
Plumb tree	Sassémenac	Strawberries	Wotáhomon
Indian corn	Sowháwmen	Beans	Mais-cusseet
Peas	------	Gourd	Whorámmok
Watermelon	Waghtiwhorámmok		
Whale	Púttap	Whale oil	Púttapapúm
Grease	Pum	Fish	Opéramac
Oyster	Apóonahac	Clam	Poquahoc

Table 5-6: Air

Sky	Ke-isk	Cloud	Pamayaúxen
Rain	Súkerun	Snow	Soáchop
Ice	Copátn	Hail	Mosécan
God	Mánto	Great god	Masakéetmúnd
Devil	Máttateáshet		
Thunder	Pataquáhamo	Lightnening	Wowosúmpa

The Languages & Origins of Indians

Table 5-7: Birds

Bird	Aswássas	Duck	Nanasecus
Gull	Arráx	Goose	Hakénah
Dove	Má-owks	Fish hawk	Manamaquas
Gull	Arráx	Goose	Hakénah
Eagle	Wéquaran	Quail	Ohócotees
Partridge	Ápacus	Whippoorwill	Whácorees

Table 5-8: Waters

River	Seépus	Ocean	Cutstúk
Bay	Petápagh		

Table 5-9: Humans & Relations Among Them

Man	Run	Woman	Squas
Husband	Ks-hamps	Wife	Keé-us
Child	Peewútstut	Grandchild	Cówhees
Boy	Macúchax	Girl	Squásses
Lad	Rungcump	Lass	Yúnksquas
Mild	Mais-cusseet	Child	Neechuntz
Father	Cws	Mother	Cẃca
Brother	Contàyux	Sister	Keéssums
Uncle	Nisséis	Aunt	Cacácas
Grandfather	Numpsoonk	Grandmother	Nánnax
I	Née	You	Kee
He	Naácum	<she>	<wéena>

Table 5-10: Bodily Parts

Head	Okéyununc	Hair	Wé-usk
Eyes	Skésuc	Nose	Cochóy
Mouth	Cúttoh	Teeth	Képut
Lips	Kussissit	Chin	Cotumpcan
Cheek	Canánno	Ear	Catáwoc
Neck	Keésquish	Shoulder	Péquan
Arm	Copút-te	Elbow	Keésquan
Hand	Coṙitché	Finger	Coṙitcheus
Nail	Cocássac	Back	Cúpsquan
Skin	Cuttaqúras	Belly	Cráckish
Hip	Corúcan	Thigh	Copómac
Knee	Cucúttuc	Leg	Coráun
Foot	Cussed	Great toe	Cumsquáusseet
Little toe	Peewasticonseet		

Table 5-11: Human Attributes

Good	Woréecan	Bad	Mattateáyuh
Ugly	Woreeco	Handsome	Neeho wuchayuk
Clever	Weáyuh	Angry [person]	Cheeáscota
Small	Peéwátsu		

Table 5-12: Human Attributes

To walk	Copumusah	To stand	Cotofer
To lie down	Cutchéepur	To sit	Kiummatap
To run	Quáquees	To break	Pẃksa
To bend	Counkarúnneman	To cut (knife)	Poquesíman
To cut (axe)	Poquatáhaman		

The Languages & Origins of Indians

Table 5-13: Indian Terms

Arrow	Neep	Tomahawk	Chékenas
Pot	Coquées	Bed	Apúnna
Blanket	Acquéewants	Axe	Ochégan
House	Weécho	Door	Squnt
Chimney	Hamánek	Wampum	Whampump
Mocassens	Mocússenus	To kill	Wúhnsa
To hunt	Peénsaac		
War	Ayutówac	Peace	Weéhsaac

Table 5-14: Numbers

1	Naqúut	2	Nées
3	Nus	4	Yaut
5	Pa/napáa	6	Nacúttah/cúttah
7	Túmpawa	8	Swah
9	Nẃre	10	Payac
11	Nápan-naquut	12	Nápan-ees
13	Nápan -ees	14	Nápan -yóut
15	Nápan -napá	16-19	Nápan-nacúttah, &c.
20	Neésun-chóg	21	Neésun-chognaquut
30	Sowunchóg	40	Yauhwunchóg
50	Yauhwunchóg	60	Nacúttahtsunchóg
70	Tumpawatsunchog, &c.	100	Noquut pasit
200	Nées pasu		

Jefferson ends: "The orthography is English. This Vocabulary was taken by Th: J. June 13. 1791 in presence of James Madison and Genl. Floyd. There remain but three persons of this tribe now who can speak it's language. These are old women. From two of these, brought together, this vocabulary was taken. A young woman of the same tribe was also present who knew something of the language." It is strange, given the centrality of the concepts fire, air, water, and earth in etiology throughout the centuries, that Jefferson did not ask for the Unquachog word for "fire."

The collection slowly grows. Jefferson tells William Linn (5 Feb. 1798) that the focus is "the names of natural objects," though he admits to insufficient success. His collection "will be [a] model expressing such objects in nature as must be familiar to every people savage or civilized."[8]

Figure 5-1: Page of Jefferson's Indian Vocabularies

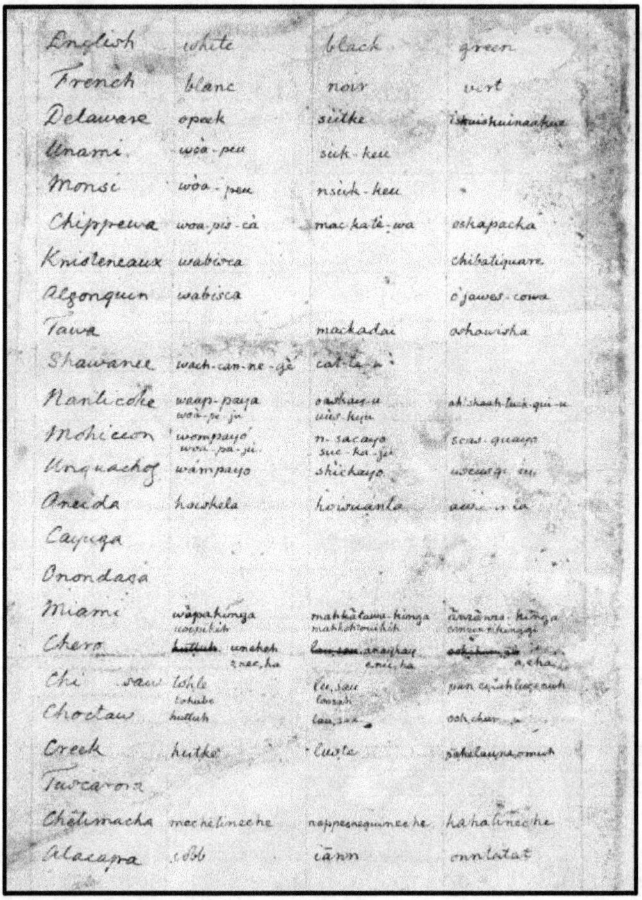

---

[8] TJ to Peter Wilson, 20 Jan. 1816.

Figure 5-1 shows a page from Jefferson's collection. He begins with the English and French for "white," "black," and "green," and lists the names of those words for various Indians' nations.

By March 1800, Jefferson has gathered up "a large collection," which he is about to print, "lest by some accident it might be lost." He waits, however, for "the Great Southern languages" of the Cherokee, Creek, Choctaw, and Chickasaw tribes. He has written to David Campbell about the Cherokee words, and he enjoins Benjamin Hawkins (14 Mar. 1800) for words from the other three tribes. He gives Hawkins a list of English words which need Creek, Choctaw, and Chickasaw equivalents. "you need not take the trouble of having any others taken, because all my other vocabularies are confined to these words, and my object is only a comparative view."

What words does Jefferson want? We can use his list from his Unquachog vocabulary as a rough guide. His interest is nowise exhaustion. His aim is "only a comparative view"—ultimately, to decide the issue of whether Eastern Asians are descendants of American Aborigines, or the converse.

On September 10, 1800, Jefferson acquires a list of Chickasaw words from Daniel Smith.

Just prior to assuming the office of the presidency of the young nation, Jefferson writes (12 Jan. 1801) to Scottish naturalist, inventor, and explorer William Dunbar (1749–1810, Figure 5-2), with whom he has begun to correspond in June 1799, to thank him for his gift of "the little vocabularies of Bedais, Jankawis and Teghas." He adds that he now has a sizeable collection. "I have it much at heart to make as extensive a collection as possible of the Indian tongues. I have at present about 30. tolerably full, among which the number radically different, is truly wonderful." He then mentions an orthographical nodus, related to the vocabularies he has received from correspondents. "Handfuls of men"—Englishmen, Frenchmen, Germans, and others—have collected the vocabularies and have distinctly preserved them. Jefferson adds that at one time he considered reducing all to one orthography—to standardize the disparate orthographies. "I soon become sensible that this would occasion two sources of error instead of one. I therefore think it best to keep them in the form of orthography in which they were taken, only noting whether that were English, French, German, or what."

Figure 5-2: William Dunbar

What precisely are those errors in reduction of all to the English orthography, he never says. In an earlier letter to David Campbell (14 Mar. 1800), he mentions the nodus of failure of English to capture certain sound of Cherokee words. That can only be the difficulty. Since it is impossible for any one European language to capture the subtle sounds of various Indian dialects, it is perhaps best not to "reduce" German, French, Italian, or Spanish lists to English—at least, that is a task that would exceed Jefferson's talents and would be too exhaustive of his time.

Upon completion of Captain Lewis' expedition to the Pacific Ocean and his list of Indians' vocabularies, and reception of news of Natives "West of the Missisipi & South of the Arcansa [River],"[9] Jefferson enjoins Indian agent and

---

[9] The Arkansas River begins in the Rocky Mountains, to the west of Denver, and moves in an east-southeasterly course through Arkansas, Oklahoma, and Arkansas, where it meets the Mississippi River.

The Languages & Origins of Indians

explorer John Sibley (1757–1837, 27 May 1805) to glean whatever vocabularies he can of those Aborigines. He already has "the vocabularies of the Attacapas & Chetimachas," north of the Arcansa.

The project of collecting Indian vocabularies—a project of some 30 years—is despoiled just after he leaves the presidency. On September 21, 1809, he writes to naturalist and physician Benjamin Smith Barton (1766–1815, Figure 5-3) of "an irreparable misfortune." Jefferson writes:

> I have now been thirty years availing myself of every possible opportunity of procuring Indian vocabularies to the same set of words: my opportunities were probably better than will ever occur again to any person having the same desire. I had collected about 50. Furthermore, had digested most of them in collateral columns and meant to have printed them the last year of my stay in Washington. But not having yet digested Capt Lewis's collection, nor having leisure then to do it, I put it off till I should return home. The whole, as well digest as originals, were packed in a trunk of stationary & sent round by water with about 30. other packages of my effects from Washington, and while ascending James River, this package, on account of it's weight & presumed precious contents, was singled out & stolen. The thief, being disappointed on opening it, threw into the river all it's contents of which he thought he could make no use. among these were the whole of the vocabularies.

Figure 5-3: Benjamin Barton Smith

Some papers were found on a muddy shore, but they were "so defaced by the mud and water" that they could not be salvaged. There was, however, one exception: Lewis' morsel of the Pani language and a fragment of another language, which could not be deciphered. The account intimates that all of Jefferson's vocabularies, including Lewis' acquisitions, were lost. Jefferson ends disconsolately, "I may make another attempt to collect, although I am too old to expect to make much progress in it."[10]

Regarding the mishap, Jefferson writes earlier to George Jefferson (18 May 1809):

> On the subject of the trunk N° 28. I am not without a hope that an interview by yourself with the drayman and Harry, the first time he goes down, may yet discover it's fate. I am anxious, not so much for the value, tho that was considerable and the assortment of paper particular, as for the instrument (Dynamometer) which it contained, the only one in America, & imported for a particular object which had not yet been fulfilled. it is well ascertained by the concurrent information of the other three boatmen who remained with the boats that but 3. trunks came to them, which were the 3. I recieved including mr Burwell's empty one. and as you saw 4. delivered the missing one must have miscarried between your warehouse & the boats. this fixes it absolutely on the drayman & Harry jointly, and an examination of them may bring the matter to light. I think it would be well to advertize the trunk, because if they disposed of the contents, their description will betray them. it may be described as "a hair trunk of about 7. or 8. feet cubic contents, labelled on a card on the top TI. N° 28. containing principally writing paper of various qualities, but also some other articles of stationary, a pocket telescope with a brass case, a Dynamometer in steel and brass[1] or instrument for measuring the exertions of draught animals, a collection of vocabularies of the Indian languages, & some other articles not particularly noted in the memorandum taken." make the reward what you think proper under 20. or 30. dollars. the value was probably about 150. dollars exclusive of the Vocabularies, which had been the labour of 30 years in collection for publication.

Jefferson is flattened by the catastrophe. His intention was, "on retiring from public business, to have digested these into some order, so as to shew, not only

---

[10] See TJ to Peter Wilson, 20 Jan. 1816, and TJ to José Correa da Serra, 26 Apr. 1816.

what relations of language existed among our own aborigines," but also to have something to say about the relationship between Eastern Asians and Native Americans.[11] There are, he tells Barton, some 73 words common to both continents. Yet the calamity forces a change of plans.

Yet despite Jefferson's account of his vocabularies in the 1809 letter to Barton, the vocabularies of Lewis were not lost. He tells Peter S. Du Ponceau (30 Dec. 1817): "If you can recover Capt Lewis's collection, they will make an important addition, for there was no part of his instructions which he executed more fully or carefully, never meeting with a single Indian of a new tribe, without making his vocabulary the 1st object." Their fate was complex, and that complex story is best left in Jefferson's own words in a subsequent letter to Du Ponceau (7 July 1820):

> The numerous vocabularies they [Lewis and Clarke] obtained of the Indian languages are to be collated and published. altho' the whole expence of the expedition was furnished by the public, and the information to be derived from it was theirs also, yet on the return of mess^{rs} Lewis & Clarke the government thought it just to leave to them any pecuniary benefit which might result from a publication of the papers, and supposed indeed that this would secure the best form of publication. but the property in these papers still remained in the government for the benefit of their constituents. with the measures taken by Govr Lewis for their publication, I was never acquainted. after his death Govr Clarke put them, in the first instance, into the hands of the late Dr Barton, from whom some of them passed to mr Biddle, and some again, I believe, from him to mr Allen. while the MS. books of journals were in the hands of Dr Barton, I wrote to him on behalf of Govr Lewis's family requesting earnestly, that, as soon as these should be published, the originals might be returned, as the family wished to have them preserved. he promised in his answer that it should be faithfully done. after his death, I obtained, thro' the kind agency of mr Correa, from mrs Barton, three of those books, of which I knew there had been 10. or 12. having myself read them. these were all she could find. the rest therefore, I presume are in the hands of the other gentlemen. after the agency I had had, in effecting this expedition, I thought myself authorised, and indeed that it would be expected of me that I should

---

[11] TJ to Peter Wilson, 20 Jan. 1816.

follow up the subject, and endeavor to obtain it's fruits for the public. I wrote to Genl Clarke therefore for authority to recieve the original papers. he gave it in the letters to mr Biddle and to myself, which I now inclose, as the custody of these papers belonged properly to the War-office, and that was vacant at the time, I have waited several months for it's being filled. but the office still remaining vacant, and my distance rendering any effectual measures, by myself, impracticable, I ask the agency of your committee, within whose province I propose to place the matter, by making it the depository of the papers generally. I therefore now forward to them the 3. volumes of MS. journals in my possession, and authorise them, under Genl Clarke's letters, to enquire for and to recieve the rest. so also the astronomical and geographical papers, those relating to zoological, botanical, and mineral subjects, with the Indian vocabularies, and statistical tables relative to the Indians. … and if it should be within the views of the historical committee to have the Indian vocabularies digested and published, I would add to them the remains of my collection. I had thro' the course of my life availed myself of every opportunity of procuring vocabularies of the languages of every tribe which either myself or my friends could have access to. they amounted to about 40. more or less perfect. but in their passage from Washington to this place, the trunk in which they were was stolen and plundered, and some fragments only of the vocabularies were recovered. still however they were such as would be worth incorporation with a larger work, and shall be at the service of the historical commee, if they can make any use of them.[12]

Not in possession of Lewis' vocabularies and with his own collection mostly annihilated, Jefferson continues to collect words from Native tribes—he mentions, for illustration, reception of vocabulary of the Nottoway tribe in the letter Du Ponceau[13]—but he makes no especial effort to do so. Vocabularies sent to him he saves and then sends to the American Philosophical Society.[14] In a late-in-life letter to Constantine Samuel Refinesque (11 Aug. 1824), he says, "it is time for me to resign to younger hands the cares of literature, and all other

---

[12] See also Megan Snyder-Camp, "'No General Use Can Ever Be Made of the Wrecks of My Loss': A Reconsidered History of the Indian Vocabularies Collected on the Lewis and Clark Expedition," *Wicazo Sa Review*, Vol. 30, No. 2, 2015: 129–39.

[13] See also TJ to JC, 16 Mar. 1814.

[14] TJ to Capt. William Clark, 8 Sept. 1816.

cares whatever, to which, while I had power, I have been always willingly subservient."

Jefferson's extant collection of 22 Indigenous languages is accessible at the American Philosophical Society.

Anthony Wallace acknowledges Jefferson's "pioneering effort" apropos of his collection and comparative study of Indian languages.[15] Jefferson set the stage for Benjamin Smith Barton's *New Views of the Origin of the Tribes and Nations of America* (1797) and *Etymology of Certain English Words and on Their Affinity to Words in the Languages of Different European, Asiatic and American (Indian) Nations* (1797) and years later Albert Gallatin's *Synopsis of the Indian Tribes of North America* (1823).

The activity of collecting Indians' vocabularies, as we have seen, was no mere avocation—a way of occupying himself in spare time. Scientific study, for Jefferson, was ever with an aim, never autotelic, hence his lifelong disdain of metaphysics, whether religious or philosophical. Jefferson's keen interest in Native American vocabularies was an effort to solve what was to him a knotty difficulty: the provenance of Native American. Noting stark similarities between Red Americans and Red Asians, Jefferson was convinced that the two peoples were of common ancestry—the etiological direction was the problem—and collected American Indian vocabularies to compare them with East Asian vocabularies to solve the problem. "The late discoveries of Captain Cook, coasting from Kamschatka to California, have proved that, if the two continents of Asia and America be separated at all, it is only by a narrow straight. So that from this side also, inhabitants may have passed into America: and the resemblance between the Indians of America and the Eastern inhabitants of Asia, would induce us to conjecture, that the former are descendants of the latter, or the later of the former."[16]

And so, given physical resemblances between American Indians and Eastern Asians, it is reasonable *prima facie* to assume common ancestry between the two: the Asians are progenitors of the Americans; the Americans, progenitors of the Asians; or there is a common ancestor of both. Given the proximity of the

---

[15] Anthony F.C. Wallace, *Jefferson and the Indians: The Tragic Fate of the First Americans* (Cambridge: Belknap Press, 1999), 146.
[16] Thomas Jefferson, *Notes on the State of Virginia*, ed. William Peden (Chapel Hill: University of North Carolina Press, 1954), 101.

two continents—they, being separated merely by a narrow straight—it is reasonable to consider only the first two hypotheses.

How would anyone decide between the two hypotheses?

Writes Jefferson: "A knowledge of their several languages would be the most certain evidence of their derivation which could be produced. In fact, it is the best proof of the affinity of nations which ever can be referred to." One has merely to catalog the number of types on each continent and their varieties of language to answer that question. "Were vocabularies formed of all the languages spoken in North and South America," says Jefferson, "preserving their appelations [sic] of the most common objects in nature, of those which must be present to every nation barbarous or civilized, with the inflections of their nouns and verbs, their principles of regimen and concord, and these deposited in all the public libraries, it would furnish opportunities to those skilled in the languages of the old world to compare them with these, now, or at a future time, and hence to construct the best evidence of the derivation of this part of the human race."[17]

First, Jefferson argues that the Eskimo should be disregarded. He notes that similarity of language and similarity of physical features shows the Eskimo to have originated from Greenland. Next, appealing to the numerous Native American tongues and comparing them to what he knows of the varied tongues of Eastern Asians, Jefferson says: "There will be found probably twenty in America for one in Asia, of those radical languages, so called because, if they were ever the same, they have lost all resemblance to each other. A separation into dialects may be the work of a few ages only, but for two dialects to recede from one another till they have lost all vestiges of their common origin, must require an immense course of time; perhaps not less than many people give to the age of the earth." The reasoning here is sound, if he has a sufficiency of relevant facts. Jefferson flatly concludes, "A greater number of those radical changes of language having taken place among the red men of America, proves them of greater antiquity."[18]

Jefferson iterates that conclusion in a letter to Ezra Stiles (1727–1795), president of Yale College, and later a founder of Brown University (1 Sept. 1786):

> I suppose the settlement of our continent is of the most remote antiquity. The similitude between it's inhabitants and those of the

---

[17] Thomas Jefferson, *Notes on Virginia*, 101.
[18] Thomas Jefferson, *Notes on Virginia*, 102.

Eastern parts of Asia renders it probable that ours are descended from them, or they from ours. The latter is my opinion, founded on this single fact. Among the red inhabitants of Asia there are but a few languages radically different. But among our Indians the number of languages is infinite which are so radically different as to exhibit at present no appearance of their having been derived from a common source. The time necessary for the generation of so many languages must be immense.

Figure 5-4: John Sibley

Nevertheless, Jefferson's conclusion, firmly stated in his *Notes on the State of Virginia* and in his letter to Stiles, is years later rescinded. "the question whether the Indians of America have emigrated from another continent," he writes on May 27, 1805, to John Sibley, Indian agent of the Northwest Territory (Figure 5-4), "is still undecided. their vague & imperfect traditions can satisfy no mind on that subject." Jefferson then discusses a collection of words, which Jefferson has never seen, that was in the possession of the late Catherine the Great of Russia. "a comparison of our collection with that will probably decide the question of the sameness or difference of origin, altho it will not decide which is the mother country & which the colony." Jefferson here is much less optimistic about precisely what any comparative study can show.

We do, it seems, have an answer to the question that so vexed Jefferson about the origins of American Natives. Native Americans migrated to America from Siberia, and that occurred, scientists believe, in at least three waves, not one. This research, DNA based, follows up and confirms a theory of Joseph Greenberg, who claims that in the first wave, Siberians, speaking "Amerind," came to North America and migrated to South America. Greenberg's conclusions are based on scrutiny of linguistic similarities and differences. Two later waves brought those who spoke Eskimo-Aleut and Na-Dene, the language of the Apache and Navajo Indians. The DNA researchers, David Reich of Harvard and Andres Ruiz-Linares of University College London and 62 other researchers across the globe, argue that their data show, *pace* Greenberg, that the second and third waves of migrators intermixed with those of the first.[19] The researchers studied DNA from 52 Native American and 17 Siberian groups in an effort to settle the question. Their data showed that there were at least three migrations of Siberians, with many reversals, though the researchers said nothing about the years of migration. Prior research indicates that at some 15,000 years ago, glaciation so lowered the waters of the oceans that there was a 1,000-mile land bridge, Beringia, between Alaska and Siberia. The first wave of explorers moved southward along the Pacific coast; the second, much smaller, greatly influenced the Natives of the far North—the Aleut-Inuits; the third, migrated toward what is today Hudson Bay. Figure 5-5 illustrates the movement across Beringia, now the Bering Strait.

Other letters of Jefferson show the number of wildly speculative hypotheses concerning Natives' languages and their origins, though those wild hypotheses were commonly entertained by prominent men of Jefferson's day: e.g., that Indians were descendants of Hebrews, Welshmen, Greeks, or Carthaginians. I offer a few illustrations.

Politician and fellow Founding Father Edward Rutledge (1749–1800, Figure 5-6) writes Jefferson on October 23, 1787, to thank him for a copy of his *Notes on Virginia*. Rutledge turns at letter's end to Jefferson's conclusion that East Asians are of North American descent. "You seem to consider the quarter of the Globe from whence America was peopled, and the Manner, as now reduced to a certainty. But, it is not so absolutely determined, as to preclude conjecture."

---

[19] Michael H. Crawford, *The Origins of Native Americans: Evidence from Anthropological Genetics* (Cambridge: Cambridge University Press, 1998).

The Languages & Origins of Indians

Figure 5-5: Siberians Migrating into the Americas

Rutledge writes of a friend, a man of large sense and learning,[20] who maintains that Native Americans have their provenance from Carthage. When the Carthaginian Hanno (fifth century B.C.) set out to explore the coast of Africa—some scholars today assert Hanno never went beyond Morocco while other claim that he found his way to Cameroon—some of his ships were blown off their course, and found their way to the Gulph of Mexico and settled in the New World. In confirmation of that theory, there is an "exact resemblance" between the people in that part of North Africa (Tunisia) and the Creek Indians. Moreover, there are "words of both, sounding alike, and conveying the same meaning."

---

[20] A certain Dr. Andrew Turnbull (c. 1720–1792), who settled in Charleston, SC, prior to his passing.

Figure 5-6: Edward Rutledge

Jefferson (18 July 1812), ever cordial, thanks his friend and politely addresses the extravagant hypothesis. "I ... see nothing impossible in his conjecture." That is, of course, far from a sure endorsement of the plausibility of the theory. Jefferson, ever curious apropos of the origins of Aborigines, turns to the subject of the ancient Carthaginian language still being used by descendants in the interior mountainous parts of Barbary. "If so, a vocabulary of their tongue can still be got, and if your friend will get one of the Creek languages, the comparison will decide."

One month earlier in a letter to John Adams (11 June 1812), Jefferson mentions two objectionable accounts of the history of the American Indians.

First, he criticizes Joseph François Lafitau's account of American Indians in his *Mœurs des Sauvages Ameriquains, comparées aux Mœurs des Premiers Temps* (1724)

> Lafitau had in his head a preconceived theory on the mythology, manners, institutions and government of the antient [sic] nations of Europe, Asia, and Africa, and seems to have entered on those of America only to fit them into the same frame, and to draw from them a

confirmation of this general theory. He keeps up a perpetual parallel, in all those articles, between the Indians of America, and the antients of the other quarters of the globe. He selects therefore all the facts, and adopts all the falsehoods which favor his theory, and very gravely retails such absurdities as zeal for a theory could anyone swallow.

Though a missionary among the Natives of the North, Lafitau, says Jefferson, depends on the writings of others in preference to his own experiences.

Second, he castigates James Adair, who maintains in *The History of the American Indians; Particularly Those Nations adjoining to the Mississippi, East and West Florida, Georgia, South and North Carolina, and Virginia* (1775), that American Indians are descendants of the Jews in that they have the same laws, usages, rites, ceremonies, sacrifices, priests, prophets, fast, festivals, and, almost, the same religion. Having familiarity only with the Indians of the South, Adair generalizes to all American Indians as if it is unquestioned that a hundred languages, each differing from many others as "Greek from Gothic," have one common prototype.

I end this chapter with a botheration. Jefferson incessantly insists on a preference for knowledge that can be put to human use, human betterment—e.g., knowing how to grow plants that are both beautiful and useful (e.g., comestible or medicinal)—so there is reason to ask why Jefferson is obsessed with answering the question about the provenance of Natives. It is manifest from several letters that he collects his varied vocabularies to answer the question of provenance. Hence there is a use to his efforts of a collection of vocabularies. Yet of what use is an answer to the question of Indians' provenance?

One possibility is to refute critics like Buffon and Raynal concerning the inferiority of the North American land and climate. If the number and variety of tribes with distinct tongues, or relatively so, in North America are far more than those in Asia—in Query XI of *Notes on Virginia* he says there are likely 20 Indian tongues for every Asian tongue[21]—then it shows North America to be a territory most fecund and of genial climate. Yet there is then the additional nodus that Jefferson curiously never addresses: Why is it that in a land fecund and with a climate generally genial, Natives have not advanced from the state of savages?

---

[21] Thomas Jefferson, *Notes on Virginia*, 102.

Chapter 6

The Morality and Aesthetic Sensitivity of Indians

"They will crayon out an animal, a plant, or a country"

Comte de Buffon's thesis of the abasement of the animals of the Americas has implications for the physical and mental excellence of Native Americans, and Jefferson's refutation of Buffon was meant to parry Buffon's verbal abasements. What, however, can be said about the moral and aesthetic sensibility of Natives? That question must also be considered, given that humans, for Jefferson, by nature, have intellectual, moral, and aesthetic faculties, each distinct from the others, and that the faculties of humans are functionally biological. Yet each of those faculties can be stultified by under- or overstimulation: e.g., exposure to metaphysical religious thinking before the mind is sufficiently mature or art being overdone (e.g., rococo in France) among a wealthy aristocracy at the expense of the penurious many.

Jefferson, as we have seen in Chapter 2, takes himself in the lengthy Query VI of *Notes on the State of Virginia* to have shown that there are no important physical differences between Indians and Whites. He has, however, heretofore said little about Indians' mental powers except to assert that they are the equals of Whites vis-à-vis mental vivacity and activity. Yet, as an out-and-out physicalist, mental vivacity and activity, for Jefferson, are dependent on physical robustness, so there is no clean severance between the physical and the mental. Consequently, if there are no glaring physical differences, we ought not to assume glaring mental differences—at least, not without sufficient data.[1]

---

[1] Thomas Jefferson, *Notes on the State of Virginia*, ed. William Peden (Chapel Hill: University of North Carolina Press, 1954), 61–62.

The cultural differences between Indians' and Whites' societies are stark and do not allow for easy appraisal of their genius in the sciences and in the fine arts and apropos of their moral sensibility.

Buffon, we have seen in Chapter 2, thought of Indians as degenerative humans. Their principal defect was a lack of sexual potency. They "lack ardor for their females," and "consequently have no love for their fellow men." In sum, all feelings of society, from the most intimate familial to interfamilial affections, are weak or nonexistent. "Hence they have not communion, no commonwealth, no state of society." Morality is reduced to physical love. "Their heart is icy, their society cold, and their rule harsh." Buffon sums, "Nature, by refusing him the power of love, has treated him worse and lowered him deeper than any animal."[2]

It is reasonable to assert that Buffon works from effect to cause. In arguing that lack of sexual potency is the cause of dearth of social sentiments and lack of tight societies, it is likely Buffon etiologically works backwards from lack of laws and loose social structure to a presumed single cause: lack of sexual potency. Because of Indians' impotency, there is for them negligible sense of morality. All is reducible, presumable, to the relative coolth and wetness of the New World.

Jefferson, in contrast, works etiologically from cause to effect. He begins with climatic sameness of North American and small Native societies and notes that Indians, having no need of laws, have no laws. Moreover, laws, being a form of coercion, are morally prohibited. "The principles of their society forbidding all compulsion, they are to be led to duty and to enterprise by personal influence and persuasion."[3] Without laws, their moral sense—all humans roughly having an equal capacity for moral sensing—is what glues together members of a tribe. As he says in a letter to Edward Carrington (16 Jan. 1787), "Public opinion is in the place of law, & restrains morals as powerfully as laws ever did."

There is nothing in Jefferson's account in Queries VI and XI of *Notes on Virginia* to intimate that Natives are naturally defective in moral sensitivity. Yet everything Jefferson writes is suggestive of cultural immaturity, due to Indians' filiopiety—that is, being mired in tradition—and Jefferson thinks that that difficulty can be overcome through miscegenation with Americans and full

---

[2] Thomas Jefferson, *Notes on Virginia*, 58–59.
[3] Thomas Jefferson, *Notes on Virginia*, 62.

exposure to American culture and with an emphasis on American education. Jefferson writes in his 1818 Rockfish Gap Report:

> what, but education, has advanced us beyond the condition of our indigenous neighbors? and what chains them to their present state of barbarism and wretchedness, but a bigotted veneration for the supposed superlative wisdom of their fathers, and the preposterous idea that they are to look backward for better things, and not forward, longing, as it should seem, to return to the days of eating acorns and roots, rather than indulge in the degeneracies of civilization. and how much more encouraging to the achievements of science and improvement, is this, than the desponding view that the condition of man cannot be ameliorated, that what has been must ever be, and that, to secure ourselves where we are, we must tread with awful reverence in the footsteps of our fathers.[4]

What does it mean to be naturally equivalent to Americans, but culturally retarded with respect to them in moral sensitivity?

Following moral-sense and moral-sentiment theorists of his day—e.g., Earl of Shaftesbury, Francis Hutcheson, Thomas Reid, Lord Kames, Adam Smith, and David Hume—Jefferson's moral sense is a natural faculty, perhaps based in the organ of the heart, for sensing actions, naturally in accord with human wellbeing, as good, and sensing actions, naturally discordant with human wellbeing, as bad. It exists from birth, as does intellect but requires cultivation through refinement by exposure to circumstances requiring moral activity and subsequent praise or blame for correct or incorrect action—*viz.*, shaping over time. Jefferson is insistent that it does not require the aid of reason to recognize right and wrong actions, but he does concede that reason must sometimes come to the assistance of the moral sense—for instance, when circumstances disallow morally correct action, as in the case of immediate riddance of slavery in the South.[5] To daughter Martha Jefferson (11 Dec. 1783), Jefferson describes the action of the moral sense as an articulated feeling—"You will feel something within you which will tell you it is wrong [or right]"—that discourages or

---

[4] Thomas Jefferson, Rockfish Gap Report, *The Scholars' Thomas Jefferson: Vital Writings of a Vital American*, ed. M. Andrew Holowchak (Newcastle upon Tyne: Cambridge Scholars, 2021), 306–13.

[5] For more, see M. Andrew Holowchak, *Thomas Jefferson, Moralist* (Jefferson, NC: McFarland, 2017).

encourages a course of action. To grandson Thomas Jefferson Randolph (24 Nov. 1808), Jefferson states he eschewed "temptations and difficulties" by asking himself what Dr. William Small, George Wythe, and Peyton Randolph would do in the same situation as his.[6]

What evidence of Natives' moral sensitivity did Jefferson see?

Figure 6-1: Indian Hunting a Buffalo

There are numerous illustrations, says Jefferson, of American Natives' bravery and address in war or on the hunt. Of their bravery and address in war we have multiplied proofs, because we have been the subject on which they were exercised." Moreover, a warrior "endures tortures with a firmness unknown almost to religious enthusiasm with us."[7] Moreover, hunting large and powerful animals like bison (Figure 6-1) required strength and large bravery. So, their courage and loyalty to their tribesmen cannot be called into question.

---

[6] Small was Jefferson's teacher at William and Mary; Wythe, his mentor in law and lifelong friend; and Randolph, a Founding Father and first president of the Continental Congress.

[7] Thomas Jefferson, *Notes on Virginia*, 60 and 62.

Again, Indians' moral affections "comprehend his other connections, weakening, as with us, from circle to circle, as they recede from the center." Beginning with family, those affections spread out, concentric circle by concentric circle, to include others, with the outermost circles being the least intimate and duty-bound.[8] Jefferson's reference to circles, concentricity implied, is clearly a reference to the ancient Stoic philosopher Hierocles,[9] who explains how Stoic integration in the cosmos occurs through 10 concentric circles that bind people locally and globally and indicate layers of moral duty.

> The first and closest circle is one that a person has drawn as though around a center—his own mind. That circle encloses the body and anything taken for the sake of the body. It is virtually the smallest circle and it almost touches the center itself. Next, the second one, further removed from the center but enclosing the first circle, contains parents, siblings, wife, and children. The third one has in it uncles and aunts, grandparents, nephews, nieces, and cousins. The next circle (4) includes the other relatives, and that is followed by (5) the circle of local residents, then (6) the circle of fellow-demes-men, next (7) that of fellow-citizens, and then (8) in the same way the circle of people from neighboring towns, and (9) the circle of fellow-countrymen. The outermost and largest circle (10), which encompasses all the rest, is that of the whole human race.[10]

A gigantic defect of Indians' moral sensibility, says Jefferson, is the tyrannical nature of Native males vis-à-vis their women. A sure sign of their moral backwardness is the drudgery of Native American women. As drudges—thinks Jefferson, and here again his stadialism comes much into play—they do the work that in a more refined society the men ought to be doing.[11] Women are not

---

[8] Thomas Jefferson, *Notes on Virginia*, 60.

[9] See TJ to George Ticknor, 8 Feb. 1816, and TJ to Nicolas Dufief, 11 Apr. 1817.

[10] M. Andrew Holowchak, *The Stoics: A Guide for the Perplexed* (London: Continuum, 2006), 75.

[11] For a fine account of the significant role of women in Native American nations, see Gail MacLeith, "'Your women are of no small consequence': Native American Women, Gender, and Early American History" in *The Practice of U.S. Women's History: Narratives, Intersections, and Dialogues,* eds. *S. Jay Kleiberg, Ellen Boris, and Vicki Ruiz* (New Brunswick: Rutgers University Press, 2007), and Susan Sleeper-Smith, *Indigenous Prosperity and American Conquest: Indian Women of the Ohio River Valley, 1690–1792* (Chapel Hill: University of North Carolina Press, 2018).

constitutionally fit for drudgery. Appreciation of the natural equality of women is shown by allowance of them to do the things that they, by nature, are best suited to do: e.g., domestic chores that are not so physically taxing.[12]

Is Jefferson here merely being culturally close-minded?

Oliver M. Spencer, roughly of Jefferson's day, relates his observations as a captive among Natives in what is today Southern Ohio. "I have often seen families travelling, and while the poor squaw, bending under the weight of a heavy load, and the girls carrying packs, or the smaller children on their shoulders, were labouring along, the lazy [male] Indian in front might be seen, with nothing but his rifle and blanket, and the boys with only a bow and arrows, or a reed blow gun."[13]

What of the sanguinariness of many Indian tribes?

Of that, Jefferson was aware. He was thus disinclined to admit Indians as allies of American militia in skirmishes or wars. That comes out, especially in Jefferson's execration of Henry Hamilton's use of Indians during the Revolutionary War and his bestial treatment of American prisoners. Jefferson writes of the barbarity of Hamilton, who was the British governor of Detroit and superintendent of Indian affairs, in a letter to William Phillips (22 July 1779):

> He who employs another to do a deed, makes the Deed his own. If he calls in the hand of the assassin, or murderer, himself becomes the assassin or murderer. The known rule of warfare with the Indian Savages is an indiscriminate butchery of men women and children. These Savages, under this well—known Character, are employed by the British nation as allies in the War against the Americans. Governor Hamilton undertakes to be the conductor of the War. In the execution of that undertaking, he associates small parties of the whites under his immediate command with large parties of the Savages, and sends them to act, sometimes jointly, sometimes separately, not against our forts, or armies in the feild, but the farming settlements on our frontiers. Governor Hamilton then is himself the butcher of Men Women and Children.

---

[12] Thomas Jefferson, *Notes on Virginia*, 60.
[13] Oliver M. Spencer, *Indian Captivity: A True Narrative of the Capture of Rev. O.M. Spencer by the Indians, in the Neighbourhood of Cincinnati* (New York: Carlton & Porter, 1835), 72.

The Morality and Aesthetic Sensitivity of Indians 81

Jefferson recommends confinement, under the strictest circumstances, for Hamilton.

Nonetheless, Jefferson says nothing of Indian sanguinariness in his *Notes on Virginia* as he does in the letter to Phillips and elsewhere, and that smacks, as it were, of agendaism. Is he so focused on refuting Buffon's assertion of Indians' barbarism that he willfully overpasses discussion of that in his book?

James Adair, in Jefferson's day, documented the bloodthirst of some Indian nations, much of which was of ritualistic significance. "Their thirst for the blood of their reputed enemies is not to be quenched with a few drops—The more they drink, the more it inflames their thirst. When they dip their finger in human blood they are restless till they plunge themselves in it." It was common to kill as many of an enemy as was possible. Women and children were not exceptions. Nonetheless, adds Adair, Natives only with large provocation waged war with other tribes. When left to themselves, they consider with the greatest exactness and foresight, all the attending circumstances of war." Retribution was a common provenance of war.[14]

Adair continues. After victory in battle, warriors return to the scene of fighting and dismember their fallen enemies. One warrior "cuts off and carries this member of the dead person, another that, as joyful trophies of a decisive victory" to be taken to their tribe. The first order, however, is to remove their scalps, as material trophies.[15]

Turning to the torture of prisoners brought to the tribe, Adair notes, "No representation can possibly [sic] be given, so shocking to humanity, as their unmerciful method of tormenting their devoted prisoner; and as it is so contrary to the standard of the rest of known world." Each, and one at a time, is stripped of clothes, tied to a stake, while his feet are covered with "bear-skin maccaseenes."[16]

When there is the signal for death, continues Adair vis-à-vis the torture of a captured warrior of another tribe,

> victims arms are fast pinioned, and a strong grape-vine is tied round his neck, to the top of the war-pole, allowing him to track around, about fifteen yards. They fix some tough clay on his head, to secure the scalp

---

[14] James Adair, *The History of the American Indians* (London: 1775), 207–10 and 379–80.
[15] James Adair, *The History of the American Indians*, 387–88.
[16] James Adair, *The History of the American Indians*, 388–89.

from the blazing torches. Unspeakable pleasure now fills the exulting crowd of spectators, and the circle fills with the Amazon and merciless executioners—The suffering warrior however is not dismayed; with an insulting manly voice he sings the war-song! and with gallant contempt he tramples the rattling gourd with pebbles in it to pieces, and outbraves even death itself. The women make a furious onset with their burning torches: his pain is soon so excruciating, that he rushes out from the pole, with the fury of the molt savage bead of prey, and with the vine fweeps down all before him, kicking, biting, and trampling them, with the greatest despite. The circle immediately fills again, either with the fame, or fresh persons: they attack him on every fide—now he runs to the pole for shelter, but the flames pursue him. Then with champing teeth, and sparkling eye-balls, he breaks through their contrasted circle afresh, and acts every part, that the highest courage, most raging fury, and blackest despair can prompt him to. But he is sure to be over-power'd by numbers, and alter some time the fire affects his tender parts.—Then they pour over him a quantity of cold water, and allow him a proper time of respite, till his spirits recover, and he is capable of suffering new tortures. Then the like cruelties are repeated till he falls down, and happily becomes insensible of pain. Now they scalp him, in the manner before described: dismember, and carry off all the exterior branches of. the body, (*pudendis non exceptis*) in shameful, and savage triumph. This is the most favourable treatment their devoted captives receive: it would be too shocking to humanity either to give, or peruse, every particular of their conduit in such doleful tragedies—nothing can equal these scenes, but those of the merciful Romish inquisition.[17]

There is never a show of pity by any members of a tribe, sums Adair. "The women sing with religious joy, all the while they are torturing the devoted victim, and peals of laughter resound through the crowded theatre—especially if he fears to die." Yet the tortured warrior "puts on a bold austere countenance, and carries it through all his pains." He whoops and recites his deeds of valor and bravery, and he shouts of revenge.[18]

---

[17] James Adair, *The History of the American Indians*, 390–91.
[18] James Adair, *The History of the American Indians*, 389–91.

The Morality and Aesthetic Sensitivity of Indians 83

Figure 6-2: Indians Torturing at the Stake

Iroquois—comprising Cayugas, Mohawks, Oneidas, Onondagas, and Senecans—of the Northwest were especially brutal, even cannibalistic. Methods of torture of captives from other tribes, for those who were not integrated into the tribe, were in general consistent. It would begin with the fingers: ripping out fingernails and cutting off some fingers to prevent captives from using a weapon. Captives would be stripped and forced to sing and dance. They thereafter would be subjected to a very slow and agonizing death, which occurred at sunrise—a test of the captives' courage and endurance. Women and children participated in the torture, which invariably involved fire. Those who were broken quickly were forthwith and shamefully executed. Eating the flesh of a dead captive usually followed, and that was practiced too by Hurons and Winnebagos. Torture and execution, ritualized, almost certainly always had religious significance. So, too, did the ritualized cannibalism, along with the drinking of blood, for the Iroquois believed that one took up the spirit of what one ate. Thus, cannibalism of a great warrior of another tribe was common in Jefferson's day,[19] though the religious significance of that act certainly went unnoticed by Adair.

---

[19] Hierosme Lalemant, *"Of the Treachery of the Iroquois,"* in *Jesuit Relations and Allied Documents: Travels and Explorations of the Jesuit Missionaries in New France, 1610–1791*, Vol. 30, ed. Reuben Gold Thwaites (Cleveland: The Burrows Brothers Company, 1899), 152–

In addition to the discussion of Indians' moral sensitivity, there is also Natives' aesthetic sense. Jefferson, again, in his *Notes on Virginia* proffers discussion of Indians' sense of beauty and sublimity. Yet before broaching that subject, there needs to be some discussion of Jefferson and his aesthetic sense.

Like many philosophers of his day—e.g., William Hogarth, Edmund Burke, Adam Smith, and Lord Kames—Jefferson makes purchase of an aesthetic sense, which is a sensory faculty, independent of reason and moral sensibility. It is, roughly, the ability to see beauty and sublimity in things exciting those sensations, as well as their opposites. Though independent of the moral sense as a faculty, when refined, it works intimately with the moral sense, in that, for illustration, the things that naturally incited feelings of moral worth also incited feelings of beauty.[20] To Thomas Law (13 June 1814), Jefferson states, "We have indeed an innate sense [aesthetic sense or taste] of what we call beautiful: but that is exercised chiefly on subjects addressed to the fancy, whether thro' the eye, in visible forms, as landscape, animal figure, dress drapery, architecture, the composition of colours &c. or to the imagination directly, as imagery, style, or measure in prose or poetry, or whatever else constitutes the domain of criticism or taste, a faculty entirely distinct from the moral one."

The fine arts for Jefferson are eight: criticism, poetry, rhetoric, oratory, gardening, architecture, painting and sculpture (treated as one), and music. Outside of some evidence of oratorical eloquence of Natives and the rhetorical skills behind them, they show signs of aesthetic excellence in painting and sculpture. Having not had exposure to European works of art, they "will often carve figures on their pipes not destitute of design and merit. They will crayon out an animal, a plant, or a country, so as to prove the existence of a germ in their minds which only wants cultivation."[21]

There is also evidence of capacity for refinement of taste as well as genius to be found in American natives' capacity for oratory, "displayed chiefly in their own councils." One instance is "of very superior luster" and challenges even Demosthenes' and Cicero's orations. It is the speech of Mingo chief, Logan (Figure 6-3).

204, and Colin G. Calloway, "American Indians: Resistance or Accommodation," in *Interpretations of American History, Patterns & Perspectives*, ed. Francis G. Couvares, Martha Saxton, Gerald N. Grob, and George Athan Billias (New York: The Free Press, 2000), 61–99.

[20] See M. Andrew Holowchak, *Thomas Jefferson, Taste, and the Fine Arts* (Wilmington, DE: Vernon Press, 2023), chap. 1.

[21] Thomas Jefferson, *Notes on Virginia*, 140.

Figure 6-3: Mingo, Chief Logan

Jefferson then tells the story of Chief Logan, who suffered injustice bravely at the hands of Whites. In spring 1774, two Shawnees committed a robbery and murder of a white inhabitant of the frontiers of Virginia. The neighboring Whites were outraged and sought retribution. And so, Col. Cresap—"a man infamous for the many murders he had committed on those much-injured people"—gathered, for revenge, some men and traveled down the Kanawha River. Espying a canoe with one man and several women and children, all unarmed, he and his men hid in the boscage at the river's bank. Upon natives alighting from their canoe, all were set on and killed. All were members of Logan's family.

That, Logan thought, was a return unworthy of the initial misdeed. Consequently, he declared war on the local Whites. In the autumn of 1774, there was a decisive battle fought at the mouth of the Kanawha River. Shawanees, Mingoes, and Delawares engaged the Virginian militia. The Whites won the battle and the Indians sued for peace. Because of the indignities he suffered, Logan thought that it was beneath him to be part of the Indians involved in negotiation. He did, however, send the following speech to be delivered to England's Lord Dunmore, then governor of Virginia.

> I appeal to any white man to say if ever he entered Logan's cabin hungry, and he gave him not meat; if ever he came cold and naked, and he clothed him not. During the course of the last long and bloody war, Logan remained idle in his cabin, an advocate for peace. Such was my love for the whites, that my countrymen pointed as they passed, and said, "Logan is the friend of white men." I had even thought to have lived with you, but for the injuries of one man. Col. Cresap, the last Spring, in cold blood, and unprovoked, murdered all the relations of Logan, not sparing even my women and children. There runs not a drop of my blood in the veins of any living creature. This called on me for revenge. I have sought it: I have killed many: I have fully glutted my vengeance. For my country, I rejoice at the beams of peace. But do not harbor a thought that mine is the joy of fear. Logan never felt fear. He will not turn on his heel to save his life. Who is there to mourn for Logan? Not one.[22]

Jefferson is abundantly aware that proffering the speech of one warrior, howsoever esteemed, does nothing to prove the oratorical skills of Indians. Yet the introduction of the speech functions much the same as his discussion of the Big Buffalo when Jefferson begins to discuss the quadrupeds of Virginia. In a climate that is avowedly inimical to biotic thriving, a climate that is wet and cold, it would be astonishing to find one singular instance of profound oratorical capacities just as it was astonishing to find the skeletal remains of an animal of the bulk of the mammoth.

Nonetheless, many Indian tribes highly prized the art of oratory. Another great Native American orator was Red Jacket (1750–1830, Figure 6-4), whose study of the persuasive elocution of Logan—he much envied Logan's skills—made him an important Iroquois chief. Enthralled by Logan's persuasiveness, "he resolved to attain if possible the same high standard of eloquence." He would be known to spend many hours in the woods where "he had been

---

[22] Thomas Jefferson, *Notes on Virginia*, 63. For the controversy of the affair of Chief Logan, see Frank Shuffleton, "Relative to the Murder of Logan's Family, *Thomas Jefferson: Notes on the State of Virginia*, ed. Frank Shuffleton (New York: Penguin, 1999), 233–64.

playing Logan." His attitude was graceful; his gestures, significant; his intonation, perfect; his pauses, effective; and his gesticulations and facial expressions, exemplary.[23] Figure 6-4 is the famous painting of Red Jacket by Robert Walter Weir. Red Jacket wear the medal of peace given to him by George Washington. In the backgrounds is the falls of Niagara. Red Jacket was very fond of this portrait.

Figure 6-4: Senecan, Chief Red Jacket

---

[23] J. Niles Hubbard, *Red Jacket and His People, 1750–1830* (New York: Burt Franklin, 1886), 53–54.

Politician and U.S. marshal Thomas Morris writes of his impression of Red Jacket: "Red Jacket was ... well formed, with an intelligent countenance, and a fine eye.... He was the most graceful public speaker I have ever know; his manner was most dignified and easy. He was fluent, and at times witty and sarcastic. He was quick and ready at reply."[24]

As W.C. Bryant notes—he was speaking at the ceremony of reinterment of Red Jacket—the chief was aided by a flexibility and sonority of the Iroquois language:

> Their language was flexible and sonorous, the sense largely depending upon inflection, copious in vowel sounds, abounding in metaphor; affording constant opportunity for the ingenious combination and construction of words to image delicate, and varying shades of thought, and to express vehement manifestations of passion; admitting of greater and more sudden variations in pitch, than is permissible in English oratory, and encouraging pantomimic gesture, for greater force of effect.[25]

Figure 6-5: Postcard 1 of Entrance to Monticello

---

[24] J. Niles Hubbard, *Red Jacket and His People*, 159.
[25] J. Niles Hubbard, *Red Jacket and His People*, 11–17.

Jefferson's interest and pride in the aesthetic capacities of Indians is evident as one enters "Indian Hall" at the entrance of Monticello. The hall was part of the "huge cabinet, wherein whatsoever the hand of man by exquisite art or engine" might be placed on display" to complement "a most perfect and general library" and "a spacious, wonderful garden" as a microcosm of "the universal nature" made private for "a learned gentleman."[26]

Figure 6-6: Postcard 2 of Entrance to Monticello

There is there an impressive number of Native American artifacts, representative of Aborigines' artistic abilities. Figure 6-5, from an old postcard in my possession, shows feathered pipes, lances, arrows and bows, painted shields, quillwork, carved figures and a male head and female head (table, bottom left),[27] tomahawk, clubs and heads of clubs, leggings, and paintings on

---

[26] From Joyce Henri Robinson, "An American Cabinet of Curiosities: Thomas Jefferson's 'Indian Hall at Monticello,'" *Winterthur Portfolio*, Vol. 30, No. 1, 1995: 43.

[27] Baron de Montlezun, after visiting Monticello, said of the heads: "Two stone busts, sculptured by the Indians, one representing a man and the other a woman. The faces are hideous and very crudely executed. They are doubtless designated for worship, and have much similarity with those divinities of the Egyptians and Orientals whose picture are seen engraved in most of the books which treat of those people." Baron de Montlezun, "A

buffalos' hides[28] to the left as one enters Monticello (South and West Walls, left to right). Horns and animals' bones are on the North Wall (Figure 6-6). The beauty of Natives' art is its simplicity—*viz.*, it abstracts little from nature. He says to Captain William Clark (12 Sept. 1825), "Those of Indian arts stand very near to nature itself."

Historian Harold Hellenbrand baldly, and incautiously, writes of "Jefferson's disdain for Indian artifacts."[29] Yet it is impossible to believe that one disdaining their artifacts would showcase them at the entrance of Monticello.

Art dealer and gallerist Ivan Karp maintains that Indian Hall merely contains "trophies of imperial conquest."[30] The notion of hegemonic white imperial conquest is tiresome and deserves no counter-remonstration.

Elizabeth Chew, president of Montpelier, states apropos of Jefferson's collection of *naturalia* and *artificialia* that as "an individual of learning, intellect, distinction, and discrimination," and with the fiscal wherewithal, Jefferson put together a "collection [that] could even suggest the individual's ability to control or contain the world, represented by the wide range of items in the collection, or at least to occupy a privileged place in the cosmos."[31] Here again we get the tiresome language of American imperialism—"to control or contain the world," though it is unclear how a collection of *naturalia* and *artificialia* shows an ability—but in an enormously watered down form—"could even suggest…."—that, in effect, makes her assertion meaningless. She does offer certain insights about the fate of Indian artefacts—many of which might have succumbed to smoke and water with a fire at Brooks Hall of Natural Science at University of Virginia.

Frenchman Eyes the Museum," *Visitors to Monticello,* ed. Merrill D. Peterson (Charlottesville: University Press of Virginia, 1993), 69.

[28] Some were given to Gov. Jefferson by dear friend and Kaskasian chief, Jean Baptiste Ducoigne (see TJ to JBD, 1 June 1781). It is not known if the one currently hanging in Monticello are of Ducoigne or of Capt. Lewis' expedition to the Pacific Ocean.

[29] Harrold Hellenbrand, "Not 'To Destroy But to Fulfil' Jefferson, Indians, and Republican Dispensation," *Eighteenth-Century* Studies, Vol. 18, No. 4, 1985: 538.

[30] Ivan Karp, "Culture and Representation," *Exhibiting Cultures: The Poetics and Politics of Museum Display,* ed. Ivan Karp and Steven Lavine (Washington, D.C.: Smithsonian, 1991), 16.

[31] Elizabeth Chew, "Thomas Jefferson's Indian Hall at the University of Virginia," *Transactions of the American Philosophical Society,* Vol. 110, No. 2, 2022: 47 and 68–72.

What of Jefferson's take of the numerous monumental and elaborate earthworks of Natives? Jefferson never visited any site other than the tumulus (burial mound) near Charlottesville—the subject of the next chapter. One cannot infer from no other visits any lack of interest in tumuli, for his interest in Italian architecture was profound, but while in Italy, he made no effort to see Italian, especially Palladian, structures. It is difficult to presume that he had no knowledge of Rev. David Jones' *Journal of a Tour into the Territory Northwest of the Allegheny Mountains* (1774), in which he writes of his experiences of tumuli, though there is no record of the book in his libraries. Yet he did own Jonathan Carver's *Travels through the Interior Parts of North America* (1778) in which Carver talks of what might be an octagonal entrenchment on the upper Mississippi River (today, near Red Wing, Minnesota).[32]

With the completion of analysis of Indians' moral and aesthetic sensibility, Jefferson, in his *Notes on Virginia*, finishes with Buffon. Jefferson, it is crucial to note, is not aiming at besting Buffon—an inordinately ambitious, and foolhardy, aim. He merely wishes to cast doubt on Buffon's claim concerning the inferiority of Indians. He aims not at an inductively strong argument. He does not have the evidence for that. Yet, he notes, natives have not yet been introduced to letters. Given full exposure to letters, naturalists will be in a better position to assess Indians' genius.

Jefferson overall acknowledges "varieties in the race of man, distinguished by their powers both of body and mind," as there are varieties in other animals. "I only mean to suggest a doubt, whether the bulk and faculties of animals depend on the side of the Atlantic on which their food happens to grow, or which furnishes the elements of which they are compounded? Whether Nature has enlisted herself as a Cis or Trans-Atlantic partisan?"[33]

The best we can do is to compare Indians now with the Germanic tribes in the days of the Roman republic, when Roman soldiers and the Roman arts first crossed the Alps. Yet that comparison has its limit, for the Germanic peoples swarmed with numbers, and "numbers produce emulation, and multiply the chances of improvement, and one improvement begets another." Still, even with the introduction of Roman science north of the Alps, it was 16 centuries "before a Newton could be formed."[34] In sum, Jefferson acknowledges the

---

[32] For more, see Roger Kennedy, "Jefferson and the Indians," *Winterthur Portfolio*, Vol. 27, Nos. 2–3, 1992: 105–21.
[33] Thomas Jefferson, *Notes on Virginia*, 63.
[34] Thomas Jefferson, *Notes on Virginia*, 63.

barbarism of Natives. Yet in time, given exposure and acclimation to the arts and sciences cultivated in Europe, Indians too, he believes, will excel in them.

Despite their barbarism, American natives "enjoy in their general mass an infinitely greater degree of happiness" than do their more civilized Europeans. Though backward in the arts and sciences, they are freer than Europeans[35]—so critical is liberty to the enjoyment of human happiness.

---

[35] TJ to Edward Carrington, 16 Jan. 1787.

Chapter 7

A Dig into an Indian Burial Mound

"The most decisive proof"

Besides his impressive collection of Indian vocabularies, the most signal instance of Jefferson's deep interest in Native Americans concerns his interest in their barrows or mounds. His analysis of their barrows also illustrates that he, at times, could be a shoddy inductivist.

After his seventeenth-century catalog of the number of Indian warriors among the Manahoacs, Monacans, and Powhatans in Query XI of *Notes on the State of Virginia*, Jefferson attends to critical discussion of Indian monuments. On a small scale, he rules out, as monuments, "arrow points, stone hatchets, stone pipes, and half-shapen images." On a large scale, there are the Native Americans' "Barrows" (tumuli or mounds), "to be found all over this country," and they are of varies sizes and some of earth and some of stones. More than any other illustration of hypothesis-testing in the *Notes on Virginia*, this episode exemplifies Jefferson's capacities for scientific marvel, acute observation, regard for minutiae, descriptive accurateness, and veridical judgment.[1]

It is known to all, thinks Jefferson, that the mounds are repositories of the dead. What is not known is their composition. He aims to settle the question of their composition.

There are three common-held hypotheses, and Jefferson gives each due scrutiny as he visits a tumulus in "his neighborhood"—"on the low grounds of the Rivanna, about two miles above its principal fork, and opposite to some hills, on which had been an Indian town."[2]

First, there is the fallen-warrior hypothesis (H_{FW}). According to H_{FW}, the mounds are constructed to cover the bones of warriors fallen in battle, just where they have fallen.

---

[1] Thomas Jefferson, *Notes on the State of Virginia*, ed. William Peden (Chapel Hill: University of North Carolina Press, 1954), 97.
[2] Thomas Jefferson, *Notes on Virginia*, 98.

Next, there is the periodic-collection hypothesis (H_{PC}). According to H_{PC}, bones of the dead are taken at intervals to a suitable spot and buried in a manner revelatory of the time of death.

Last, there is the sepulcher hypothesis (H_S). According to H_S, the barrows are sepulchers for towns, once on or near the grounds, which contain the bones of the dead, placed upright and next to each other, in a manner that reveals the time of death.[3]

The mound near Monticello, he notes, "was of spheroidal form, of about 40 feet diameter at the base, and had been of about twelve feet altitude, though now reduced by the plow to seven and a half" from a dozen or so years of farming. Around the base of the spheroid is a ditch, five feet wide by five feet deep, where the earth for the barrow has been taken.[4]

Jefferson then digs into several parts of the barrow and finds bones buried from six inches to three feet below.

> These were lying in utmost confusion, some vertical, some oblique, some horizontal, and directed to every point of the compass, entangled, and held together in clusters by the earth. Bones of the most distant parts were found together, as, for instance, the small bones of the foot in the hollow of a scull, many sculls would sometimes be in contact, lying on the face, on the side, on the back, top or bottom, so as, on the whole, to give the idea of bones emptied promiscuously from a bag or basket, and covered over with earth, without any attention to their order.[5]

Sculls, jaws, teeth, arms, legs feet, and hands, he notes, exist in great number. There are few ribs and vertebrae. Jefferson also describes several items evident of infant burial: e.g., the teeth of an infant, an infant's scull, two rib bones (each from a different infant), and an infant's jaw, without teeth having been cut.[6] Jefferson's keen attentiveness to the last item deserves to be in his own words.

> This last furnishing the most decisive proof of the burial of children here, I was particular in my attention to it. It was part of the right-half of the under-jaw. The processes, by which it was articulated to the

---

[3] Thomas Jefferson, *Notes on Virginia*, 97–98.
[4] Thomas Jefferson, *Notes on Virginia*, 98.
[5] Thomas Jefferson, *Notes on Virginia*, 98.
[6] Thomas Jefferson, *Notes on Virginia*, 98–99.

temporal bones, were entire; and the bone itself firm to where it had been broken off, which, as nearly as I could judge, was about the place of the eye-tooth. Its upper edge, wherein would have been the sockets of the teeth, was perfectly smooth. Measuring it with that of an adult, by placing their hinder processes together, its broken and extended to the penultimate grinder of the adult. This bone was white, all the others of a sand color.[7]

Jefferson's elation on finding bones of infants is certainly due to recognition that he can rule out one hypothesis, H_{FW}, and the indiscriminate placement of bones is disconfirmatory evidence for H_S, which demands that the bones be placed upright.

Ruling out two of three hypotheses is not offering confirmatory evidence of the remaining hypothesis, and so, Jefferson is not content to embrace the third merely by virtue of eliminative reasoning. He seeks additional evidence.

Jefferson next makes a perpendicular cut into the body of the barrow to examine its internal structure to glean more information about the barrow. The cut is some three feet from the center and wide enough for a person to "walk through and examine its sides." At the bottom are bones. Above the bones are stones. Thereafter a "large interval of earth, then a stratum of bones." On one end, four strata of bones are found. On the other, three strata are discovered, though they are not commensurate with those on the other end. The lowest bones show the most decay; the highest bones, the least. There are no indications of wounds from battle.[8] The number of bodies in the barrow Jefferson approximates to be one thousand.

There is an abundance of data: (1) the number of bones, (2) their confused position, (3) bones placed in different strata, (4) the incommensurability of strata on different ends, (5) the amount of decay being commensurate with depth of inhumation, and (6) the existence of infant bones. Jefferson concludes:

> Every one will readily seize the circumstances above related, which militate against the opinion, that it covered the bones only of persons fallen in battle; and against the tradition also, which would make it the common sepulcher of a town, in which the bodies were placed upright and touching each other. Appearances certainly indicate that it has

---

[7] Thomas Jefferson, *Notes on Virginia*, 99.
[8] Thomas Jefferson, *Notes on Virginia*, 99.

derived both origin and growth from the accustomary collection of bones, and deposition of them together; that the first collection had been deposited on the common surface of the earth, a few stones put over it, and then a covering of earth, that the second had been laid on this, had covered more or less of it in proportion to the number of bones, and was then also covered with earth.[9]

Thus, the six data militate for H_{PC}, and they militate rather decisively against H_{FW} and H_S.[10]

Before ending his account of the tumulus near Monticello, Jefferson tells of a party of Indians passing through the woods in the area of the mound some 30 years ago. He was then a teen-aged boy. The Natives divagated some six miles from the high road to pay their respects with expressions of sorrow and then returned to the high road.[11]

Jefferson ends by mentioning two other barrows: one in the low grounds of the southern Shenandoah River, near Staunton, and the other just a few miles north of Wood's Gap in the Blue Ridge Mountains. The last is a large heap of stones.[12]

What might strike readers of Query XI of *Notes on Virginia* is any mention by Jefferson of the religious significance of the tumuli. The mounds and each of the hypotheses he entertains, before deciding on the periodic-collection hypothesis for the one he has visited and studied, have some religious or spiritual significance, and Jefferson nowhere in his book says anything about the religiosity or spirituality of Native Americans other than his passing comment of the party of Indians visiting the mound he investigated to pay respects to the dead. That is astonishing, even if Jefferson himself thought little of religious sectarianism.

Jefferson, prompted by John Adams, does address the issue of Indians' religiosity in a letter to Adams (11 June 1812). After dismissing the inaccurate accounts of Lafitau, Jefferson proffers his own sentiments on the "priests" of Indians.

---

[9] Thomas Jefferson, *Notes on Virginia*, 99–100.
[10] For Thomson's account of this process in his commentary on Jefferson's book, see Charles Thomson, "Notes on *Notes on Virginia*" (Appendix I), in Thomas Jefferson, *Notes on the State of Virginia*, ed. Frank Shuffleton (New York: Penguin, 1999), 215–16.
[11] Thomas Jefferson, *Notes on Virginia*, 100.
[12] Thomas Jefferson, *Notes on Virginia*, 100.

In the solemn ceremonies of the Indians, the persons who direct or officiate, are their chiefs, elders and warriors, in civil ceremonies or in those of war; it is the head of the cabin in their private or particular feasts or ceremonies; and sometimes the matrons, as in their corn feasts. ... The true line of distinction seems to be, that solemn ceremonies, whether public or private, addressed to the Great Spirit, are conducted by the worthies of the nation, men or matrons, while conjurers are resorted to only for the invocation of evil spirits. The present state of the several Indian tribes, without any public order of priests, is proof sufficient that they never had such an order. Their steady habits permit no innovations, not even those which the progress of science offers to increase the comforts, enlarge the understanding, and improve the morality of mankind. Indeed, so little idea have they of a regular order of priests, that they mistake ours for their conjurers, and call them by that name.

There are two other botherations with Jefferson's account of Natives' burial mounds. First, the burial mounds are of varied compositions—sometimes of earth and sometimes of stones—but he fails to expatiate. Is it merely that in some areas, stones are readily available while in others they are not? We note also Jefferson's mention of separation of layers in the spheroidal mound he investigates by stones and a coving or earth, with the amount of stones and earth roughly proportionate to the number of bodies to be covered. Finally, what is also significant, given that Jefferson is typically a careful inductivist, is that Jefferson is silent about what his excavation of *one* burial mound is supposed to show. Does he think that by showing the mound he has excavated to be confirmatory of the Periodic Collection Hypothesis, that conclusion might be applied to all other mounds in North America? That seems likely, given his prefatory comment that it was "obvious to all" that such tumuli were repositories of the dead."

On July 25, 1813, lawyer, explorer, and author Henry Marie Brackenridge (1786–1871, Figure 7-1) writes Jefferson to tell him how his *Notes on Virginia* inspired him to make a study of all the barrows he could find along or near the Ohio and Mississippi Rivers. "From examination and reflection, something like hypothesis, has taken the place of the vague wanderings of fancy." He sums his disclosures in a lengthy letter to Jefferson. Brackenridge's disclosures show that Jefferson's comments on the study of his sole barrow are preliminary, incomplete.

Figure 7-1: Henry Marie Brackenridge

In the valley of the Mississippi, says Brackenridge, there are traces of two distinct races of Natives—one being more ancient than the other—with the most recent leaving behind more traces of its existence than the least recent. Both practiced subsistence agriculture without pasturage. Game was sufficiently numerous in the nearby woods.

Through interaction with the interloping Whites, continues Brackenridge, the population of those Natives diminished, as the Whites' towns were palisaded and some enclosed as much as 100 acres. Throughout the valley, there were numerous Indian burial mounds, evidence of the most ancient period. "I have reason to beleive that their antiquity is very great. The oldest Indians have no tradition as to their Authors or the purposes for which they were originally intended, yet they were unconsciously formerly in the habit of using them for one of the purposes for which they were at first designed to wit as places of defence."

Brackenridge proffers a list of 15 barrows found along the Mississippi and Ohio Rivers. Of each, he made a study, inasmuch as his time allowed for a study (spelling, Brackenridge's).

1. At Great creek, below Wheeling
2. At Pittsburgh
3. At Marietta
4. Cincinati

5. New Madrid—one of them 350 feet diameter at the base

6. Bois [Brule] bottom, 15 miles, below St. Genevieve

7. At St. Genevieve

8. mouth of the Marameck

9. St. Louis—one with two Stages another with three

10. mouth of the Missouri

11. on the Cohokia River—in two groups

12. twenty miles below—two groups also, but the mound of a smaller size—on the back of a lake formerly the bed of the river

13. near Washington (M.T.) 146 feet in height

14 At Baton Rouge and on the [Manac] bayou one of the mounds near the lake is chiefly composed of shells. the inhabitants have taken away great quantities for the purpose of making lime

15. The mound on Black river—of two stages,—with a group around it

At each of the 15 spots, there are "groupes of mounds," indicative of a large town or city. Yet over a vast stretch between the Ohio, Mississippi, Missouri, and Illinois Rivers, there is the center of this large race of Natives. In the plains between the Arkansas and St. Francis Rivers, there are barrows "numerous and some verry large." Some points of note are that there are two large mounds among the others, that those large mounds, are of many stages, that the smaller mounds are symmetrically situated around the two larger mounds, and that "the cardinal points" (the two large mounds or some specific features of the set up?) are readily spotted. Sums Brackenridge, "Such are the appearances of Antiquity in the western country, which I consider as furnishing proof of an ancient and numerous population," similar in customs and manners to the inhabitants of New Spain—which comprised. at the time, roughly the Spain-owned territories in North America to the west and south of Louisiana—given the structural and organizational similarities in the mounds.

Brackenridge then offers an analysis of the trifunctionality of the mounds in New Spain: as temples, as fortresses, and as mausoleums.

Where there were tumuli in New Spain, there were "numerous steeples"—there were some two thousand in and around the four great cities of early "Mexico"—evidence of a large population. "Architecture was perhaps too much in its infancy to enable them to build to any great height, a mound was therefore raised, and a building erected on the top."

Places of worship were thus established. There are numerous instances in antiquity, adds Brackenridge, of high places as functionally religious. "This prevailed amongst all nations, and probably the first edifice dedicated to the Deity was an elevation of earth, the next step was the placing a temple on it, and finally churches & mosques were built with steeples. This has prevailed in all countries: it may be considered the dictate of Nature."

Such places of worship also functioned, says Brackenridge, as fortresses. In times of attack, as when Cortes assaulted the Incas, the Natives could retreat to the towers.

> They were enabled from the position, form, and the tower on the top, to defend themselves in these places to great advantage. Placed from the bottom to the top of the mount, by gradations above each other, they appear'd (as Solis in his animated Style expresses it) to constitute "a living hill"; and at first, judging only from the experience of their own wars, they fancied themselves impregnable.

A third function was that a mound was a repository for the dead: a mausoleum. "What is remarkable, all nations in their wars have made the last stand in the edifices consecrated to their Gods, and near the tombs of their Ancestors."

Brackenridge sums: "The <u>Adoratorio</u> of New Spain, like all works of the kind answered the three purposes, of the temple, the fortress and the mausoleum. Can we entertain a doubt but that this was also the case with those of the Mississippi [basin]?"

There can also be little doubt, continues Brackenridge, that the ages of Indian mounds are very great. The reasoning is metempirical: The mounds indicate much labor; much labor indicates many laborers; and many laborers indicates advancement to some degree in the arts. Brackenridge also thinks that there must be traces of the use of stone and brick. "The great mound of Cohokia, is evidently constructed with as much regularity as any of the Teocalli of new Spain, and was doubtless cased with brick or stone, and crowned with buildings, but of these no traces remain." That mound might be as old as Egypt's pyramids, adds Brackenridge. There are decaying stones at the mound by St. Louis.

Brackenridge then assails the querulous European philosophers. "The philosophers of Europe with a narrowness and Selfishness of mind have endeavoured to depreciate every thing which relates to it. They have called it the New world, as though its formation was posterior to the rest of the habitable globe." Yet the land itself shows no traces of being newer than that of Europe and the number of Indian languages is "greater perhaps than in all the rest of the world." Prior to use of letters and the inventions of the mariner's compass, gunpowder, and printing, the Mexican and Peruvians were perhaps the most advanced of all humans. Brackenridge would publish his observations in *Voyage to South America* (1820), a copy of which was sent to Jefferson,[13] and *Recollections of Persons and Places in the West* (1868).

Having received Brackenridge's missive, Jefferson replies brachylogously (20 Sept. 1813): "I have read with pleasure the account it gives of the antient mounds & fortifications in the Western country. I never before had an idea that they were so numerous. presuming the communication was meant for me in my relation with the Philosophical society, and deeming it well worthy their attention, I have forwarded it to them, and with my thanks for the information it contained." Jefferson is perhaps overwhelmed by Brackenridge's data.

While Brackenridge's assessment of Natives' barrows is more studied than Jefferson's, his is much too narrow. The Natives who now occupy the Americas, as we have seen, likely came to the continents as early as 15,000 years ago and in three or more waves. It is foolish to group all such persons from that time till Jefferson's day as one kind of people with certain core customs that have survived the millennia. Much happens over millennia. What we can say is that Jefferson has given us an early study of one tumulus and the favorable reception of his *Notes on Virginia* has motivated others after him to correct and expand on his preliminary observations.

Jefferson was likely intentionally conservative and cautious concerning his conclusions about the barrow he had visited and examined. He was aware of numerous other mounds of varied sizes and likely aware at least of the possibility of different functions, though he says merely "that they were repositories of the dead, has been obvious to all." Finding his tumulus near Monticello to be a burial mound merely confirms the generalization that all were burial mounds—an illustration of sloppy single-shot inductivism. In the 1770s, George Washington, during his days as a surveyor, saw the enormous Grave Creek Mound (as early as 1,000 B.C.) south of what is today Wheeling, West Virginia. Missionaries such as David Zeisberger (1772) and Rev. David Jones (1774) captured in writing their impressions of such mounds.

---

[13] See Henry M. Brackenridge to TJ, 5 Feb. 1820.

Figure 7-2: Hopewell Mound Group by Chillicothe

David Jones, in his book *A Journal of Two Visits Made to Some Nations of Indians in 1772 and 1773*, writes this about what is today called Hopewell Mound Group, just north of Chillicothe, Ohio (Figure 7-2):

> North of this town [Chillicothe] are to be seen the remains of an old fortification, the area of which may be fifteen acres. It lies near four square, and appears to have had gates at each corner, and in the middle likewise. From the west middle gate, went a circular entrenchment including about ten acres, which seems designated to defend on all quarters. This circle included a spring. ... 'Tis evident to all travelers that this country has been inhabited formerly by a martial race of mankind enjoying the use of iron, for such entrenchments, as appear in various places, could not have been made otherwise: but of this part of antiquity, we shall remain ignorant.[14]

It is strange that Jefferson, by the time of writing his *Notes on Virginia*, is silent about other mounds and the possibility of other functions, such as fortification and worship. He certainly read Adair, whose argument that Natives are descendants of Jews, we saw Jefferson rejects. Adair begins the final chapter of his book with certain "General Observations on the North American Indians",

---

[14] David Jones, *A Journal of Two Visits Made to Some Nations of Indians in 1772 and 1773* (Burlington, NJ: Isaac Collins, 1774), 41.

and he begins with Natives' "great mounds," some of which, he says, are garrisons.[15]

Jefferson is also skeptical about the possibility of the use of iron or bricks in early Indians' history. When Ezra Stiles of Yale College informs Jefferson (8 May 1786) through enclosure of a drawing of "works of Earth in Lines of Circumvallation found at Muskingham [River] on Ohio [River] ... with Bricks"— and the drawing is about "ancient ages"—by a certain Gen. Parsons (Figure 7-3), Jefferson replies (1 Sept. 1786) with cool skepticism: "Intrenchments of earth they might indeed make; but brick is more difficult. The art of making it may have preceded the use of iron, but it would suppose a greater degree of industry than men in the hunter state usually possess. I should like to know whether General Parsons himself saw actual bricks among the remains of fortification. I suppose the settlement of our continent is of the most remote antiquity."

And so, while Jefferson allows for the possibility of the "ancient ages" of Indians being a state more sophisticated and civilized than their current state, he awaits definitive evidence before embracing that possibility. If the builders of the ancient barrows were more advanced, then either the Indians of Jefferson's day are unrelated to them or there needs to be some explanation for their declination of culture.

Figure 7-3: Parsons' Drawing of Ohioan Archeological Site

---

[15] James Adair, *The History of the American Indians* (London: 1775), 377.

Stiles' reference is to what is today a large archeological site at the confluence of Muskingum and Ohio Rivers. The site contains the Conus (right-center on the site in Figure 7-4), the Capitolium (a pyramidal mound with three paths to its summit; Figure B in the 50-acre enclosure), the Quadranaou (a 180-feet long and 32-feet wide mound with four paths to its summit; Figure A in the 50-acre enclosure), and the Sacra Via (a walled pathway that led to the Muskingum River; lower left of 50-acre enclosure).

Figure 7-4: Layout of Marietta's Site, Squier and Davis, 1838

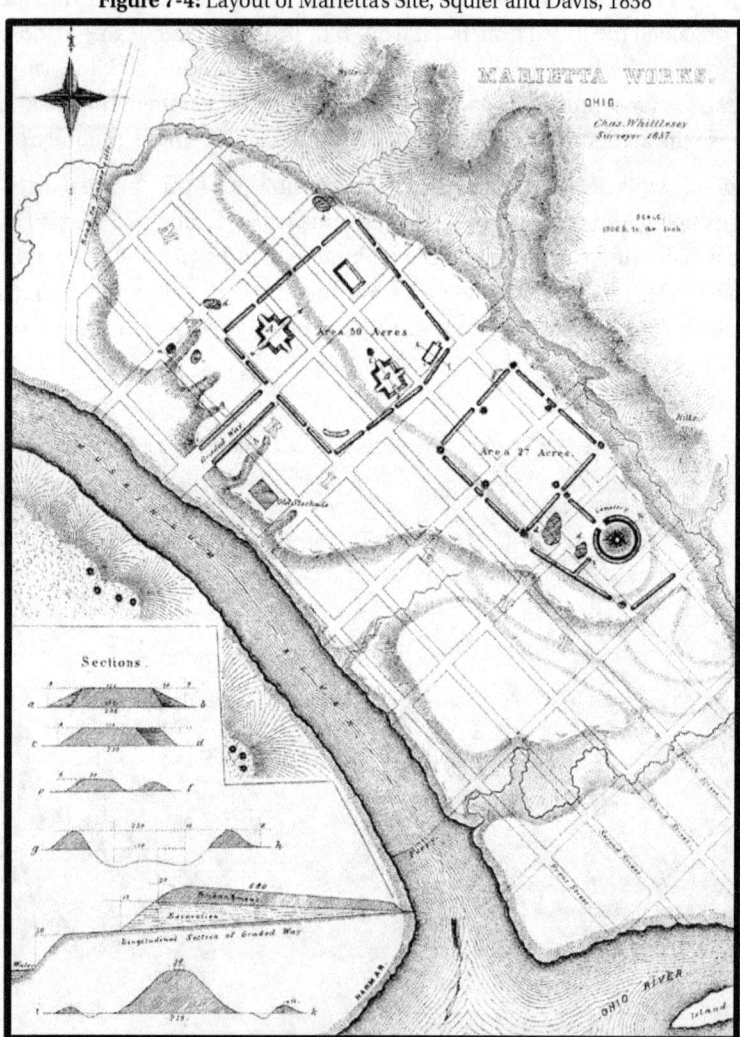

Why was Jefferson skeptical at the time of writing *Notes on Virginia* given exposure to some evidence that his views of Natives being mired in the stage of hunting and gathering throughout their lengthy tenure in North America?

Anthony Wallace states that Jefferson's silence is dissimulation. "Given that the prime purpose of the *Notes* ... was to attract European investment," mention of "massive Indian fortifications and the slaughter of thousands of combatants" would be a poor way to entice Europeans to come to or invest in the jejune country.[16]

Wallace's explanation cannot be sustained. The prime purpose of the *Notes* was *not* to attract European investment. Jefferson initially intended the publication of only 200 copies to be sent to friends, fellow republicans, and students at William and Mary College, but was forced to authorized general publication of the book, given unauthorized publication of a poor French translation of it.[17]

Figure 7-5: Mounds at Poplar Forest

What we do know is that from the time of Jefferson's skepticism in the 1786 letter to Stiles, his skepticism slowly faded. He became receptive to a degree of early Indian architectural sophistication that he, in 1786, thought was impossible. "It is probably, though not certain," writes Roger Kennedy, "that he [Jefferson] was acquainted with the reports of [others] Harris, Heart, and Jones" on the tumuli. He thus was likely familiar with Benjamin Barton's 1787 account

---

[16] Anthony F.C. Wallace, *Jefferson and the Indians: The Tragic Fate of the First Americans* (Cambridge, MS: The Belknap Press, 1999), 136.
[17] M. Andrew Holowchak, *Thomas Jefferson's* Notes on the State of Virginia: *A Prolegomena* (Wilmington, DE: Vernon Press, 2023), chap. 2.

with a diagram of the Marietta complex. If he was acquainted with the reports of others on Indians' use of geometry—squares, rectangles, circles, and semicircles—at sites with mounds, it might even be that Jefferson's use of mounds at Poplar Forest (arrows, Figure 10-5) was inspired by Natives' tumuli.[118]

---

[18] Roger Kennedy, "Jefferson and the Indians," *Winterthur Portfolio,* Vol. 27, Nos. 2/3, 1992: 117.

PART II
Thomas Jefferson's Indian Policy

Chapter 8

British & Early American Indian Policy

"To advance the happiness of the Indians"

The first part of this book was chiefly philosophical and expiscatory, inasmuch as my aim was to illustrate Jefferson's enormous interest in the study of Native Americans. That is what set him apart from other presidents of his day. He had a love of Indians and an appreciation for their *ethnoi*. Yet his political policies toward them, as we shall see, were mostly a continuation of those policies, amicable but unfavorable to Natives, of the two presidents before him. The chief question I aim to answer in Part II is this: Why did Jefferson, who had a deep respect for Native Americans, not adopt as president policies that differed from predecessors (and successors)—that were more favorable to the interests of Indians?

This chapter, as the title implies, is a brief sketch of American Indian policy prior to Jefferson's presidency.

There is this story, circa 1885, about Blackfoot Chief Crowfoot's interaction with a trader, who in some effort to impress the chief, spreads numerous one-dollar bills in the ground. The trader explains that the money has the same worth of the Indians' buffalo robes and states that the chief would have all the paper on the ground should he sign a treaty. Crowfoot then takes a handful of clay, makes a ball out of it, and places it over a fire. The clay is undisturbed. "Now put your money on the fire and see if it will last as long as the clay," says Crowfoot. The white man replies, "No, my money will burn because it is made of paper." The chief sniggers and says," Your money is not as good as our land, is it? The wind will blow it away; the fire will burn it; water will rot it. But nothing will destroy our land. You don't make a very good trade." Crowfoot then picks up a handful of sand from the river bank, hands it to the white man, and adds, "You count the grains of sand in that while I count the money you give for the land." The white man says, "I would not live long enough to count this, but you can count the money in a few minutes." Crowfoot replies: "Our land is more valuable than your money. It will last forever. It will not perish as long as the sun shines and the water flows, and through all the years, it will give life to men and animals, and therefore we cannot sell the land. It was put there by the Great Spirit, and we cannot sell it because it does not really belong to us. You can count your money and burn it with a nod of a buffalo's head, but only the Great Spirit can count the grains of sand and the blades of grass on these plains."[1]

American frontiersmen were unrelenting in their quest for arable lands and often acquired them by illicit personal transactions with Indians. Transactions for small parcels of land were frequently, though not always, equitable. Natives cherished iron products, glassware, firearms, and liquor—the last two goods created enormous problems for white settlers and the U.S. government as well as for Indians—and often traded away parcels of land for them. Large parcels of land were generally exchanged through some measure of coercion, though such transactions sometimes occurred when Indians were inebriated. On far too many occasions, Americans merely settled illegally on Natives' lands to the dismay of the Natives. When the government—though it did this too infrequently due to limited manpower and money—intervened and forced the white settlers from Indians' lands, the relocated Whites often again removed to the same lands from which they were removed when the governmental threat was gone.

Moreover, there was a mammoth difficulty about who was authorized to negotiate with the Indians for goods or land. Indians, prior to the Revolutionary War, sold lands to federal authorities, delegates from states, and individuals from England, France, and the Netherlands. Figure 8-1 shows British claims on the eastern coast and in upper Canada, French claims west of the Appalachian Mountains and on the eastern Canadian coast, and Spanish possession of Florida.

That, of course, led to monumental confusion about matters of legality. England, wishing to dominate the exchange of goods with Indians, aimed to make Natives dependent on British goods and thereby wrested control from the individual colonies, whose interactions with Indians were skimble-scamble, as each colony had its own regulations, and each tried to undercut all others in Indian trading.

After the British victory in the Seven Years' War (aka, French and Indian War, 1756–1763; Figure 8-2), the British government, through the Royal Proclamation of 1763, established definite boundaries for the colonies and thereby allowed for Indians to occupy lands beyond the colonies. It also prohibited governors and

---

[1] "Native Americans Describe Traditional Views of Land Ownership," *Social History for Every Classroom*, CUNY: The Graduate Center, https://shec.ashp.cuny.edu/items/show/1543, accessed 2 June 2023.

British & Early American Indian Policy   111

high officials of a colony from surveying lands beyond their colony, and it mandated that all transactions of land were affairs of the British government. It prohibited transactions west of the Appalachian Mountains. Any transactions were to be conducted through designated representatives of England.

Figure 8-1: British, French, and Spanish Land Claims in Early North America

The nodus of boundaries had become of singular significance. Natives were ever anxious about the westerly migration of white interlopers and they were insistent that something must be done to stop or slow the movement.

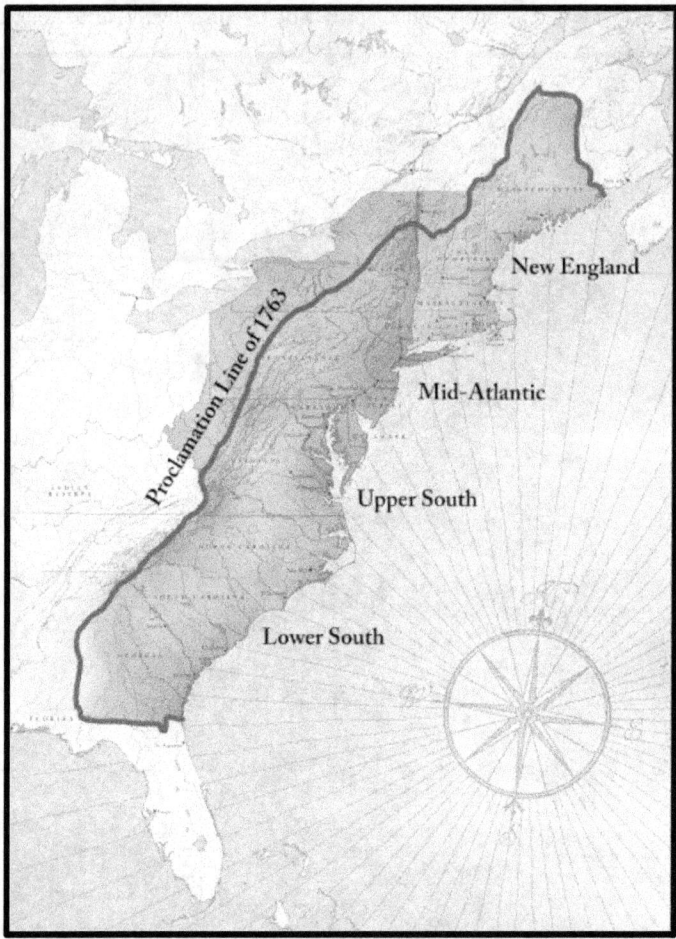

Figure 8-2: Boundaries with Proclamation of 1763

From the British perspective, the Appalachian line was provisional—*viz.*, established to quell the whooping for war of the Indians. The British government was having enough difficulties with the intransigent Colonists. Wrote Sir William Johnson, agent of Indian affairs in the North, in 1764: "Ascertaining and defining the precise and exact Boundaries of the Indian

Lands is a very [sic] necessary, but a delicate point. ... The Six Nations, Western Indians, etc [sic], having never been conquered, either by the English or French nor subject to the Laws, consider themselves as a free people. ... It will require a good deal of caution to point out any boundary, that shall appear to circumscribe their limits too far."[2]

Yet it was impossible for the British government to enforce the strictures of the proclamation. They had spread thin their military through the protracted war with France and the Indians, and there was little money to enforce the decree, which the government estimated would cost some 20 thousand pounds per year. Moreover, French settlers in the region ultramontane were not willfully ready to give up their lands or trade routes. Again, though the war had ended, the Indians that fought with the French in a losing effort continued to skirmish with the British. Last, what was to prevent adventurous British colonists from venturing beyond the mountains and dealing with the Natives howsoever they might please? As a consequence, in 1768, England formally returned regulation of trade with Natives to its individual colonies. Said the Lords of Trade of the impossibility of regulating trade with the Natives, of various *ethnoi*, "No one general plan of Commerce & Policy is or can be applicable to all the different Nations of Indians of different interests and different situations."[3] That would be an enduring problem after the Revolutionary War.

Trade between what would become the U.S. government began on July 12, 1775, when the Continental Congress established a committee for "procuring goods and carrying on the Indian trade." The following year, the government set up trading houses. Yet there was at the time no governmental prohibition, by the individual states or by the Continental Congress, against private traders.[4]

Relations between Colonists and Natives were strained during the Revolutionary War, as Natives tended to partner with the British, whose interest was mostly the lands along the Atlantic coast so that communications with the mother country could be smooth. For instance, John Stuart, British Superintendent to the Indian Department in the South, urged the Choctaws

---

[2] Francis Paul Prucha, *American Indian Policy in the Formative Years: The Indian Trade and Intercourse Acts 1790–1834* (Cambridge: Harvard University Press, 1962), 19. Johnson in the same year, negotiated the Treaty of Fort Niagara through wampum with 24 separate First Nations (Canadian Natives).
[3] Francis Paul Prucha, *American Indian Policy in the Formative Years*, 23.
[4] Edgar B. Wesley, "The Government Factory System among the Indians, 1795–1822," in *Mississippi Valley Historical Review*, VI, 1919, 489*f*

and Chickasaws to join the British in fighting the Colonists. "It is the declared intention of the Rebels to possess themselves of your Lands; it also becomes your duty and interest to unite yourselves with other nations for your mutual defense and protection and to attach yourselves firmly to the King's cause, to whose goodness and protection you have been and are so much indebted."[5]

In Virginia, the issue had been settled by the adoption of a constitution in 1776. That constitution mandated that "no purchases of lands shall be made of the Indian natives, but on behalf of the public, by authority of the General Assembly"[6] of Virginia. That was a proviso also suggested by Jefferson[7] and adopted at the Constitutional Convention.

During the Revolutionary War, the Continental Congress put forth the Articles of Confederation (1777), which did little to settle affairs with Indians. Article IX says, "The United States, in congress assembled, shall also have the sole and exclusive right and power of … regulating the trade and managing all affairs with the Indians, not members of any of the states; provided that the legislative right of any state, within its own limits, be not infringed or violated."[8] Just what constraints did the vague qualifying clause, "provided that…," impose?

The U.S. Constitution 10 years later was not much clearer. The Commerce Clause (Article I, Section VIII) reads, "The Congress shall have Power … To regulate Commerce with foreign Nations, and among the several States, and with the Indian Tribes."[9] Though the wording here, too is vague, the advance is singular: Only the U.S. Congress has the power to negotiate with Indians. That step was fiscally singular, and sound. Assuming ownership in 1786 of lands west of the Appalachian Mountains, the federal government hoped to solve its considerable debt, incurred during the Revolutionary War.[10] Yet the U.S. government generally lacked the power to enforce fully its authority due to the

---

[5] Francis Paul Prucha, *American Indian Policy in the Formative Years*, 27.

[6] "The Constitution of Virginia," Encyclopedia Virginia, https://encyclopediavirginia.org/entries/the-constitution-of-virginia-1776/, accessed 10 May 2023.

[7] Thomas Jefferson, Draft Constitution for Virginia, *Thomas Jefferson: Writings*, ed. Merrill D. Peterson (New York: Library of America, 1984), 343.

[8] Articles of Confederation, National Archives, https://www.archives.gov/milestone-documents/articles-of-confederation, accessed 12 May 2023.

[9] Constitution of the United States, *National Archives*, https://www.archives.gov/founding-docs/constitution, accessed 12 May 2023.

[10] Reginald Horsman, "American Indian Policy in the Old Northwest, 1783–1812," *The William and Mary Quarterly*, Vol. 18, No. 1, 1961: 36.

large expense of a standing army, which eventually would be needed, in part, to enforce its Indian policies.[11] Loss of parochial control over dealings with Natives and increases in federal taxes were large botherations for the individual states. And so, frontiersmen, wishing to have tracts of Western lands, often merely ignored the mandates of the federal government and settled illegally on Indians' lands or purchased them directly from Aborigines despite the stricture of the new constitution. The federal government merely did not have the money to enforce its policies.

Thus, after the Revolutionary War, the U.S. government claimed the sole right to negotiate with Natives. The rationale, in effect, was the right of conquest. Most Native tribes, because of the continual encroachments of Colonial frontiersmen in their lands, sided with the British in the war. And so, after having won the war, there was little incentive by the federal government to deal fairly with Indians. That was evident in the boundaries drawn up by Americans. As Francis Prucha states: "The Indians had been on the losing side in the war. They could with justice be treated as a conquered nation and their land be taken from them by right of conquest."[12]

The government's Indian policy from 1783 to 1786 was disastrous because it was based on the right of conquest. The territorial sovereignty ceded by England in 1783 at the end of the Revolutionary War was presumed by the Congress to surcease Natives' claim to the lands. Natives, who had become accustomed to being treated as rightful owners of their lands, disavowed that policy and resisted it.[13]

Thomas Jefferson, as we shall see in chapter 10, consistently championed a policy of dealing justly with the Indians. In Jefferson's proposal on the Western Territory in 1784, he begins thus in his plan for partitioning parcels of land into states, "Resolved that the territory ceded or to be ceded by the Individual States to the United States whensoever the same shall have been purchased of the Indican Inhabitants & offered for sale by the U.S. shall be formed into distinct States."[14] Acquisition of Natives' lands would be through fair purchases.

---

[11] Washington approved the bill for a standing army on September 29, 1789.
[12] Francis Paul Prucha, *American Indian Policy in the Formative Years*, 32–33.
[13] Reginald Horsman, "American Indian Policy in the Old Northwest, 1783–1812," *The William and Mary Quarterly*, Vol. 18, No. 1, 1961: 39.
[14] Thomas Jefferson, Report on Government for Western Territory, *The Scholars' Thomas Jefferson*, ed. M. Andrew Holowchak (Newcastle upon Tyne, Cambridge Scholars, 2021), 30.

Jefferson's notion of peaceful and just acquisition of Natives' lands by governmental authorities would find its way into the Northwest Ordinance (1787), which marked a decisive change in the U.S. government's policy. Article III states, "The utmost good faith shall always be observed towards the Indians; their lands and property shall never be taken from them without their consent; and in their property, rights and liberty, they never shall be invaded or disturbed, unless in just and lawful wars authorized by Congress; but laws founded in justice and humanity shall from time to time be made, from preventing wrongs being done to them, and for preserving peace and friendship with them."[15] The right of conquest became the right of purchase.

Why was there a sea change of policy?

One of the issues was certainly American compunction, if only subconscious. With continued westward encroachment of American settlers, there were sanguinary responses by Indians. The Northwest Territory, granted to the United States as part of the Treaty of Paris after the Revolutionary War (1783), which in effect nullified the British "proclamation line" established with the earlier Treaty of Paris (1763), is a fine illustration. Native Americans, who were free to occupy the land by the Royal Proclamation (1763) of the lands beyond the Appalachians, now found American frontiersmen interloping and claiming their lands. Indian tribes of the Ohio and Illinois Countries—e.g., the Shawnee, Miami, Delaware, Potawatomi, Wabash, and Illinois—formed a provisional confederacy to confront the problem of encroachment and skirmishing, if not warring, began in 1785.

To avoid warring with the Indians due to the unending encroachment of Americans in Natives' lands, the U.S. Continental Congress made a study of the nodus of Natives' intransigency. In 1786, a U.S. Congressional Committee weighed the cost of war with the cost of purchasing the lands from the Aborigines. To counter the aggression of the who had joined and gathered for war—Henry Knox, U.S. Secretary of War, argued that the country would need to appropriate some 3,000 men for two years and at a cost of two million dollars. Yet, he figured that Americans could eschew the wrath of the Indians and buy their lands for 20,000 dollars.[16] That was, in a commonly used colloquialism

---

[15] Northwest Ordinance, 1787, *Milestone Documents*, https://www.archives.gov/milestone-documents/northwest-ordinance, accessed 25 June 2023.

[16] Anthony F.C. Wallace, *Jefferson and the Indians: The Tragic Fate of the First Americans* (Cambridge, MS: The Belknap Press, 1999), 165–70.

today, a no-brainer. Consequently, purchasing the lands of Indians became the policy in 1787, and it would be the policy thereafter.

The change of policy did not eschew war. There would be a protracted war of some 10 years in the Northwestern Territory, and a large victory for the confederation of nations when they defeated Gen. Josiah Harmar at the Miami village Kekionga and near Fort Miami, off Maumee River in 1790 (Figure 8-3).[17]

Figure 8-3: Gen. Harmar's Defeat

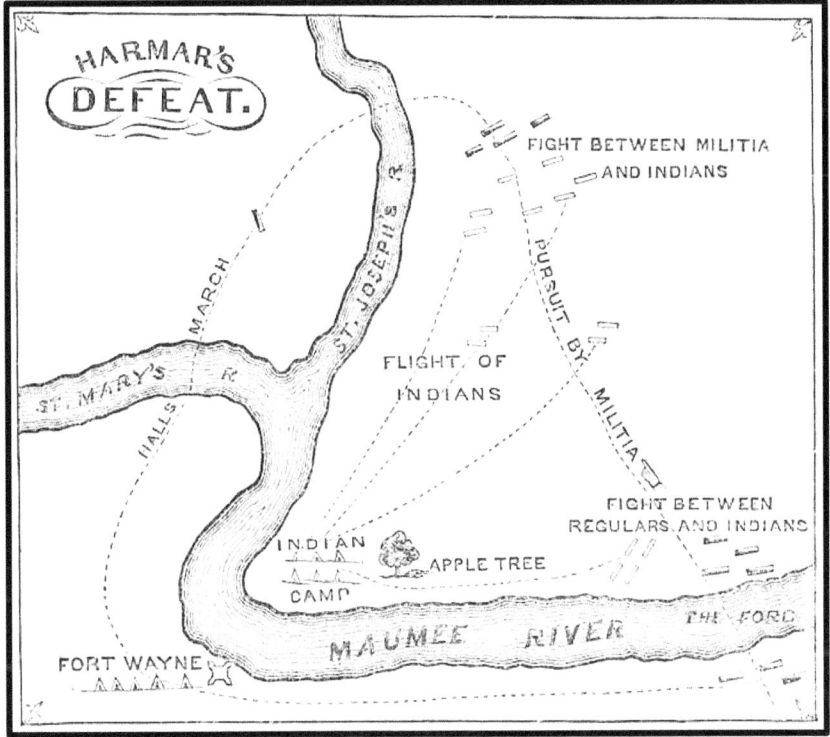

In conjunction with a change of policy, the Congress, consistent with the U.S. Constitution, also decreed that only it, as an agency of the federal government, had the power "to regulate Commerce ... with the Indian Tribes"—a decision upheld by the Supreme Court in *Johnson v. McIntosh* (1823), and a decision that

---

[17] Wiley Sword, *President Washington's Indian War: The Struggle for the Old Northwest, 1790–1795* (Norman, OK: University of Oklahoma Press, 1985), 84–109.

was written and delivered by Chief Justice John Marshall. Marshall argued that discovery of the lands gave title to the discovering nation and excluded all other European nations from purchasing lands from the American Natives. In establishing the regulations between the discovering nation and the Indians, the latter's rights were "to a considerable extent, impaired." They had a right to occupy the land, to possess it, and to use it as they wished, but they lost the right to "complete sovereignty, as independent nations." He sums, "Their power to dispose of the soil at their own will, to whomever they pleased, was denied by the original fundamental principle, that discovery gave exclusive title to those who made it."[18]

The Natives, it is not astonishing to note, were unimpressed by the Congress' concession that they could, if they wished, sell their lands to the government—a needless formal expression of what was apparent to them. What, however, gave the U.S. government the right to dictate how the Indians would sell their land and to whom? Natives often sold land to individuals and would continue to do so, should they so choose.

There was also the problem of territorial governors in the frontiers—especially prominent after the Louisiana Purchase. When governors were put into place, their authority was questioned. Territorial governors often knew too little about Indians' culture, so agents with significant experience with Indians were appointed to act as go-betweens. Territorial governors were also asked to administrate and superintend Natives' affairs, but they were not empowered to make significant decisions. When they did, they were in the main answerable to the U.S. secretary of war.

When Jefferson was president, he gave the governorship of Mississippi Territory to William Charles Cole Claiborne—a post he would hold for two years. At that time, Benjamin Hawkins, a man intimately knowledgeable of the affairs of Southern Natives, was an agent of Indians' affairs south of the Ohio River since George Washington's administration. While Hawkins was answerable to Claiborne, Claiborne was answerable to Henry Dearborn, the secretary of war.[19] Yet urgency often required action before awaiting instructions through the chain of command—that is, from the secretary of war. The chain of command was complicated by appointments of regional agents—e.g., Return J. Meigs as agent to the Cherokee in Tennessee from 1801 to 1823. For instance, agents could not

---

[18] Stuart Banner, *How the Indians Lost Their Land* (Cambridge: Belknap Press, 2005), 178–88.

[19] Anthony F.C. Wallace, *Jefferson and the Indians*, 210–11.

enforce the acts concerning trade or intercourse without military backing and military backing could only be had by a decision from the secretary of war. That often was temporally inefficient. Moreover, some states, Southern states especially, considered the federal government's say as final arbiter to be unconstitutional and significant of heavy-handed government.[20]

Difficulties concerning regulation of American and Indian affairs were addressed by President George Washington with passage of Trade and Intercourse Act (22 July 1790), which attempted to regulate governmental policies between officials and Natives beyond the Appalachian Mountains. The territories south of Ohio River were especially contested. Virginia, North Carolina, and Georgia made claims to extensive parcels of land to the West and through actions on such claims, those states were continually fighting with Indians in such territories.[21] This act was an attempt at a pacific and conciliatory approach to Indian policy. It also mandated that independent traders with Aborigines be licensed and that any purchase of Indians' lands had to be sanctioned by the federal government.

Washington was, in the main, sympathetic to the plight of Native Americans, and he also recognized Americans' need of more arable land. He aimed to solve the problems between Americans and Indians or at least ameliorate the tensions between them. Washington writes in October 1791 of the indispensability of "impartial dispensation of justice" for Native Americans. "A system corresponding with the mild principles of religion and philanthropy, towards an unenlightened race of men, whose happiness materially depends on the conduct of the United States, would be as honorable to the National character as conformable to the dictates of sound policy.[22] There is, of course, a heavy paternalistic tone to his sentiments, as Natives' happiness "materially depends" on the actions of the federal government. That paternalistic tone, dictated by Americans' perception of Natives' barbarity, would never be a part of U.S. policy.

Washington was following the lead of his Secretary of War, Henry Knox (1750–1806, Figure 8-4). As we have seen, Knox recognized the legitimacy of Indians' claims to the western lands, yet he argued economically, not humanitarianly. As

---

[20] Anthony F.C. Wallace, *Jefferson and the Indians*, 211.
[21] Editors, "U.S. Congress: An Act to Regulate Trade and Intercourse with the Indian Tribes," https://www.encyclopedia.com/history/encyclopedias-almanacs-transcripts-and-maps/us-congress-act-regulate-trade-and-intercourse-indian-tribes, accessed 14 May 2023.
[22] Merritt B. Pound, *Benjamin Hawkins: Indian Agent* (Athens: University of Georgia Press, 1958), 160–61.

we have seen, he decided that a policy of paying for Natives' lands was cheaper than constant skirmishes and wars—the right of conquest. Washington agreed. "The Indians ... will ever retreat as our Settlements advance upon them and they will be as ready to sell, as we are to buy; That it is the cheapest as well as the least distressing way of dealing with them, none who are acquainted with the Nature of Indian warfare, and has ever been at the trouble of estimating the expence of one, and comparing it with the cost of purchasing their Lands, will hesitate to acknowledge."[23]

Figure 8-4: Henry Knox, Secretary of State

---

[23] George Washington to James Duane, 7 Sept. 1783.

That policy would be fleshed out—and given a gilded gloss—two years later in Washington's Fourth Message to Congress (3 Dec. 1793).

> Next to a rigorous execution of justice on the violators of peace, the establishment of a commerce with the Indian nations, on behalf of the United States, is most likely to conciliate their attachment. But it ought to be conducted without fraud, without extortion, with constant and plentiful supplies; with a ready market for the commodities of the Indians, and a stated price for what they give in payment and receive in exchange. Individuals will not pursue such traffic, unless they be allured by the hope of profit; but it will be enough for the United States to be reimbursed only.[24]

Washington's Fourth Message would be the policy that Jefferson, upon assuming the presidency early in 1801, would continue. That commerce would be fruitfully conducted through establishing trading houses—the "factory system." That system allowed for a superintendent of Indian trade (e.g., Hawkins, south of the Ohio River), contractors and depositories in the port cities, and factors to run trading posts.

Natives traded eagerly for cloth and thread, hats, looking glasses, combs, saddles, rifles, locks, kettles, spoons, penknives, and fishhooks.[25] Trading posts allowed for exchanges on credit, but that was generally discouraged by Hawkins, because his interactions with Indian chiefs found them often deeply in debt with independent traders. Trading on credit was new, and Indians, who, like others first introduced to trading on credit, merely did not grasp the implications of trading on credit—a method often used to steal lands from them by running them deeply into debt. Washington's rationale was to undercut esurient private traders, whose methods of "equal" exchange placed profit ahead of justice; to remove British traders from the frontiers; and to prevent tensions between Natives and Americans that might lead to costly wars. The factory system, revisited every three years when a new Trade and Intercourse Act was put into place, was successful early on but ultimately faltered, as it, designed to address current difficulties and give at least the

---

[24] George Washington, "George Washington to the United States Senate and House of Representatives" (3 Dec. 1793), *Founders Online*, https://founders.archives.gov/documents/Washington/05-14-02-0306, accessed 26 May 2023.

[25] Merritt B. Pound, *Benjamin Hawkins*, 199, 203, and 206.

appearance of governmental action pursuant to Natives' needs, was in essence a stopgap.[26]

Thus, with the shift of U.S.'s Indian policy from right of conquest to right of purchase with the Northwest Ordinance of 1787 and the first Trade and Intercourse Act, Natives were granted the right to their occupied lands and boundaries between Natives' lands and Whites' lands were established. Also, the federal government was empowered as the sole agent for acquiring Natives' lands, for regulating trade between Natives and Whites, and for punishing Americans who acted criminally toward or as agents of exchange with Natives.[27] The system, one can readily see, was not efficient.

To address problems with the Trade and Intercourse Act of 1790, there would be the Trade and Intercourse Act of 1793, and further acts in 1796, 1799, and 1802. That there was a need for revisions and additions to prior acts shows the nodi of federal regulation of Indian policy. Further acts established more trading posts, mandated licensing of private traders, set more or "cleaner" boundaries for Natives' territories, created laws against American intrusions in Indians' affairs, placed more agents to regulate Americans' and Indians' concerns, and proffered enticements for Indians wishing to civilize.[28]

The largest and most persistent problem, already noted, was that many unlicensed frontiersmen merely ignored the directives of the federal government. How could they be enforced by the jejune nation? In October 1818, the Missouri Baptist Association pleaded thus to Congress about unlicensed American traders: "They are, generally speaking, men who have no principle but gain; and being at a distance from the restraints of civilized manners, they give full scope to their corrupt propensities. To gratify these, they defraud the Indians of their property, corrupt their morals, debauch their manners, and consequently, increase the wretchedness of those already miserable people, and prejudice their minds against our Government, our citizens, and our manners, and lead them to have the most contemptible ideas of our civilization, and religion."

Such wild miscreants cared nowise about fines, for they had no property to lose. They cared nowise for territorial prohibitions, for if forbidden in one area, they would merely move to another. Moreover, they were almost never brought

---

[26] Francis Paul Prucha, *American Indian Policy in the Formative Years*, 88–91.

[27] Editors, "An Act to Regulate Trade and Intercourse with the Indian Tribes."

[28] Anthony F.C. Wallace, *Jefferson and the Indians*, 212–13, and Francis Paul Prucha, *American Indian Policy in the Formative Years*, 50.

to justice. The machinery of justice in the frontiers was brittle, inefficient, and corrupt. "Distances were too great, the time lag too long, and the difficulties of arranging for witnesses [were] too serious to provide an effective deterrent or remedy for the illicit traffic."[29] During Jefferson's presidency, for illustration, a delegation of Indians situated along the Missouri River complained to Jefferson about the problem of distance. "You tell us that your children of this side of the Mississippi hear your Word, you are Mistaken, Since every day they Rise their Tomahawks over your heads. You may tall your white children on our lands, to follow you orders, and do not as they please, for they do not keep your word. Our brothers who came here before told us you had ordered good things to be done and sent to our villages, but we have seen nothing, and your waged men think that truth will not reach your ears."[30]

The difficulty of miscreant frontiersmen would not improve much over time. One Indian agent in 1831 had this to say about mandating licenses: "Grating license to traders is, at present, a mere farce; any person, no matter how depraved, can produce a license, and every provision of law is violated under it." The aim of a trader was to monetize and he could not monetize without ignoring the laws. Exchanges, including whiskey, were common. If a licensed trader eschewed whiskey in his transactions, he would lose out to those who did not. "Thus the Intercourse Law, as custom has rendered it, only serves to retain bad men among the Indians & is productive of much injury to the tribe & to the government."[31]

The frontiersmen's lust for arable land drove speculators to invest. "Such is the rage for speculating in, and forestalling the Lands of the No. West side of Ohio," says George Washington to Jacob Read (3 Nov. 1784), "that scarce a valuable spot within any tolerable distance of it, is left without a claimant. Men in these times, talk with as much facility of fifty, a hundred, and even 500,000 Acres as a Gentleman formerly would do of 1000 acres. In defiance of the proclamation of Congress, they roam over the Country on the Indian side of the Ohio, mark out Lands, Survey, and even settle them. This gives great discontent to the Indians, and will unless measures are taken in time to prevent it, inevitably produce a war with the western Tribes." As an illustration of the American frontiersmen's longing for Natives' lands, after the Treaty of Hopewell

---

[29] Francis Paul Prucha, *American Indian Policy in the Formative Years*, 71 and 73.
[30] Donald Jackson, *Letters of the Lewis and Clark Expedition with Related Documents, 1783–1854*, Vol. 1 (Urbana: University of Illinois Press, 1978), 285.
[31] Francis Paul Prucha, *American Indian Policy in the Formative Years*, 97.

(1785) between the U.S. government and the Cherokees, Chickasaws, and Choctaws[32]—the treaty was made in large part to establish boundaries between Indian tribes and U.S. lands for settlement by Whites—frontiersmen in South Carolina engaged in unprovoked outrages against the Cherokees simply to acquire their fertile lands.[33] That was typical of what was happening everywhere. Governmental prohibitions were merely idle threats.

Figure 8-5: William Augustus Bowles

---

[32] See Charles J. Kappler (ed.), *Indian Affairs: Laws and Treaties,* Vol. 2 (Washington: Government Printing Office, 1904), https://archive.ph/20120710111224/http://digital.library.okstate.edu/kappler/Vol2/treaties/che0008.htm, accessed 24 February 2024.

[33] Francis Paul Prucha, *American Indian Policy in the Formative Years,* 39.

There were numerous treaties throughout the decades that professed to protect the natives' lands, but the federal government often at least implicitly acknowledged the impossibility of taking justificatory action. Thus, in the Treaty of Holston (1791), conducted by Governor William Blount (1749–1800) of the Southwest Territory, the U.S. government decreed, *inter alia*, that anyone who settled on Cherokees' lands forfeited governmental protection, and "the Cherokees may punish him, or not, as they please." The federal government, because it could not act in most instances, pledged inaction—pledged to turn a blind eye to Cherokees' acts of revenge. The treaty stipulated also that the federal government would award presents to the Cherokees to encourage agrarianism.[34] Yet in this instance, we see another nodus. Land speculation was highly profitable, and Blount was no disinterested representative of Indians' affairs. He was a "heavily invested speculator" in Americans' settlement of Western lands.[35] Thus, by failing to do his job, he would largely monetize.

There were also influential independent troublemakers. Marylander William Augustus Bowles (1763–1805, Figure 8-5), who fought with the British in the American Revolution, was *soi-disant* "Chief and Director General of the Creeks" and caused many problems for Hawkins, who specialized in the Creeks' affairs. In interactions with the Creeks, Bowles told them that they, as members of an independent nation—the policy of the federal government beginning with Washington was to treat each tribe as an independent nation and equal partner in trade—were not obliged to obey decrees of the U.S. government. He even advised them in a formal proclamation to remove all federal Indian agents from their lands. Hawkins writes late in 1799 to the Governor James Jackson of Georgia of that scalawag: "Mr. Bowles he is near the mouth of this [Apalachicola] river from whence he continued to pour forth his threats against the affairs of the U.S. in this department. ... I find it an arduous undertaking with a few assistants to make the impressions I wish on the minds of my red charges which are scattered over a wild country of at least three hundred miles square and to fit them to be good neighbors, [when] I am assisted by Bowles and other mischief makers, who are by every opportunity poisoning the minds of the Indians with their abominable lies and misrepresentations."[36]

---

[34] Henry Knox, "Enclosure: Report, 17 January 1792," *Founders Online*, National Archives, https://founders.archives.gov/documents/Washington/05-09-02-0273-0002, accessed 4 June 2023.
[35] William H. Masterson, *William Blount* (Baton Rouge: LSU Press, 1954), 186–87.
[36] Merritt B. Pound, *Benjamin Hawkins*, 191–92.

Bowles, who likely had the patronage of the British government, posed a large threat to Hawkins' authority. After putting together an army of some 300 Seminoles, he assailed and captured the Spanish held Fort St. Marks (Fort San Marcos de Apalache) on May 20, 1800. Bowles escaped arrest by staying and causing trouble in Spain-occupied Florida (Figure 8-6). President Jefferson's Secretary of War, Henry Dearborn, enjoined Hawkins to arrest Bowles should he be found on American soil, which occasionally happened when he aimed to stir up resistance among the Creeks. "Should Bowles at any time come within the limits of the United States, every exertion must be made to apprehend him."[37]

Figure 8-6: Spain-Occupied Florida, West and East c. 1800

[37] Merritt B. Pound, *Benjamin Hawkins*, 193.

In addition to Bowles, there were other scalawags and opportunists who used the Indians to their advantage. British trader William Panton used to his monetary advantage the presence of Spain in the Floridas. He won over Spanish Governor Vicente Manuel de Cespedes of St. Augustine and was allowed to bring into the Floridas certain English merchants to deal in trade with the Natives and to undersell American merchants. In 1784, Panton, Leslie & Company and Mathew and Stother were allowed entry into the Floridas. They soon established stores in St. Augustine and St. Marks for the Upper Creeks, stores in Pensacola and Mobile for the Choctaws and Chickasaws, and even a store far to the west on Spain-owned land at Chickasaw Bluffs on the Mississippi River. Though no enemy of the U.S. government, for reasons of business—and Panton became an inordinately wealthy man through interaction with Spain—he was partnered with Spain and certainly encouraged the Indians in the South to prefer Spain to the United States, but he was no enemy of the United States, like Bowles, whom he considered a "mad dog and even offered one man a reward for killing Bowles.[38]

The story of Bowles is one instance of the existence of numerous British traders, many of whom established themselves in the Northwest Territory after the British drove out the French in 1763 at the conclusion of the French and Indian War. In 1792, the senior officer of Fort Knox, J.F. Hamtramck, reported that British traders from Michilimackinac were underselling American traders and giving alcohol to the Natives. Francis Prucha notes, "It was through the influence of the traders that the Indians fought with the British against the Americans in the war [of 1812]."[39]

An additional problem was the lack of regulation concerning Indians. The number of Indian nations, each with different customs and traditions, was just too large for there to be an "Indian policy," justly serviceable to all. That was obvious by a need for a new Trade and Intercourse Act every three years. The Trade and Intercourse Acts, throughout the years tended to deal with Indians in the aggregate, and that created more problems than it solved.

All such nodi were redoubled with the Louisiana Purchase of 1803. When the federal government purchased from France much land west of the Mississippi River, nodi with Natives decupled. That is one large reason why Jefferson's

---

[38] Merritt B. Pound, *Benjamin Hawkins*, 195–96.
[39] Francis Paul Prucha, *American Indian Policy in the Formative Years*, 68–69 and 77.

Indian policy acquired a significance and political centrality that Washington's could never have had.

It is worth adding here something about John Adams' Indian policy, for he was president between Washington and Jefferson. That policy was roughly a continuation of Washington's, yet Adams underscored his political obligation to place the needs of Americans ahead of Indians.[40] He says to members of the Cherokee Nation (27 Aug. 1798) in reply to their worries about "a certain Zachariah Cox, and others, from carrying an armed force into your country, to take possession of a part of it." Adams divagates and reminds the Cherokees of a trading store erected at Tellico to give the Cherokees needed and cheap goods. He adds, "As I have looked upon it as a part of my duty to attend to your interests, I am also under the strongest obligations to hear the complaints and relieve, as far as is in my power, the distresses of my white children, citizens of the United States." The implicit message is Adams' obligations to Americans trump those of his red children. That was certainly very likely the same with Washington's policy, though never made explicit.

Overall, the early American Indian policy prior to Jefferson's presidency was Knox's policy: "Indian tribes possess the right of the soil of all lands within their limits, respectively, and ... they are not to be divested thereof, but in consequence of fair and bonafide purchases, made under the authority, or with the express approbation of the United States."[41] That policy would dictate the government's interaction with Natives during the early nineteenth century.

The question of what made a transaction "fair and bonafide" was thorny and difficult to answer. As we shall see, the U.S. government consistently treated Natives like children in desperate need of fatherly succor to decide what was in their best interest—even the prominent Indian agent Thomas McKenney, who fought hard for Natives to be treated with dignity, advocated a policy of acting in their best interest because they were "nothing but children"[42]—yet they

---

[40] Usner maintains that Adams' views on Indians is reducible to four "themes": They were merely military allies or enemies in the fight for independence; references to them are chiefly in political writings; Adams' policies were mostly a carry-over from those of Washington; and Adams had little interest in the origins and customs of Indians. Daniel H. Usner, "'A Savage Feast They Made of it': John Adams and the Paradoxical Origins of Federal Indian Policy," in *Journal of the Early Republic*, Vol. 33, No, 4, 2013: 607–41.
[41] Anthony F.C. Wallace, *Jefferson and the Indians*, 167.
[42] Bernard Sheehan, *The Seeds of Extinction: Jefferson Philanthropy and the American Indian* (New York: W.W. Norton & Company, 1973), 153.

granted them equal sovereignty when it came to transactions of trade that involved Aborigines deeding over their lands to representatives of the federal government.

Chapter 9

Philosophical Interlude

"A doubt has been suggested…"

For many Americans, there was the question of whether Native Americans had an above-board claim to rightful ownership of land in North America. What gave any person a rightful claim to a parcel of land? Most American Indians did not farm lands; most were hunters and gatherers. Through hunting and gathering, Indians took from the land but did not fix themselves to it and did not, in the eyes of Americans who wanted to take their lands, use it in any meaningful—i.e., efficient—sense. Indians were merely squatters. Could squatters claim ownership of any parcel of land?

The Indians' perspective was, in many instances, radically different. Some Natives looked on farming—digging into a parcel of land—to be desecration through disembowelment of that land. That was a signal of dishonor to the Great Mother, Earth. Men were to live off nature, not change or carve up nature.

The reality was that Europeans had been sailing to new lands—e.g., the Americas, Africa, and Australia—populating those lands and displacing the Natives of those lands. Did Europeans have a right to do that?

That question was essentially a question of the right of ownership of property, and it was addressed by British philosopher John Locke (1632–1704, Figure 9-1). Locke writes famously in Book II of *Second Treatise on Government*, "Whatsoever … [a man] removes out of the state that nature hath provided, and left it in, he hath mixed his *labour* with, and joined to it something that is his own, and thereby makes it his *property*. It being by him removed from the common state nature hath placed it in, it has by this *labour* something annexed to it, that excludes the common right of other men."[1] Thus, a man has a right to a parcel of land that prohibits other men from such a claim once he works that land. Improving the land through that work (e.g., farming it or building on it) is implied.

---

[1] John Locke, *Second Treatise of Government* (Indianapolis: Hackett Publishing Company, Inc., 1980), V.27.

Note also that Locke mentions leaving the state of nature, in which ownership of property is moot.

Figure 9-1: John Locke

How did Locke's sentiments apply to Native Americans?

It is first noteworthy that Indians, in the main, have not left the state of nature, so they have no legitimate claim to their lands. Second, most have not "mixed their labour" with their lands, and so they cannot claim to have joined something of themselves to their lands.

Many years later, Swiss lawyer and political theorist Emmerich de Vatel (1714–1767) addresses the issue of human habitation of the globe and the possibility of appropriation of sparsely inhabited lands by another country. With small numbers of humans in occupation of the earth, all could freely live and forage and hunt for food. Yet, when the human race soon "became extremely multiplied," there was a need to cultivate the soil to produce food

Philosophical Interlude

sufficient for human numbers. Thus, humans, because of their increase in number, were forced to fix themselves to plots of land.[2]

Vatel moves to the "celebrated question, to which the discovery of the New World has principally given rise." Can a nation legally take possession of "a vast country, in which there are none but erratic nations, incapable by the smallness of their numbers, to people the whole?" Appropriation can only be proportioned to usage. Thus, "their unsettled habitation in those immense regions cannot be accounted a true and legal possession; and the people of Europe, too closely pent up at home, finding land of which the savages stood in no particular need, and of which they made no actual and constant use, were lawfully entitled to take possession of it, and settle it with colonies." It follows that "interloping" inhabitants of a country can take legal possession of a large parcel of land, when the natives are not putting that land to full usage.[3] That is an argument that would be iterated and reiterated for decades by Americans on behalf of misappropriating Indians' lands.

Figure 9-2: Governor John Sevier

---

[2] Emmerich de Vatel, *The Law of Nations, or Principles of the Law of Nature, Applied to the Conduct and Affairs of Nations and Sovereigns* (Philadelphia: P. & J.W. Johnson & Co., 1856), 97–98.

[3] Emmerich de Vatel, *The Law of Nations*, 99–101.

John Sevier, Tennessee's first governor (tenure, 1803–1809, Figure 9-2), followed Vatel: "By the law of nations, it is agreed that no people shall be entitled to more land than they can cultivate. Of course, no people will sit and starve from want of land to work when a neighboring nation has much more than they can make us of."[4] This appeal, and a very commonly used argument, was to Indians' selfishness.

We should not ignore the force of religious arguments on dispossessing Natives of their lands. Puritan John Winthrop (1587–1640) said: "The whole earth is the lords Garden & he hath given it to the sonnes of men, with a general Condition, Gen: 1.28. Increase & multiply, replenish the earth & subdue it. ... For the Natives of New England, they inclose noe land neither have any settled habitation nor any tame cattle to improve the land by, & soe have noe other but a natural right to those countries Soe as if we leave them sufficient for their use wee may lawfully take the rest, there being more than enough for them & us." That general line of thinking was followed by other religionists—e.g., Lewis Cass and Thomas Hart Benton—in early America.[5] It was also followed by politicians. Governor George Gilmer (1790–1859) of Georgia says: "Treaties were expedients to which ignorant, intractable, and savage people were induced without bloodshed to yield up what civilized peoples had a right to possess by virtue of that command of the Creator delivered to many upon his formation—be fruitful, multiply, and replenish the earth, and subdue it."[6]

In one instance in what is now Northern Alabama, American frontiersmen settled on land owned by the Chickasaws and north of the Tennessee River. Return Jonathan Meigs, who was an Indian agent of Tennessee, removed 284 families, though some 5,000 families remained. Early in 1809, the settlers pleaded to new president James Madison and to the Congress: "To gratify a heathen nations Who have no better right to this land than we have ourselves; and they have by estimation nearly 100,000 acres of land to each man of their nation and of no more use to government or society than to saunter about upon like so many wolves or bares, whilst they who would be a supporter to government and improve the country must be forsed even to rent poor stoney ridges to make a support or rase their famelies on whilst there is fine fertile

---

[4] Robert H. White, *Messages of the Governors of Tennessee*, Vol. 1 (Nashville: Tennessee Historical Commission, 1952–1959), 58.
[5] Francis Paul Prucha, *American Indian Policy in the Formative Years: The Indian Trade and Intercourse Acts, 1790–1834* (Cambridge: Harvard University Press, 1962), 240–41.
[6] George Gilmer, *Journal of the House of Representatives of the State of Georgia*, 1830, 13.

countrys lying uncultivated, and we must be debared even from inJoying a small Corner of this land."[7] Natives, so the argument says, have abundantly more land than they need, are antagonistic to the federal government, and do not improve their land. Natives are also "heathens"—*viz.*, not god-fearing—and that was an argument that was decisive in the minds of many Americans, though we must note that it never became part early American Indian policy by the U.S. government. And so, the argument intimates, while Natives might have claimed a right to the land by primacy, primacy was trumped by ill usage of that land and by the barbarity of the Natives.

John Quincy Adams (1767–1848), who would follow as president after James Monroe, agreed. A huntsman might forage 1000 miles in search of prey, but that gives him no right of ownership. "Shall the liberal bounties of Providence to the race of man be monopolized by one of ten thousand for whom they were created? Shall the exuberant bosom of the common mother, amply adequate to the nourishment of millions, be claimed exclusively by a few hundreds of her offspring? Shall the lordly savage not only disdain the virtues and enjoyments of civilization himself, but shall he control the civilization of a world?"[8] The argument, implicit, again concerns the aborigines' inefficient use of land and their barbarity. By allowing them the privilege of ownership of their lands, Americans are letting barbarity trump civility. Indians, thus, are retardants of civilization. Only efficient usage of land, thinks Adams, offers a right to ownership. Nomadic peoples have no right to land, and so too the Natives' claim to ownership is suspect.

What was the Native American view of land?

Here, I reiterate that there is no one Indians' view of their lands because the number of their nations was too large, and they differed often radically in their customs and manner of living. That does not prohibit certain rough observations, however, on how Natives, in general viewed land.

The Indians' view of land was typically different from their white interlopers, often spiritual, and so plowing the land was not necessarily improving it. Says one anonymous Native circa 1880: "You ask me to plow the ground. Shall I take

---

[7] Francis Paul Prucha, *American Indian Policy in the Formative Years*, 162.

[8] "A Brief History of Land Transfers between American Indians and the United States Government," *Clarke Historical Library,* https://www.cmich.edu/research/clarke-historical-library/explore-collection/explore-online/native-american-material/native-american-treaty-rights/land-transfers, accessed 6 May 2023.

a knife and tear my mother's bosom? You ask me to cut grass and make hay and sell it and be rich like white men. But dare I cut off my mother's hair?" Again, there is this quote from Lakota warrior Sitting Bull in the late nineteenth century: "I wish all to know that I do not propose to sell any part of my country, nor will I have Whites cutting our timber along the rivers, more especially the bark. I am particularly fond of the little groves of oak trees. I love to look at them, because they endure the wintry storm and the summer's heat, and—not unlike ourselves—seem to flourish by them."[9]

Nonetheless, the policy of the federal government from the time of Washington and for over two decades beyond Jefferson's second term was that Natives had rightful ownership on the lands on which they hunted, and so the U.S. government had no right of appropriation through conquest, irrespective of many Indian nations siding with the British in the Revolutionary War. That policy, we have seen, was shaped by Knox, who argued very likely more from fiscal considerations—the costliness of continued warfare with Aborigines—than from above-board concern for Indians' welfare. The financial cost of acquisition of lands by conquest, if undertaken, would be much greater than merely purchasing such lands. Moreover, there would be no human cost through American lives lost—at least, theoretically.

Over time, U.S. policy would be informed by the U.S. Supreme Court. Let us consider the singular Supreme Court case of *Fletcher v. Pleck* (1807), which did not directly involve Indians, but had implications for their claim to lands and is illustrative of the duplicity involved in purchasing Natives' lands.

Robert Fletcher bought land from John Peck, which was part of 35 million acres (now Alabama and Mississippi) claimed by Georgia after the Revolutionary War in an Indian reserve. Georgia then quadrapartitioned the land, which it sold to separate companies in 1795 as the Yazoo Land Act, approved by Georgian legislation. Yet formal approbation occurred through bribery by the speculators. Almost all the legislators who approved the sale were bribed. When they learned of the bribery, Georgians were furious and demanded action. Consequently, when up for reelection, many members of the legislature were removed and replaced by new members. The new legislation voided the sales.[10]

---

[9] "Native Americans Describe Traditional Views of Land Ownership," *Social History for Every Classroom*, CUNY: The Graduate Center, https://shec.ashp.cuny.edu/items/show/1543, accessed 2 June 2023.

[10] Stuart Banner, *How the Indians Lost Their Land* (Cambridge: Belknap Press, 2005), 171.

Philosophical Interlude 137

Yet the speculators had in the meantime sold much of the purchased land to investors like Peck, who claimed that he had a right to the land he had purchased. He, after all, was merely an innocent victim of the salacious speculators.

In the ravelment, the case landed in the U.S. Supreme Court. Fletcher's lawyers argued that the sale was invalid, due to speculators selling land that was not rightly theirs. They maintained that the land belonged to the United States; Peck's lawyers, to Georgia. Yet Fletcher, in collusion with and not antagonistic to Peck, hoped to lose: that is, he hoped that the court would decide in favor of Peck—who had as the prominent lawyers John Quincy Adams, Joseph Story (soon-to-be member of the Supreme Court), and Robert Goodlow Harper (an eminent lawyer), while Peck was represented by the alcoholic Luther Martin, who was paid in effect to lose the case.[11]

The Supreme Court, led by John Marshall (1755–1835, Figure 9-3), voted that the Georgian congress acted unconstitutionally, for "impairing the Obligation of Contracts." Citing Article 1, Section 10, it judged that even if the transaction was illegal, the law could not be repealed.[12]

Figure 9-3: Justice John Marshall

---

[11] Stuart Banner, *How the Indians Lost Their Land*, 171.
[12] Stuart Banner, *How the Indians Lost Their Land*, 172.

No person involved in the kerfuffle was bewilderingly incentivized to concern himself with the Indians' claim that it was their land that was illegally sold. The issue was here between Georgia as an individual state and the U.S. government.

Even so, the issue of the Cherokees' right to the land was brought up toward the end of the argument of one of Peck's representatives and likely by one of the justices. "A doubt has been suggested whether this power extends to land to which the Indian title has not yet been extinguished."[13]

A lawyer of Peck began his vitriolic counter-remonstrance in a Lockean manner: "What is the Indian title? It is a mere occupancy for the purpose of hunting. It is not like our tenures; they have no idea of a title to the soil itself. It is overrun by them, rather than inhabited. It is not a true and legal possession."[14]

Two prominent justices, Marshall and William Johnson, gave discordant views on the Natives' claim to the lands. For Justice Marshall, the question concerned whether the land belonged to the federal government or to Georgia. The local Natives could merely claim "Indian title"—a term never explained but implicitly considered to be something less than what a White or a group of Whites could claim.[15] Justice William Johnson disagreed. Marshall, he said, was whiffle-waffling. The Indians either owned or did not own the land. There could be no Indian title as a middle position—a quasi-ownership or sort-of ownership.[16]

Thomas Jefferson expressed his views on the Georgian affair to book-peddler Samuel Whitcomb, Jr., in 1824. Whitcomb came to Monticello to try to entice the aging sage to a purchase of some book. After his visit with Jefferson, the peddler wrote: "He is decidedly opposed to the Georgian Claim. Says she [Georgia] is the most greedy of land of any State in the Union. That the Indians are under no obligation to sell these lands, that they have an original title to them."[17]

Marshall would, in 1823, expatiate on "Indian title" in *Johnson v. McIntosh*. Indians had both "a legal as well as a just claim" to the land, but they could not claim ownership, just a right to occupancy—again, Indian title. Commenting on the philosophical aspects of the issue, Marshall adds: "We will not enter into

---

[13] Stuart Banner, *How the Indians Lost Their Land*, 172.

[14] Stuart Banner, *How the Indians Lost Their Land*, 172.

[15] "A Brief History of Land Transfers between American Indians and the United States Government."

[16] Stuart Banner, *How the Indians Lost Their Land*, 171–72.

[17] Samuel Whitcomb, Jr., "A Book Peddler at Monticello," in *Visitors to Monticello*, ed. Merrill D. Peterson (Charlottesville: University Press of Virginia, 1993), 94.

the controversy whether agriculturalists, merchants, and manufacturers, have a right, on abstract principles, to expel hunters from the territory they possess. Conquest gives a title which the Courts of the conqueror cannot deny, whatever the private and speculative opinions of individuals may be, respecting the original justice of the claim." [18] Marshall's use of "possess," given his expiscation of "Indian title," is odd. The argument from conquest is also odd, as it is, in a manner of speaking, self-serving. Conquest, it seems, overrules, or at least negates, justice. Marshall's solution to the Indian problem was, in effect, a return to the policy prior to Washington's administration. Pragmatics trumps philosophy. Americans need Indians' lands and will eventually take them, so there is no need of philosophical shilly-shally.

Marshall's argument was not decisive. Not all Indians were hunters and gatherers, and that was known to almost all who had significant interactions with Natives. Christian missionaries had done much work in introducing Native Americans to the plow. Georgian Indians were especially draw to husbandry. Marshall's problem—and this was a perennial problem for the federal government—was that he lumped together all Indian nations as if they comprised across the continent a culturally homogenous group such that a solution to a problem with one nation could, with equal justice apply to all others.

Yet that fact was expediently overlooked. The issue was Americans' ever pressing need for Indians' lands. With the population of Whites steadily increasing, those numbers and the need of land to farm increasingly required willy-nilly removal of the Indians to the west of White territories. John Weaver notes that frontiersmen used property rights to their advantage. "Extraction of wealth from frontiers benefited from a tension, remarkable and fateful, between defiant private initiatives and the ordered, state-backed certainties of property rights." While laws for acquisition were in place in states or the federal government, frontiersmen, motivated by self-interest, often ignored those laws.[19] Terry Anderson and Peter Hill in *The Not So Wild, Wild West* add that laws tended to favor much frontiersmen at the expense of the Natives, though homesteaders were often granted too little land for profitable farms, and lawmakers often knew too little about those lands about which they were making laws. Lawmakers and Indians—"Indians invested in establishing

---

[18] "A Brief History of Land Transfers between American Indians and the United States Government."

[19] John C. Weaver, *The Great Land Rush and the Making of the Modern World, 1650–1900* (Montreal: McGill-Queen's University Press, 2003). 4.

property rights when it was economical to do so"—because of vastly limited resources, tended to exercise caution apropos of property rights, their distribution, and their enforcement in proportion to the value of a property. Nonetheless, Anderson and Hill maintain, in keeping with the title of their book, that exchanges between Indians and American frontiersmen prior to the Civil War tended to be "mutually wealth-enhancing."[20]

Figure 9-4: General Andrew Jackson

With the purchase of the Louisiana Territories in 1803 during Jefferson's first term as president of the United States, the Congress passed a law, deemed cromulent, that encouraged Jefferson to have Natives swap land east of the Mississippi River, needed for the bloating American population, for lands west

---

[20] Terry L. Anderson and Peter J. Hill, *The Not So Wild, Wild West: Property Rights on the Frontier* (Stanford: Stanford University Press, 2004), 34–52.

of the Mississippi River. The argument of Congress was that there was aplenty land in North America, and so conflict could be gamely eschewed, so long as Indians agreed to remove, and if needed, to remove again, ever in a westerly direction. They were, after all, not rooted to the land, as were the interloping Americans, who farmed it and engaged in manufacture on it. If Natives wished not to vacate their lands—Creek and Cherokee Indians were especially averse to removal—they would be "enticed" to vacate them. Those enticements usually came at the urgings of lawless Westerners, who were in proximity of Natives' lands and whom the federal government could not police.

By the presidency of Andrew Jackson (1829–1837, Figure 9-4), there was little choice for Indians. When Creek Indians of Georgia told representatives of the U.S. government in 1828 that they refused to remove themselves, they were given a chilly dilemma over which to mull. That amounted to forfeiture of a way of life or extinction. "If you wish to quit the chase, to free yourself of barbarism, and settle down in the calm pursuits of civilization and good morals, and to raise up a generation of Christians, you had better go." If not, "you must be sensible that it will be impossible for you to remain for any length of time in your present situation as a distinct Society or Nation, within the limits of Georgia. Such a community is incompatible with our System and must yield to it."[21]

Jackson's presidency coincided with another landmark case, *Cherokee Nation v. Georgia* (1831). The U.S. Supreme Court, in that case, decided the issue of the "independent" status of Indian nations, hitherto treated like any other foreign nation (e.g., France, Italy, or Portugal). Cherokee Chief John Ross and lawyer William Wirt defended the Cherokee Nation, which was suing Georgia for attempting to annihilate the Cherokee Indians. Chief Justice John Marshall, consistent with his earlier notion of "Indian title," summed the majority opinion of the court":

> Though the Indians are acknowledged to have an unquestionable, and, heretofore, unquestioned right to the lands they occupy, until that right shall be extinguished by a voluntary cession to our government; yet it may well be doubted whether those tribes which reside within the acknowledged boundaries of the United States can, with strict accuracy, be denominated foreign nations. They may, more correctly be denominated domestic dependent nations. They occupy a territory to which we assert a

---

[21] "A Brief History of Land Transfers between American Indians and the United States Government."

title independent of their will, which must take effect in point of possession when their right of possession ceases. Meanwhile, they are in a state of pupilage. Their relation to the United States resembles that of a ward to his guardian.[22]

That decision, exceptionally paternalistic, would be overturned one year later by the Supreme Court in *Worcester v. Georgia* (1932).

Andrew Jackson's presidency marked a decided shift in federal government's Indian policy. He passed through Congress the Indian Removal Act (28 May 1830), which removed, from 1830 to 1850, some 60,000 Natives from some 20 tribes to lands west of the Mississippi. Southern tribes settled mainly in the arid regions of Oklahoma; northern, mainly in Kansas. Thousands died from disease, starvation, and exposure to the elements *in transitu*, in what is today known as the Trail of Tears (Figure 9-5).[23]

Figure 9-5: Trail of Tears

It should be obvious that the policy of westward removal was a short-term solution and, even so, a bad one. The American population swelled, and many Americans, in time, wished to move to the West Coast, California especially,

---

[22] *Cherokee Nation v. Georgia, 30 U.S. 1, Justia: U.S. Supreme Court,* https://supreme.justia.com/cases/federal/us/30/1/, accessed 20 June 2 -23.
[23] Guenter Lewey, "Were American Indians the Victims of Genocide?" *History,* 2004, https://web.archive.org/web/20170815233620/https://www.commentarymagazine.com/articles/were-american-indians-the-victims-of-genocide/, accessed 7 May 2023.

Philosophical Interlude 143

during the "Gold Rush" (1848–1855). In removal, they would pass through Natives' lands, thereby making roads and encroaching on the removed Indians. The future was clear: Natives, in the "state of pupilage," had little choice but to become part of the "System." If they refused, ….

I have more to say of Jackson' Indian policy as well as the policies of Madison, Monroe, and Adams before him, in the appendix.

The next three chapters expiscate and critically assess Thomas Jefferson's Indian policy, which would become one of the focal issues of his presidency because of his attempts to implement his political philosophy and the many new problems with Aborigines on account of the Louisiana Purchase.

Chapter 10

Thomas Jefferson's Indian Policy in Gist

"This ideas might be so novel…"

As I mention in the preface, I am, by choice and by inclination, more of a philosopher than a historian, and as a philosopher, my disposition is analytical. And so, I seek conceptual clarification and exactness of understanding. In this chapter, I turn to Thomas Jefferson's Indian policy. In doing so, I seek answers to these questions. What was Jefferson's early view of Natives' right to land? Also, with the explosive American populational growth ever necessitating acquisition of new lands and the removal of Native peoples farther and farther into the West—the U.S. population was some 2.5 million in 1776, some 5.3 million, and some 11 million in 1825[1]—did Jefferson believe that Indians could intermix with Americans without blighting the offspring? Finally, was Jefferson's Indian policy significantly different from his presidential predecessors and successors, as Anthony Wallace suggests? Answers to those questions are the focus of this chapter.

It is fitting, to begin with Anthony Wallace's thesis, what I shall dub the Subtle Muscularity Thesis (SMT), in his book on Jefferson and the Indians. To grasp the policy, we must first grasp the avowed psychopathy of the man behind the policy.

Wallace's Jefferson is deeply paranoic. Jefferson had a "deeply controlling temperament" and possessed a "willingness to trample on civil liberty and use force to achieve national goals." He justified his titanolatry by a "relentless moralism"—his amaranthine tendency to give his actions a moral slant, while his aims were typically self-interested, not other-interested.[2] And so, references to "the liberty of 'the people'" were instead veiled references—more appositely, projections—concerning his own fears of persecution by others. He longed ever

---

[1] Matt Rosenberg, "U.S. Population Throughout History," *ThoughtCo*, https://www.thoughtco.com/us-population-through-history-1435268, accessed 20 May 2023.

[2] Anthony F.C. Wallace, *Jefferson and the Indians: The Tragic Fate of the First Americans* (Cambridge: Belknap Press, 1999), 15.

for personal freedom, but as a false prophet, he projected and marketed that as political liberalism. Lusting after control, he feared being controlled by others. Thus, Jefferson gave his self-interested Indian policy a moral gloss. He "projected his private drama onto a national, indeed a global, scene, demanding liberty for the downtrodden everywhere, to the point of being prepared to force freedom on the unwilling."[3] Thus, his vision of a global "empire of liberty," the subject of the final chapter, was reducible to personal paranoia, and so, despite the fact that Jefferson's policy was nearly identical to Henry Knox's policy with Washington, there was an intensity or psychopathological urgency to it because of Jefferson's deeply unbalanced, paranoic mind. (I say more on Wallace's thesis in my appendix.)

If we follow the thread of the SMT, we expect to find—by close analysis of Jefferson's letters, messages, or addresses, or even of the actions of federal agents during his tenure as president—evidence of narcissism and paranoia that spills into actions much to the detriment of Native Americans, *pace* Knox, and much to Jefferson's own benefit.

Prior to Wallace, there is Bernard Sheehan's more subtle Naïve Philanthropic Thesis (NPT) in *Seeds of Extinction: Jeffersonian Philanthropy and the American Indian* (1973). Sheehan argues that there was momentum to the actions of American revolutionists who successfully threw off the British yoke to begin their own experiment of confederated government of the 13 states. With the overthrow of the British yoke, Americans were in no mood to let uncivilized Natives ruin their experiment.[4] That is the milieu that Jefferson inherited, and that inheritance limited what Jefferson could do on behalf of the Indians.

While, for Sheehan, Jefferson theoretically adds nothing to his Indian policy that was not in place prior to his presidency, he did concretize the policies, essentially experimental, of predecessors. "Jefferson led the age, not because his ideas were original, but because they represented a consensus." Indian agents such as Benjamin Hawkins, Return Meigs, and Thomas McKenney and under the direction of Secretary of War Henry Dearborn, were given a consistent policy that was essentially in some sense philanthropic—though for Sheehan there is a built-in polarity to the term—and that was a policy that successors could readily adopt. The policy, though not original, had a

---

[3] Anthony F.C. Wallace, *Jefferson and the Indians*, 15–16.
[4] Bernard Sheehan, *Seeds of Extinction: Jeffersonian Philanthropy and the American Indian* (New York: W.W. Norton & Company, 1973), 5–8.

significance that only Jefferson, qua champion of liberty and of science, could give it.⁵

Yet Jeffersonian policy, which necessitated obliteration of Indian culture in the process of civilizing Natives, was oversimple. It was intolerant of failure: It could not accommodate refusal of Indians both to adopt American culture and to intermix with Americans. If Jefferson committed any crime, says Sheehan, it was that of naïveté. He may have been motivated by an "excess of goodwill, but not the intentional inflicting of pain on a less powerful people."⁶

To assess the theses of Wallace and Sheehan, I turn to Jefferson's writings.

As early as 1784, Jefferson writes in some notes, consistent with the early American policy, that Americans have the preemptive right, not the occupational right, to Indians' lands. "Prender of possession, and assumption of boundary, by the Jus gentium of America, gives a right of *preemption* against all nations and individuals but not of *occupation* against the native inhabitants."⁷ In the same year, he gives formal expression to that preemptive policy in his Report on Government for the Western Territory.⁸ Some eight years later, Jefferson, as Washington's secretary of state, writes to Secretary of War, Henry Knox (26 Aug. 1790), of the Treaty of Hopewell—three treaties with the Cherokee, Chickasaw, and Choctow nations from 1785 to 1786. "The Cherokees were entitled to the sole occupation of the lands within the limits guaranteed to them. The state of N. Carolina, according to the jus gentium established for America by universal usage, had only a right of preemption of these lands against all other nations. It could convey then to it's citizens only this right of preemption, and the right of occupation could not be united to it till obtained by the U.S. from the Cherokees. … The claimants of N.C. then and also the Cherokees are exactly where they would have been had neither the act of cession nor that of acceptance been ever made; that is, the latter possess the right of occupation, and the former the right of preemption." Jefferson's position is clear, and it is not John Marshall's position of Indian title—a sort of quasi-ownership. Natives have the right to live on the lands they occupy; the U.S. is first in line should the Natives wish to part with them.

---

⁵ Bernard Sheehan, *Seeds of Extinction*, 7–11.
⁶ Bernard Sheehan, *Seeds of Extinction*, 11–12.
⁷ Thomas Jefferson, "Notes Concerning Boundaries, [1784?]," *Founders Online,* https://founders.archives.gov/documents/Jefferson/01-06-02-0369-0002, accessed 4 June 2023.
⁸ Thomas Jefferson, Report on Government for Western Territory, *The Scholars' Thomas Jefferson,* ed. M. Andrew Holowchak (Newcastle upon Tyne, Cambridge Scholars, 2021), 30

What of the issue of miscegenation?

My critical examination of the first part of this book shows, I trust that Jefferson thought that Indians could intermix with white Americans without blighting the offspring. Unlike Blacks, with whom miscegenation would taint the offspring from the European perspective,[9] there is never the suggestion in any writing that intermixing would taint the offspring should it occur. As governor of Virginia and especially during his presidency, Jefferson ever encouraged peaceable interaction between Americans and Natives (Figure 10-1), adoption of American ways by Natives, and gradual miscegenation. Miscegenation was quietly encouraged, but only on condition of Indians adopting the ways of Americans.

Figure 10-1: Trade between Whites and Reds

---

[9] Jefferson writes, "The improvement of the blacks in body and mind, in the first instance of their mixture with the whites, has been observed by every one, and proves that their inferiority is not the effect merely of their condition of life." Thomas Jefferson, *Notes on the State of Virginia*, ed. William Peden (Chapel Hill: University of North Carolina Press, 1954), 141. He ingeminates that sentiment in a letter to Edmund Coles (25 Aug. 1814): "Their amalgamation with the other color produces a degradation to which no lover of his country, no lover of excellence in the human character can innocently consent."

Jefferson was largely optimistic about the intellectual capacities and civilizing tendencies of Indians. To miscegenate, they would have to meet certain criteria. First, they would have to abandon their nomadic, hunt-and-gather lifestyle, which was largely thought to be the cause of their barbarism, and then they would have to become farmers. Next, they would need some grasp of American law, with an emphasis on individual ownership of land. Third, with a turn to agriculture and a much smaller need for land for sufficiency, Indians would have to sell unused land to the federal government to be used mostly for new American settlers for the growing American population. Last, they would need a general, American education—conversion to Christianity for most, though not for Jefferson, deemed crucial to that education. It was presumed by most who aimed to civilize the Natives that civilizing and Christianizing were mutually entailing: A civilized life was Christian, and Christian life was civilized. As those conditions show, there was never the suggestion that there was much, if anything, worth salvaging of Indians' cultures.

Why, then did miscegenation not occur?

The commitment to agriculture for Jefferson was key, since more efficient use and improvement of land, private property, selling surplus lands to the government, and American education would follow seriatim.[10] Jefferson writes to Southern Indian agent Benjamin Hawkins (9 Feb. 1803) in a letter that expresses neatly his program of miscegenation. The message is Aboriginal

---

[10] Indians in general did not take so easily to American education, for most merely did not see the need for reading, writing, and elementary math, and education in American culture. Natives functioned for centuries without them. In 1744, for instance, Virginian delegates offer Onondaga chief, Canasatego, an education at William and Mary for Onondaga braves. Canasatego replies: "You, who are wise, must know that difference. Nations have different Conceptions of things; and you will therefore not take it amiss, if our Ideas of this kind of Education happen no to be the same with yours. We have had some Experience of it; Several of our young People were formerly brought up at the College of the Northern Provinces; they were instructed in all your Science; but, when they came back to us, they were bad Runners, ignorant of every means of living in the Woods, unable to bear either Cold or Hunger, knew neither how to build a Cabin, take a Dear, or kill an enemy, spoke our Language imperfectly, were therefore neither fit for Hunters, Warriors, nor Counsellors; they were totally good for nothing. We are however not the less oblig'd by your kind Offer, tho' we decline accepting it; and, to show our grateful Sense of it, if the Gentlemen of Virginian will send us a Dozen of their Sons, we will take Care of their Education, instruct them in all we know, and make *Men* of them." Alexis de Tocqueville, *Democracy in America*, trans. Gerald Bevan (New York: Penguin Classics, 2003), 383.

esurience, their greediness: They will learn to do more with less and in becoming Americanized, they will affect a "coincidence of interests.

> I consider the business of hunting as already become insufficient to furnish clothing and subsistence to the Indians. The promotion of agriculture, therefore, and household manufacture, are essential in their preservation, and I am disposed to aid and encourage it liberally. This will enable them to live on much smaller portions of land, and indeed will render their vast forests useless but for the range of cattle; for which purpose, also, as they become better farmers, they will be found useless, and even disadvantageous. While they are learning to do better on less land, our increasing numbers will be calling for more land, and thus a coincidence of interests will be produced between those who have lands to spare, and want other necessaries, and those who have such necessaries to spare, and want lands.

Hawkins is to instill in the Indians "a sense of the superior value of a little land, well cultivated, over a great deal, unimproved," captured succinctly by the formula, "to do better on less land." There is urgency to the intimations in the letter. Napoleon has become the autocrat of France, and Jefferson, wanting to acquire the New Orleans' lands, is worried about France's ownership of the Louisiana territories.

Jefferson next turns to a bewildering analogy of hunter and hunted—bewildering because it shows plainly his frame of mind upon crafting the letter. The natives ought to adopt the policy of a hunted animal, amputating and leaving behind to the hunter the parts for which he is pursued, thereby escaping from the hunt. There is an element of disanalogy, he notes. In this instance, the American "hunters" are not asking the Indian "hunted" for anything useful to the Indians, though what is useless to the hunted is preeminently useful to the hunters. Disanalogy notwithstanding, Jefferson's use of such an analogy intimates that the exchange between Americans and Indians is nowise even or equal. Americans have the power, and with power comes leverage, though not right.

There follow Jefferson's thoughts on miscegenation, "The ultimate point of rest & happiness for them is to let our settlements and theirs meet and blend together, to intermix, and become one people." By doing so, they will merely be following "the natural progress of things," which makes resistance senseless. By intermixing and identifying with Americans, Indians will eschew "the many casualties which may endanger them while a separate people." Jefferson's reasoning here is in keeping with the stadialism of his day (chapter 1). There are the options of intermixing and Americans adopting Indians' ways, of intermixing and Indians adopting Americans' ways, and of intermixing and forming a sort of mixed culture. Only the former, Jefferson thinks, benefits all. Jefferson then asks Hawkins to exercise caution in his interactions with the Natives. "This idea [of intermixing] may be so novel as that it might shock the Indians, were it even hinted to them," so Hawkins is enjoined to keep the notion to himself. Disclosure will likely lead to heightened hostilities.[11]

There was nothing in principle objectionable to Americans about intermixing with Natives, so long as it was on the formers' terms. The generally unobjectionable, often lauded marriage of John Rolfe with Pocahontas is evidence.[12] What Whites did find objectionable, in the main, was marriage between an Indian male and white female.[13] Why was that the case? It the former instance, the American male would (ideally) civilize the Indian female; in the latter case, the American female would be barbarized by the Indian male.

Having thought through the plan in the letter to Hawkins, Jefferson is convinced of its "moral" soundness. He proposes to assuage both land-hungry Americans and Native Americans, soon to be introduced to a better way of life. Hawkins, when circumstances are propitious, is periodically to convince Indians to part with lands to assuage American adventurers, in need of land. Jefferson asks Hawkins to work, especially with the intransigent Creeks in the South.

---

[11] Jeffersonian dissembling is not unique to him. Jedidiah Morse, for instance, in his "Report on Indian Affairs," advocates dissembling vis-à-vis "learning them [Indians] to cultivate the soil." It is aidful and instructive to teach Indians the rudiments of husbandry, but not to insist that they must learn husbandry because that must be their future. Jedidiah Morse, *A Report to the Secretary of War of the United States on Indian Affairs, Comprising a Narrative of a Tour Performed in the Summer of 1820* (New Haven: S. Converse, 1822), 58–59.

[12] Jefferson himself, according to the testimony of a book-peddler, Samuel Whitcomb, Jr., who visited Monticello in 1824, and failing to make any sale, found himself embroiled in an engaging conversation with the former president. When talking about the Indians, Jefferson related that "both his daughters married descendants of Pocahontas." Whitcomb argues that Jefferson seemed very proud of that fact. Samuel Whitcomb, Jr., "A Book Peddler at Monticello," in *Visitors to Monticello*, ed. Merrill D. Peterson (Charlottesville: University Press of Virginia, 1993), 95.

[13] Bernard Sheehan, *Seeds of Extinction*, 178.

There is nothing stated here particularly attractive to the Creeks or any Natives—Jefferson is dangling a grape-leaf before the face of a hungry fish-eating puffin—and Jefferson intimates that Indians might be indignant about the offer of miscegenation and integration if it should be made explicit, so it is likely that Jefferson thinks it will only be obvious to Indians that integration with Americans is an advantageous thing, a harbinger to their future happiness, only when it happens.

The nodus of the unattractiveness of integration with Americans Jefferson must foresee. He mentions in a 1787 letter to Madison (Jan. 30) that living without laws in small communities might be the happiest manner of living—"it is problem, not clear in my mind, that the 1st condition [living like Indians] is not the best"—but it is inconsistent with any significant amount of population. There is a degree of liberty in such small societies that cannot be had in larger ones. What cannot be had in small societies is any degree of science and the arts. Moreover, the happiness Jefferson suggests in the letter to Hawkins seems mostly to be the result of the eschewal of "many casualties" that they would suffer were they to refuse integration.

Figure 10-2: Indian Males' Hunting Lifestyle

Though Jefferson's Indian policy was right-intended—at least, following Sheehan, we can agree that he had the best interest of Natives in mind—there were innumerable cultural snags, which Jefferson should have fully anticipated but did not. Those which I have mentioned in the prior chapter I here ignore.

First, the abandonment of Native males' hunting lifestyle (Figure 10-2) for one of husbandry was not without elephantine cultural consequences. Since in Indian communities, women were the farmers, when there was farming, and males were the warriors and hunters, it was an act of great emasculation for a hunter/warrior, ever exposed to parlousness and great dangers, to adopt the role of farmer—a womanly task. "Hunting, war and manly pursuits were best fitted to them."[14] Furthermore, there was certainly volatility in husbandry, as Jefferson learned, usually from afar, through experiences with his own properties. Agricultural surpluses were not always easily transported to markets, and markets did not always need farmed goods—especially during the embargo (1807), when farmed goods were in superabundance. Moreover, the weather did not always cooperate and not all land was equally arable. The nodus of poorly arable land was a special problem, as Americans ever sought to dispossess Natives of their most fecund and functional lands. Thus, some amount of hunting was a means of ensuring Natives' subsistence, given the precariousness of husbandry. And so, there was, in principle, no reason for Natives to abandon hunting completely. Skins and furs were much wanted commodities. American frontiersmen, knowing that, often hunted. That noted Jefferson's imploration was very likely not to eradicate all hunting by Natives, but most hunting to free up land that could be cleared for agriculture. Jefferson, too, hunted and enjoyed his guns.[15]

Second, the proposed change from an economics of shared prosperity—the Indians' way of life—to one of individual prosperity through the privatization of goods and leadership based on wealth—the American way of life—was a cultural tsunami that, if adopted, would have to drown out all traces of Indians' culture in little time. Older tribesmen, filiopietistic and meritocratic, valued leadership based on excellence: bravery and success in hunting and war as well as callidity in trade and eloquence in diplomacy. Conversion to a society which

---

[14] J. Niles Hubbard, *Red Jacket and His People, 1750–1830* (New York: Burt Franklin, 1886), 289–90. Anthony F.C. Wallace, *Jefferson and the Indians*, 298.
[15] See Arthur Scherr, "'Have Gun(s), Will Travel": Thomas Jefferson, Gun Ownership and Military Affairs," *The Elusive Thomas Jefferson: Essays on the Man behind the Myths* (Jefferson: McFarland, 2017), 163–90.

placed acquisition above merit, howsoever attractive that might have seemed to younger Indians, was a sea-change for Natives—a manner of living that was greed-driven, and womanly.

The olive branches offered by agents of the federal government, under the direction of Jefferson, were not always so attractive to Indians willing to integrate. Many tribal members were drawn to the American way of life not because it was seen as more fruitful or better, but because they recognized rightly that there was no possibility of preservation of Indians' ways. Americanized Europeans were surely moving westward, and swiftly so, and forcing Aborigines to move even further westward, and it was only a matter of time before there would be no place to which to remove. Those olive branches presaged the demise of their way of life. Overhill Cherokee chief, Old Tassell (d. 1788), argues with cogency: "You say, Why do not the Indians till the ground and live as we do? May we not, with equal propriety, ask, Why the white people do not hunt and live as we do? ... The Great God of Nature ... has given each their lands under distinct considerations and circumstance; he has stocked yours with corn, ours with buffalo, yours with hog, ours with bear; yours with sheep, ours with deer."[16]

Third, Natives were suspicious about and irked by the persistent pressure on them to sell their lands to the government or those persons with governmental sanction. Buyers were remorseless and unrelenting.

Already in possession of Senecans' breathtakingly beautiful land east of Genesee River in Western New York, Whites sought the land west of that river. Thomas Morris (1771–1849), son of Robert Morris, signer of the Declaration of Independence, obtained a preemptive right to that property in 1791. Morris soon met with a delegation of Natives. Col. Wadsworth of Connecticut was the U.S. commissioner, William Shepard was the commissioner of Massachusetts, New Yorker William Bayard represented the Holland Company, and Robert Morris was represented by his son Thomas and Col. Williamson. Noteworthy sachems of the nearby tribes were Cornplanter, Farmer's Brother, Little Beard, Little Billy, and Red Jacket. Morris offered 100,000 dollars. The Natives, led by Red Jacket, rejected the offer as they were ill-disposed to part with the handsome land for any amount of money. Knowing that transactional decisions could be influenced by warriors and women—warriors defended the land, and women gave birth to warriors—Morris later approached key women

---

[16] Anthony F.C. Wallace, *Jefferson and the Indians*, 303.

with gifts of beads, blankets, brooches, and other desirable items and promises of their needs being met throughout their lives. Morris' appeal to the woman proved fructiferous, and Morris gained the lands he sought.[17]

In 1810, David Ogden of the Ogden Company purchased the preemptive right to the remainder of the Senecans' lands—i.e., the five reservations upon which the Senecans lived—and the Ogden Company (est. 1821) even pressed them to sell those lands. Red Jacket enjoined Thomas Ludlow Ogden to look to Joseph Ellicott of the Holland Land Company, for "he has lands enough to sell." Red Jacket, of course, realized that Ogden, having purchased the right of preemption, would not rest until he had acquired the remainder of the Senecans' lands. Ogden's bid was unsuccessful, but he would not relent.[18]

The last snag, though one which was not formally part of Jefferson's policy, was religious. Christianizing the Indians was especially difficult. Christianity, the uptake of which was seen as essential for integration into white culture, Indians found to be a strange religion. Axial concepts—such as original sin, the fall of man, a triune God, and the coming and second coming of Christ—furhoodled them.

Aborigines also found puzzling the vast number of denominations of Christianity, which boasted of being one religion. Says the silver-tongued Red Jacket of the Iroquois in 1828 to a Massachusetts' missionary who came to convert the Natives: "You say there is but one way to worship and serve the Great Spirit. If there is but one religion, why do white people differ so much about it? Why do you, not all agree, as you can all read the book [the Bible]? … We also have a religion which was given to our forefathers and has been handed down to us their children. We worship that way. It teaches us to be thankful for all the favors we receive, to love each other, and to be united. We never quarrel about religion." Since the Great Spirit made a religion for Whites and another for Indians, Indians aim not to take from Whites their religion, and Whites ought not to take from Natives theirs.[19] The exchange with the missionary was one of Red Jacket's greatest speeches.

---

[17] J. Niles Hubbard, *Red Jacket and His People, 1750–1830* (New York: Burt Franklin, 1886), 161–95.
[18] J. Niles Hubbard, *Red Jacket and His People*, 279.
[19] Red Jacket, "Red Jacket Defends Native American Religion," *History Matters*, https://historymatters.gmu.edu/d/5790, accessed 6 July 2023.

Natives were put off by white Christians' duplicity: How little the precepts of Christianity shaped Whites' behavior. Black Hawk of the Sauk Nation says in 1833, "The Whites may do bad all their lives, and then if they are sorry for it when about to die, all is well! But with us, it is different: we must continue throughout our lives to do what we conceive to be good." Red Jacket used the behavior of Whites as evidence of the inadequacy of the religion. A good religion will produce good people, but Whites were deceitful, esurient, and uncaring of the plight of Reds.[20]

Most Indian nations were deeply spiritual and that spirituality found its way into almost all Natives' daily activities. Consequently, riddance of their own spiritual ways for embrace of Christianity was to many Natives a very poor exchange.

We have seen in chapter 8 the complexities of the U.S. government ensuring the Natives that its intentions were guileless. The reason is that they, Jefferson included, were not guileless. Of the numerous treaties ratified with Natives, almost all contained some clause for Indians to capitulate some parcel of land—the choicer, the better—to the American government in exchange for the federal government attending to Indians' problems with Whites—problems that were typically created by Whites. General Philip Schuyler writes on July 29, 1783, "As our settlements approach their country, they must from the scarcity of game, which that approach will induce to, retire farther back, and dispose of their lands, unless they dwindle comparatively to nothing, as all savages have done, who gain their sustenance by the chace [*sic*], when compelled to live in the vicinity of civilized people, and thus leave us the country without the expence of a purchase, trifling as that will probably be."[21] Washington replies in a letter to fellow member of the Continental Congress James Duane (7 Sept. 1783), "My Sentiments with respect to the proper line of Conduct to be observed towards these people coincides precisely with those delivered by Genl Schuyler so far as he has gone in his Letter of the 29th July to Congress."

The Trade and Intercourse Acts and the numerous treaties with Indian nations or alliances of nations were intended to quell Natives' unrest and reassure them of the federal government's sincere interest in their wellbeing. Such laws, ultimately, were mere lip service. Fleshed out by Justice John Marshall in 1923, in

---

[20] J. Niles Hubbard, *Red Jacket and His People*, 228–29.
[21] Reginald Horsman, "American Indian Policy in the Old Northwest, 1783–1812," in *The William and Mary Quarterly*, Vol. 18, No. 1, 1961: 37.

Johnson v. McIntosh, [22] Natives' right of occupancy was ultimately at the discretion of the "discovering" peoples: British turned Americans. Thus, the axial principle of the U.S. government was that as Americans swept into Indians' lands, Indians would be removed to the West. Francis Paul Prucha sums: "Its interest was primarily that this process should be as free of disorder and injustice as possible. The government meant to restrain and govern the advance of the whites, not to prevent it forever." [23] Thus, the federal government wanted American expansion to be orderly but not to be mostly free of injustice. There merely needed to be some appearance of justice to the Indians.

Figure 10-3: Shawnee, Chief Tecumseh

Seeing the government's duplicity, many Natives were not ensorcelled by Jefferson's promise of being able to do more with less land and with less work. They noticed that the U.S. government, in dealing with individual tribes, was

---

[22] For more on John Marshall and Native Americans, see Robert J. Miller, "American Indian Influence on the United States Constitution and Its Framers," *American Indian Law Review*, Vol. 18, No. 1, 1993: 138–41.

[23] Francis Paul Prucha, *American Indian Policy in the Formative Years: The Indian Trade and Intercourse Acts 1790–1834* (Cambridge: Harvard University Press, 1962), 186.

pursuing, as it were, a divide-and-conquer scheme. Tecumseh (1768–1813, Figure 10-3), the warrior turned chief, proposed to fellow Indians a scheme to prevent the facile acquisition of Indians' lands by Americans. He maintained that Natives' lands belonged to all Natives in common and so future treaties with individual tribes could only be ceded with the consent of all tribes. He would work with some success to confederate Indian tribes.[24]

Yet here lack of centralization and being scattered relatively thinly over vast distances made impossible confederation. For illustration, after the Battle of Fallen Timbers (1794, Figure 10-4), in which the Indian tribes of north of Ohio River with British succor fought for the territory ceded to the U.S. by England after the Revolutionary War—i.e., the Northwest Indian War (1785–1795)—the loose-knit confederacy of tribal nations fell apart, and most of what is today Ohio was ceded to the U.S. in the Treaty of Greenville (1795) and many of the Aborigines therein were displaced.

Figure 10-4: Battle of Fallen Timbers

In sum, despite Jefferson's favorable views of the Indians' nature though decades of study of them—that is, the potential for genius and fecund imagination of Native Americans—the exigencies of his presidential office

---

[24] John Sugden, *Tecumseh: A Life* (New York: Henry Holt and Company, 1997), 42–44.

demanded that his own political policies concerning Indians were not much more than a continuance of the policies of his predecessors, Washington especially. *Pace* Anthony F.C. Wallace, there is no evidence of presidential muscularity, subtle or unsubtle, based on paranoia. In agreement with Bernard Sheehan, Jefferson's policy was right-intended, given his purchase of Enlightenment progressivism, shown by his stadialism (chapter 1), but somewhat naïve. The two glaring defects of his policies were these: failure to see Indians' intransigence vis-à-vis U.S. policies from the Natives' perspective (covered fully in the final chapters)—he was too wedded to Enlightenment progressivism for that—and failure to address Indians' various *ethnoi* from the perspective of the various manifestations of their profound spirituality. Had he come to terms with Indians' spirituality, he might have altered significantly his presidential policies, to which I next turn.

Chapter 11

Jefferson's Indian Policy in Praxis

"The stream of overflowing population"

American Indians became over time much distrustful of Americans' overtures—President Jefferson's included. The chief reason for distrust was that everything always seemed to hinge on treaties that centered on cessation of lands to the U.S. government, and Indians generally tended, often by "persuasion"—populational losses through constant skirmishes with frontiersmen or with other Indian nations or heavy debts that could not be paid—to cede their lands to or through the government. That was, in effect, the U.S. government's solution to the perpetual problem of interloping American frontiersmen.

It is unlikely that early governmental officials gave much thought to the permanency of the "solution" of relocation of Natives beyond the Appalachian Mountains, as white settlers constantly encroached on Indians' lands. It was a workable expedient, but it was no solution. As Americans too removed beyond the Appalachians, there was a need for more and more treaties to purchase Indians' lands and to encourage them to move even farther to the West. That, of course, created hostilities with Natives who occupied those lands, as different Indian nations were forced into smaller spaces, and it further thinned the number of Indians, considered in the aggregate. According to the Iroquois chief, Red Jacket: "They [Whites] are driving us on toward the setting sun. They would shut us in, they would close up the path to our brethren at the west."[1]

Jefferson was quite unlike other governmental officials in one key respect. Because he continually studied Natives, he ever saw the picture from above. Whites were violently and inevitably moving into Natives' lands, and there was nothing that the federal government, or any agency, could do to stop them. The only course of action for the federal government would be to make the inevitable as smooth as a violent process could be. Writes Reginald Horsman:

---

[1] J. Niles Hubbard, *Red Jacket and His People* (New York: Burt Franklin, 1886), 63.

"For the land problem there was no real solution. The rapidly expanding American population could no more be expected to ignore the rich, sparsely settled lands to the west than could the Indians be expected to yield them without a struggle. The American government could make the process less painful, but it could not solve the basic dilemma."[2] Jefferson, as the 1803 letter to Benjamin Hawkins shows, added something to the policy. That was the on-the-quiet encouragement of something that was already occurring to some extent on the American frontier: *viz.*, the intermixing of red with white blood.[3]

Miscegenation was not a complete solution for Jefferson. He certainly did not envision that all, most, or even many Indians would willingly intermix with Whites. He clearly thought of that solution as partial. That he cautioned Hawkins not to make explicitly known that goal shows that he understood that it would have been unpalatable to Indians—that is, that had it been made explicit; it would likely have led to greater tensions between the Americans and Aborigines. Following the plan of Knox, Jefferson grasped that the U.S. Indian policy of continual westerly removal would inevitably lead to a disintegration of Indian culture. Natives of one nation would ceaselessly be pushed together in the West with Natives of other nations, thereby causing intertribal tensions which would lead to wars, force tribal intermixing, and result in rapid declination of the number of Natives. As Jefferson's lists of seventeenth- and eighteenth-century charts of Indian nations show, that was already occurring at an alarming rate. At the writing of Jefferson's *Notes on the State of Virginia*, there was nearly complete disintegration of the once-powerful Chickahominies, Pamunkeys, and Mattaponis in Virginia.

And so, though Thomas Jefferson's Indian policy formally differed nowise from Knox's policy, under President Washington, there were, however, two informal differences: Jefferson tacitly and largely encouraged miscegenation and he much more aggressively, especially given the implications of the Louisiana Purchase, pushed for the acquisition of Natives' lands.

How did Jefferson arrive at his policy?

I answer that question in this chapter by looking first at Jefferson's first five presidential addresses, then at letters/addresses to Indian chiefs and delegates,

---

[2] Reginald Horsman, "American Indian Policy in the Old Northwest, 1783–1812," *The William and Mary Quarterly*, Vol. 18, No. 1, 1961: 45.

[3] Thomas Jefferson, *Notes on the State of Virginia*, ed. William Peden (Chapel Hill: University of North Carolina Press, 1954), 61.

and last at a singular letter during the first presidential term to Governor William Henry Harrison. While all governmental policies had at day's end acquisition of Indians' lands, Jefferson, I maintain, was exceptionally acquisitive of Natives' lands.

Jefferson's Annual Messages show a pattern: interact respectfully with Indians, establish clear boundaries between Natives' and Americans' lands, create integrity through just commerce with Indians, and acquire as much land as possible from the Natives.

In his First Annual Message (8 Dec. 1801), Jefferson speaks of successes in introducing Natives to husbandry and American ways. "they are becoming more and more sensible of the superiority of this dependence for clothing and subsistence over the precarious resources of hunting and fishing; and already we are able to announce, that instead of that constant diminution of their numbers, produced by their wars and their wants, some of them begin to experience an increase of population." The message bespeaks a campaign by Indian agents to convince tribal leaders of the superiority of the American way of life: It yields more with less effort and greater yield leads to happiness and to populational increase.

Jefferson's Second Annual Message (15 Dec. 1802) tells of fixing the boundaries of American and Natives' lands. For that to occur, there needs to be prompt settlement of all rights and claims by Americans to lands, and that was a continual and knotty problem. Jefferson writes of Indians' "monopoly which prevents population." The reference is to a manner of living that requires scattering themselves over large expanses of land. In keeping with his first message, Jefferson iterates that a more efficient usage of land will lead to a diminution of tensions between tribes. Fixing the boundaries between tribes, too, will result in a diminution of tensions between them. The boundaries between Aboriginal tribes were natural and never clean.[4] "The white man's mode of running lines and of measuring land, he did not comprehend or appreciate," says J. Niles Hubbard. Those acres and roods were determined by man, not by the Great Spirit. "But when the line was made by a creek, river, or maintain, he understood it, and it harmonized better with his views of fitness

---

[4] As Charles Thomson notes, Natives used natural boundaries—e.g., rivers or mountains—to determine their lands. That imprecise approach led to continual skirmishes and wars between nations. Charles Thomson, "Notes on *Notes on Virginia*" (Appendix I), in Thomas Jefferson, *Notes on the State of Virginia*, ed. Frank Shuffleton (New York: Penguin, 1999), 213.

in dividing up the surface of this great earth."[5] A creek that separated one tribe from another for instance, could be flooded by a freshet and have diverted its course, and thereby lead to a territorial dispute between the two tribes.

In his Third Annual Message (17 Oct. 1803)—the Louisiana Purchase here has been completed—Jefferson speaks of the urgency of "establishing trading houses" for Native Americans. Yet unlike the unregulated practices of frontiersmen aimed at bilking the Natives, prices of goods at U.S. trading houses will be so moderated that sellers will neither gain nor lose. The aim is to win Indians' trust and goodwill and to secure peace. Jefferson is clearly responding to numerous reports of inflated prices for needed or desired American goods with the aim of incurring Indians' debts to facilitate the selling of their lands. Government-backed trading stations, not aiming at a profit, we have seen, were merely a continuation of Knox's policy. The aim here was to win the trust of Aborigines and monopolize trade with them for the future benefit of the U.S. government.

Jefferson begins his Fourth Annual Message (7 Nov. 1804) by noting that there has been large success in establishing boundaries. "With the Indian tribes established within our newly-acquired limits, I have deemed it necessary to open conferences for the purpose of establishing a good understanding and neighborly relations between us" (Figure 11-1). He states that Indians are, in the main favorably disposed toward Americans, so now is the time to secure the Natives' trust through honest intercourse with them. As he does in his Third Message, he proposes "a uniform course of justice toward them," which will "better their condition." The aim is to render Americans "so [sic] necessary to their comfort and prosperity, that the protection of our citizens from their disorderly members will become their interest and their voluntary care." In such a way, there will be no need for military force to protect American interests. Natives will see that Americans' interests are also theirs.

Jefferson, in his Fourth Annual Message, also mentions "an important relinquishment of native title [that] has been received from the Delawares" on the east side of the Mississippi River. "That tribe, desiring to extinguish in their people the spirit of hunting, and to convert superfluous lands into the means

---

[5] J. Niles Hubbard, *Red Jacket and His People, 1750–1830* (New York: Burt Franklin, 1886), 166. For more on Red Jacket, see Arthur Caswell Parker, *Red Jacket: Seneca Chief* (University of Nebraska Press, 1951), and Robert G. Koch, "Red Jacket: Seneca Orator," in *The Crooked Lake Review,* March 1992, https://crookedlakereview.com/articles/34_66/48mar1992/48koch.html, accessed 15 Jan. 2023.

of improving what they retain, have ceded to us all the country between the Wabash and Ohio, south of, and including the road from the rapids towards Vincennes, for which they are to receive annuities in animals and implements for agriculture, and in other necessaries." Annuities often entailed pledge of a yearly sum of money—say, 600 dollars—for a tribe to spend as they pleased on American goods.

The land, Jefferson adds, is lush and logistically vital. "This acquisition is important, not only for its extent and fertility, but as fronting three hundred miles on the Ohio, and near half that on the Wabash." With the land ceded to the federal government, any produce passing on the Ohio and Wabash Rivers will no longer pass "in review of the Indian frontier." That, with the cession heretofore made with the Kaskaskias, "nearly consolidates our possessions north of the Ohio, in a very respectable breadth, from Lake Erie to the Mississippi." The Piankeshaw Indians, he adds, have a legitimate claim to the land ceded by the Delaware Indians, so Jefferson states that it is best "to quiet that [botheration] by fair purchase also." The suggestion seems to be that whenever Indians are in possession of lands, there will be disputes and skirmishes. They can be resolved by dispossessing Indians of their lands.

Figure 11-1: Pontiac Speaking to Natives

In his Second Inaugural Address (5 Mar. 1805), Jefferson notes that, with the acquisition of the Louisiana Territory, the Indian problem has decupled. He begins in a manner most politic—by commiserating with their plight.

> Endowed with the faculties and the rights of men, breathing an ardent love of liberty and independence, and occupying a country which left them no desire but to be undisturbed, the stream of overflowing population from other regions directed itself on these shores; without power to divert, or habits to contend against, they have been overwhelmed by the current, or driven before it; now reduced within limits too narrow for the hunter's state, humanity enjoins us to teach them agriculture and the domestic arts; to encourage them to that industry which alone can enable them to maintain their place in existence, and to prepare them in time for that state of society, which to bodily comforts adds the improvement of mind and morals.

There is nothing expressed that exculpates the intrusive Americans, but nothing either that necessarily inculpates Americans. The "stream of overflowing population" is too great to be stopped. Americans can only go with the direction of the current, while Natives are too impuissant to dam or divert the powerful stream. Its movement is relentless. As things stand, Indigenes now merely occupy too little land to be effective hunters, so morality dictates that the encroaching Americans offer education in "that industry [husbandry] which alone can enable them to maintain their place in existence." However, they will, in time, enjoy bodily comforts and see marked perfections in "mind and morals."

Jefferson turns to a significant albatross: filiopietistic Aborigines who shun reason and progress for the safety of the prejudice of the past. Those "anti-philosophers" fear loss of status in the new order of things. "These persons inculcate a sanctimonious reverence for the customs of their ancestors; that whatsoever they did, must be done through all time; that reason is a false guide, and to advance under its counsel, in their physical, moral, or political condition, is perilous innovation; that their duty is to remain as their Creator made them, ignorance being safety, and knowledge full of danger; in short, ... among them is seen the action and counteraction of good sense and bigotry." The language and argument are like those used against filiopietistic Federalists.[6]

---

[6] E.g., TJ to Thomas Paine, 18 Mar. 1801.

Jefferson, in his Fifth Annual Message (3 Dec. 1805), again propagandizes, and the emphasis is on gain of Indians' lands. "Our Indian neighbors ... are becoming sensible that the earth yields subsistence with less labor and more certainty than the forest, and find it their interest from time to time to dispose of parts of their surplus and waste lands for the means of improving those they occupy and of subsisting their families while they are preparing their farms." He mentions purchase of lands "between the Connecticut Reserve and the former Indian boundary and those on the Ohio from the same boundary to the rapids and for a considerable depth inland." The Chickasaws and Cherokees have ceded through sale "the country between and adjacent to the two districts of Tennessee." The Creeks have sold to the government "the residue of their lands in the fork of Ocmulgee up to the Olcofauhatche." Those three purchases are singular. First, they bring together "disjoined parts of our settled country" and thereby allow for secure, safe transportation of goods. Second, they place in American hands "the whole of both banks of the Ohio from its source to near its mouth." Thus, "the navigation of that river is thereby rendered forever safe to our citizens settled and settling on its extensive waters." He closes with the attractiveness of the purchase of land in Georgia from the Creeks. That, too, has been for some time particularly interesting to the State of Georgia. Once again, Jefferson's statements strongly intimate that all lands east of the Mississippi River are best settled by Americans.

There are next President Jefferson's messages or letters to Indians.

In a letter (3 Nov. 1802) to Handsome Lake (1735–1815), a Senecan spiritual leader of the Iroquois and half-brother of the Senecan chief Cornplanter, Jefferson begins with congratulations that his brother and the great chief sees "the ruinous effects which the abuse of spirituous liquors" on Indians "who have voluntarily gone into these fatal habits." He adds, "I am authorized by the great council of the United States to prohibit them."

Jefferson quickly slips into a discussion of the purchase of available land, but he cunningly tempers his eagerness with certain "qualifications." His approach, in today's psychological terms, is door-in-the-face. "We, indeed, are always ready to buy land; but we will never ask but when you wish to sell; and our laws, in order to protect you against imposition, have forbidden individuals to purchase lands from you; and have rendered it necessary, when you desire to sell, even to a State, that an agent from the United States should attend the sale, see that your consent is freely given, a satisfactory price paid, and report to us what has been done, for our approbation."

There is then an address of a messy transaction Handsome Lake has earlier discussed with Jefferson. The president, thus, explains the nuts and bolts of ownership of property. When a delegation of Iroquois came forth to sell to the state of New York certain small parcels of land, Jefferson sent a trustworthy federal agent to oversee the transaction—*viz.*, to ensure that the transaction was voluntary and that a fair price was paid for the land. While ownership of property is a human right, says Jefferson, so too is the right to sell. "The right to sell is one of the rights of property. To forbid you the exercise of that right would be a wrong to your nation."

In response to Handsome Lake's objection that every sale of land brings harm to his people, Jefferson replies, "Nor do I think, brother, that the sale of lands is, under all circumstances, injurious to your people." In a society founded on hunting, much game requires a large forest. Husbandmen, however, need little land to thrive. "A little land well stocked and improved, will yield more than a great deal without stock or improvement." Thus, "going into a state of agriculture, it may be as advantageous to a society, as it is to an individual, who has more land than he can improve, to sell a part, and lay out the money in stocks and implements of agriculture, for the better improvement of the residue." And so, Jefferson enjoins Handsome Lake to reconsider the selling of land. When it is voluntary and justly transacted, and it is in "the interest of your nation."

This letter is noteworthy. It indicates just how foreign is the concept of private property to Indians—a people unfamiliar with the notions both of seeing land as a commodity to be exchanged under certain circumstances and of distinct and artificial (man-made) boundaries on lands.[7] The cultural differences concerning how Aborigines and how Americans viewed land show plainly that Indians were not capable of voluntary and equitable transactions concerning its sale any more than Americans were capable of apprehending Indians' view that land was neither something to be violated through plowing or clearing nor something for one person to own to the exclusion of another.

---

[7] Natives did have personal possessions, but tribal members generally respected the privacy of other members. Oliver M. Spencer notes, while a young captive of Indians near Cincinnati, that Aborigines merely placed a small log against their door to let others know that they were they were not inside. There was no need of "bolts or locks." The same respect was shown with "possessions" of one tribe in the wilderness by another friendly tribe. Oliver M. Spencer, *Indian Captivity: A True Narrative of the Capture of Rev. O.M. Spencer by the Indians, in the Neighbourhood of Cincinnati* (New York: Carlton & Porter, 1835), 66.

Over one year later, Jefferson writes to the members of a delegation from the Choctaw Nation (17 Dec. 1803), who have come to visit him in Washington. The Choctaw were a Native American people who were originally rooted in what are now Alabama and Mississippi. They were mostly allies with Colonists during the Revolutionary War and the War of 1812, yet were forced to move westward, roughly today's Oklahoma, in the early 1930s with the Indian Removal Act (chapter 9).[8]

Jefferson bids his "brothers" to accept the friendship of Americans. "Born in the same land, we ought to live as brothers, doing to each other all the good we can, and not listening to wicked men, who may endeavor to make us enemies. By living in peace, we can help and prosper one another; by waging war, we can kill and destroy many on both sides; but those who survive will not be the happier for that. Then, brothers, let it forever be peace and good neighborhood between us."

Jefferson quickly turns to the acquisition of Choctaws' lands. The children of the 17 American states are like "leaves of the trees, which the winds are spreading over the forest." Yet though the people are many, they are also just. "We take from no nation what belongs to it. Our growing numbers make us always willing to buy lands from our red brethren, when they are willing to sell."

There are also confusion concerning lines of properties and plaints concerning Americans encroaching on Natives' lands. "The lines established between us by mutual consent, shall be sacredly preserved, and will protect your lands from all encroachments by our own people or any others. We will give you a copy of the law, made by our great Council, for punishing our people, who may encroach on your lands, or injure you otherwise. Carry it with you to your homes, and preserve it, as the shield which we spread over you, to protect your land, your property and persons." As we have seen in prior chapters, Jefferson is vaunting about laws that can nowise be effectively enforced.

Jefferson then addresses the subject of the large Choctaw debt, which is so hefty that it can be paid only by sale of lands. "The sum you have occasion for, brothers, is a very great one. We have never yet paid as much to any of our red brethren for the purchase of lands. You propose to us some on the Tombigbee and some on the Mississippi. Those on the Mississippi suit us well," says an esurient Jefferson. "We wish to have establishments on that river, as resting

---

[8] Howard Zinn, "As Long as Grass Grows or Water Runs": *A People's History of the United States, 1492–Present* (New York: HarperCollins, 2003), 126.

places for our boats, to furnish them provisions, and to receive our people who fall sick on the way to or from New Orleans, which is now ours. In that quarter, therefore, we are willing to purchase as much as you will spare." He then proposes to send agents to settle on a price for the Mississippi lands.

The next item of discussion is the American gift of a trading store on Choctaws' lands. "We never meant to ask land or any other payment for them," says Jefferson. "The store which we sent on was at your request also; and to accommodate you with necessaries at a reasonable price." The Choctaws now want the store, certainly the cause of their hefty debt, to be removed. Jefferson states that the secretary of war will assist in that and other matters of urgency.

There is much to unpack in the letter. First, emphasizing that Americans are "born in the same land," Jefferson wishes to show that they, too, have a right to occupy it. The metaphor of Americans spreading leaves is meant to show their great number and the ineluctability of their westerly migration. American "largesse" is underscored by the gift of the store of American goods "at a reasonable price"—prices so reasonable that the Choctaws have fallen into a desperately deep debt. Here, we again see Natives' massive unfamiliarity with private property and purchases based on credit. We also see Jefferson's habitual door-in-the-face maneuver: We want Indians' land, but only "when they are willing to sell."

On January 10, 1806, Jefferson addressed the Chiefs of the Cherokee Nation, who, too had paid a visit to him at Washington. Jefferson's message in gist is "to cultivate the earth and to avoid war." He assumes here the role of father to his Cherokee children, riven by ambivalence concerning their future.

Jefferson begins with encouraging words. American efforts to civilize the Cherokees have not been bootless. "It has been like grain sown in good ground, producing abundantly." The Cherokee, each enclosing his land and each learning to use plows and hoes, are becoming successful farmers. Jefferson sees handsome specimens of cotton cloth, cattle and hogs for slaughter, and horses to ease the moil of labor. Soon mills to grind the corn will be needed.

The president follows with a schoolmasterly lecture on the benefits of private property.

> When a man has enclosed and improved his farm, builds a good house on it and raises plentiful stocks of animals, he will wish when he dies that these things shall go to his wife and children, whom he loves more than he does his other relations, and for whom he will work with

pleasure during his life. You will, therefore, find it necessary to establish laws for this. When a man has property, earned by his own labor, he will not like to see another come and take it from him because he happens to be stronger, or else to defend it by spilling blood. You will find it necessary then to appoint good men, as judges, to decide contests between man and man, according to reason and to the rules you shall establish. If you wish to be aided by our counsel and experience in these things we shall always be ready to assist you with our advice.

With the introduction of private property, there begin complexities—needs of laws and of a judiciary system—and it is easy to see the Cherokee chiefs not seeing any advantages to being like white men.

Jefferson then addresses a large difficulty: the bellicosity of the young Cherokees. Young Cherokees on one side of the Mississippi River crossing it to battle with young Cherokees on the other side. "The Mississippi now belongs to us. It must not be a river of blood. It is now the water-path along which all our people of Natchez, St. Louis, Indiana, Ohio, Tennessee, Kentucky and the western parts of Pennsylvania and Virginia are constantly passing with their property, to and from New Orleans." Fighting on the Mississippi River must decrease, or it will eventually lead to war with Americans. Figure 11-2 shows the location of Cherokees, prior to their forced westerly migration beyond the Mississippi River, in what are today upper Northwestern Georgia, upper Northeastern Alabama, lower Southeastern Tennessee, and lower southwestern North Carolina.

Nearly one year later, President Jefferson addresses a delegation from the Wolf and People of the Mandan Nation (30 Dec. 1806), who have settled lands up the Missouri River. Jefferson acknowledges the pluck of the Natives for having undertaken such a long and arduous journey to Washington. "The journey which you have taken to visit your fathers on this side of our island is a long one, and your having undertaken it is a proof that you desired to become acquainted with us." The long trip is also a measure of their desperation.

Jefferson begins again with a statement of the rightful claim of ownership of North American lands. "We are descended from the old nations which live beyond the great water, but we and our forefathers have been so long here that we seem like you to have grown out of this land. We consider ourselves no longer of the old nations beyond the great water, but as united in one family with our red brethren here." The sentiment here is that the American Whites are the chthonic equals of the American Reds, for "we seem ... to have grown out of this land"—a meet conceit. The notion of "one family" shows no aversion to intermixing.

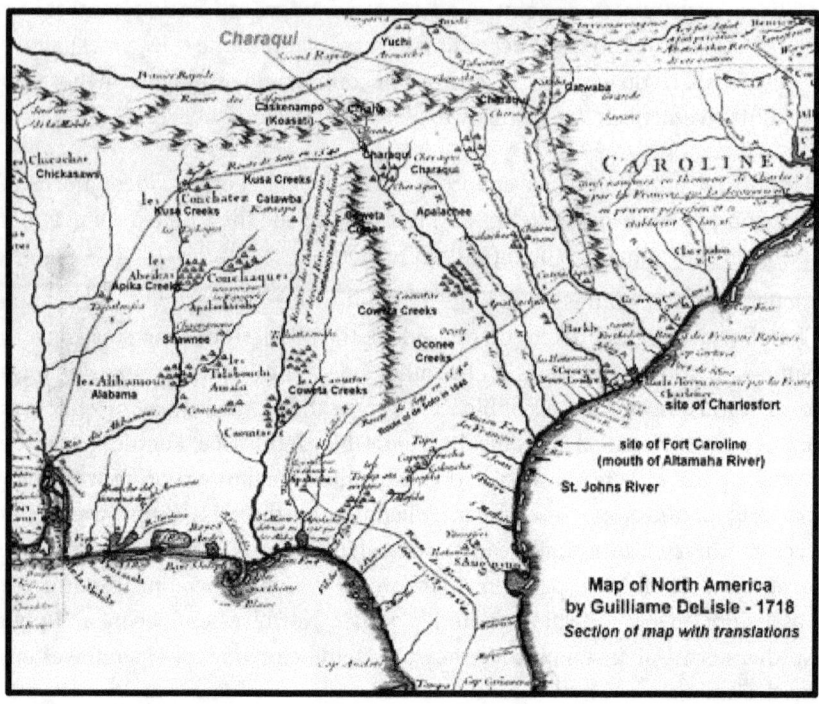

Figure 11-2: Map of North America, DeLisle, 1718

Yet the political move is Jeffersonian posturing. That notion of equality soon evanesces. The French, English, and Spanish, Jefferson notes, have granted that the land between Canada and Mexico is American. The erstwhile claimants to American territories will never return. Jefferson sums, "We are now your fathers; and you shall not lose by the change." The tone is paternalistic, though softly so, but there can be no equality where a relationship is in any degree paternalistic.

With Spain's withdrawal from the waters of the Missouri and Mississippi Rivers, Jefferson expresses his felt desire of "becoming acquainted with all my red children beyond the Mississippi, and of uniting them with us", just as Americans have done with Natives east of the great river. To facilitate acquaintance, Jefferson talks of the mission of Captain Lewis, "one of my own family, to go up the Missouri river to get acquainted with all the Indian nations in its neighborhood, to take them by the hand, deliver my talks to them, and to inform us in what way we could be useful to them." Jefferson then promises to establish trading houses for the benefit of both Americans and the Wolf and Mandans.

Jefferson ends with "important advice." He says that "all red men are my children," and so, all must live in peace. There must be neither wars between Indian nations nor wars between Indians and Whites. Eschewal of war will lead to time spent in fruitful pursuits: the making of clothing and preparation of food. The Wolf and Mandans will sleep peacefully in cabins and never again worry about being killed or carried away by other Indian nations. "You will live in plenty and in quiet," and consequently, their number will increase. That is the advice the Great Father has given to his "red brethren" to the east of the Mississippi River.

Jefferson enjoins the delegates to go farther east, to the cities of Baltimore, Philadelphia, and New York, and see their new "friends" on the east, at the shore of the Atlantic Ocean, and then, if they are willing, to travel south and north. "We will provide carriages to convey you and a person to go with you to see that you want for nothing. By the time you come back the snows will be melted on the mountains, the ice in the rivers broken up, and you will be wishing to set out on your return home." The expectation is that the Natives will be overwhelmed by what they see in the great American cities and talk about the superiority of white culture to the members of their tribes.

In a passage just prior to ending his address, Jefferson appeals to the moral sentiments of the Wolf and Mandans in language chock full of appeals to sincerity and truthfulness and of natural metaphors that certainly resonate with the Northwestern Natives:

> My children, I have long desired to see you; I have now opened my heart to you, let my words sink into your hearts and never be forgotten. If ever lying people or bad spirits should raise up clouds between us, call to mind what I have said, and what you have seen yourselves. Be sure there are some lying spirits between us; let us come together as friends and explain to each other what is misrepresented or misunderstood, the clouds will fly away like morning fog, and the sun of friendship appear and shine forever bright and clear between us.

Finally, there is a singular letter (27 Feb. 1803) to Governor William Henry Harrison (1773–1841, Figure 11-3) of the Indiana Territory,[9] not even three weeks after his letter on February 9 to Benjamin Hawkins, examined in the prior chapter. The letter is "unofficial and private," because Jefferson wishes to share with the governor "a more extensive view of our policy respecting the Indians." The confidential nature of the letter is forced upon Jefferson by the demands of his country's first office and the urgency he expresses in it is due to the mounting hostilities between France and England and Jefferson's concerns about French aims in North America.

Figure 11-3: Governor William Henry Harrison

The letter, in general, follows the overall pattern of the letter to Hawkins weeks earlier, studied in the prior chapter. The most universal aim "is to live in perpetual peace with the Indians." That can be done by just and liberal American interactions with them to secure their trust.

Jefferson's advice to Harrison is fivefold.

---

[9] For more on Harrison, see Robert M. Owens, "Jeffersonian Benevolence on the Ground: The Indian Land Cession Treaties of William Henry Harrison," in *Journal of the Early Republic,* Vol. 22, No. 3, 2002: 405–35.

Jefferson's Indian Policy in Praxis

The first step concerns persuasion: "to draw them to agriculture, to spinning & weaving." The former is achievable insofar as their hunting spaces have been largely reduced. With the men taking up husbandry, the woman can be readied for milder domestic chores, "which are exercised within doors."

The second step concerns withdrawal. Because an agricultural lifestyle is much preferable to hunting and warring, Indians will gleefully "withdraw themselves to the culture of a small piece of land." Having withdrawn to their private plots of land, they will recognize the superfluity of "their extensive forests."

The third step concerns awareness. Seeing the superfluity of their forests, Natives will be willing "to pare them off from time to time in exchange for necessaries for their farms & families."

The fourth step concerns reinforcement. The federal government will establish trading houses to give Natives the sort of needed goods for flourishing in husbandry. The use of such goods will reinforce what Jefferson has ever been preaching to Natives: how to do more and live better with less land.

Yet the fifth step, however, is nefandous. No longer is the government pushing a moderate purchase of goods at a just price; it is intentionally running Indians into deep debts by pushing for excessive purchase of goods. "To promote this disposition to exchange lands which they have to spare & we want, for necessaries, which we have to spare & they want, we shall push our trading houses, and be glad to see the good & influential individuals among them run in debt." When those cannot be paid, Indians will be forced to sell their lands. The *modus operandi* is, at first, to sell many goods at prices so low—covering overhead and not profit is the goal—so that independent traders, even the most unscrupulous, cannot compete with trading houses, and the Natives will necessarily trade at those and no other, posts. When that happens, governmental traders will entice Natives to acquire much beyond their means of recompense and, thus, ponderously heavy debts that can only be settled by ceding lands to Americans.

Next, there comes a most intriguing expression of Jefferson's Indian policy: integration or disintegration.

> in this way our settlements will gradually circumscribe & approach the Indians, & they will in time either incorporate with us as citizens of the US. or remove beyond the Missisipi. the former is certainly the termination of their history most happy for themselves. but in the whole course of this, it is essential to cultivate their love. as to their fear, we

presume that our strength & their weakness is now so visible that they must see we have only to shut our hand to crush them, & that all our liberalities to them proceed from motives of pure humanity only. should any tribe be fool-hardy enough to take up the hatchet at any time, the seizing the whole country of that tribe & driving them across the Missisipi, as the only condition of peace, would be an example to others, and a furtherance of our final consolidation.

As I note in *Dutiful Correspondent,* the passage is astonishing for its extraordinary, even ferocious, ambivalence. [10] Jefferson ping-pongs from statement to statement to express sentiments first of tenderness and then of execration. Readers are fronted with intermixing or extermination, love versus fear, American strength versus Indian weakness, and pure American humanity versus crushing American cruelty. There is first the nefarious notion of circumscription and suffocation of Indians. Jefferson then turns to the heroic notion of cultivating their love. Yet that is a queer fear-founded love, for seeing American strength and their weakness, Indians too will see that a mere closure of a hand is sufficient to annihilate them, so American generosities have been granted only through "pure humanity." Finally, the passage ends infamously. Any Indian nation that chooses to "take up the hatchet" will lose its lands and be driven to the west of the Mississippi River—in general, far beyond the river. The plan overall is to have full possession of the lands around the Mississippi River "from it's mouth to it's Northern regions." Jefferson's panic here, of course, is due to the uncertainty of France's designs at the time of the letter, in North America.

Jefferson then proffers specific instructions about how to deal with the remnants of depleted Indian nations. Most importantly, Jefferson gives Governor Harrison suggestions for how to finagle lands from the Choctaws, Cahokias, Piorias, Kaskaskias, Poutewatamies, and Kickapoos.

while we are bargaining with the Kaskaskias, the minds of the Poutewatamies & Kickapoos should be soothed & consiliated by liberalities and sincere assurances of friendship. perhaps by sending a well qualified character to stay some time in [Kaskaskian chief] Decoigne's village as if on other business, and to sound him & introduce the subject by degrees to his mind & that of the other heads of families,

---

[10] M. Andrew Holowchak, *Dutiful Correspondent: Philosophical Essays on Thomas Jefferson* (Lanham, MD: Rowman & Littlefield, 2013), 239–40.

inculcating in the way of conversation all those considerations which prove the advantages they would recieve by a cession on these terms, the object might be more easily & effectually obtained than by abruptly proposing it to them at a formal treaty.

Jefferson has instructed Harrison concerning a "system" that will "best promote the interests of the Indians & of ourselves" and have as its end consolidation of "our whole country into one nation." The matter is urgent, even desperate. "The occupation of New Orleans, hourly expected, by the French, is already felt like a light breeze by the Indians," who look upon the French as their liberators. "Under the hopes of their protection, they will immediately stiffen against cessions of land to us." Jefferson bids Harrison to act speedily to gain as much land from the Southern Indians as is possible. The future of the American nation might be at stake.

The addresses, messages, and letters covered in this chapter seem to show that Thomas Jefferson's views on Native Americans are very "presidential," very Adamsian (chapter 8). His thoughts and deeds are not those of a philosopher, who seeks solutions to problems between Americans and Indians that are equally just to both parties, but those of his jejune country's first citizen, whose politic solutions are to benefit chiefly those persons that have elected him to his nation's presidency. As president, he wishes to acquire from Natives as much of their land as they are willing to release—the choicer, the better. Lands around the major rivers are paramount. That policy has an urgency early in 1803, due to the Napoleonic crisis. If he has, at some point, to encourage shady practices to encourage Natives to part with lands, he is willing to do so.

Chapter 12

Indians in Jefferson's "Empire for liberty"

"Reduce within limits too narrow for the Hunter's state"

At the end of chapter 11, I intimate that Jefferson, as president, was more politician than a philosopher when it came to Native Americans. He had a decided pro-American policy that disfavored the first inhabitants of North America. That which was needed for the preservation of Indian culture, Indian land, was at every viable opportunity to be taken. I use "taken" instead of "purchased" because, as I have shown, purchases were likely seldom fully willful and equitable. Though Jefferson customarily employed such language, as we have seen, he often felt the need to explain such language from a private-property perspective, not fully graspable to Indians, unaccustomed to the privatization of goods and to strict partitioning of land.

The addresses, messages, and letters covered in chapter 11, show Thomas Jefferson's views on Native Americans to be very "presidential." His thoughts and deeds are not those of a philosopher—of a man who looks at events from above and who seeks solutions to problems between Americans and Indians that are equally just to both parties—but those of his jejune country's first citizen, whose solutions are to benefit chiefly those persons that have elected him to his nation's presidency. As president, he wishes to acquire from Natives as much of their land as they are willing to release—the choicer, the better. Lands around the major rivers are paramount because of their fertility and the ease of transport of farmed goods. If he has, at some point, encouraged fishy practices to encourage Natives to part with lands, he is, at times, willing to do so.

Yet the story I aim to show in this final chapter, is essentially philosophical, not political. Jefferson has an investment in a philosophical experiment about the government of and for the people. The westerly spread of Americans over the continent will, he hopes, be the spread of a form of republicanism, Jeffersonian, that will be unique in the history of humanity—a republicanism based on equality and liberty that is so just that it will spread to Europe and, hopefully in time, to all parts of the world. He sees his presidency as the provenance of that experiment—an experiment essentially involving human thriving, human happiness. For the success and spread of Jeffersonian republicanism, Natives' barbarism must be eradicated, and the influence of coercive, aristocratic governments must be removed, inasmuch as possible, from North America. Civilizing the Indians is a needed part of the program; so, too, is acquiring Indians' lands.[1]

Jefferson, I have shown in other writings, which cover more fully Jefferson's notion of "empire for Liberty" and discuss more fully the relevant secondary literature,[2] had a clear vision for America's future. Jefferson envisioned a country, spread out from the Atlantic to the Pacific Oceans, which was liberty-loving and Jeffersonian-republican: citizen-based, with a thin federal government that chiefly directed foreign affairs and with succor of citizens' rights. Indians posed a threat not because the worry that Americans willingly intermixing with barbaric Aborigines might taint the offspring—he did not think Natives to be naturally deficient in body or mind—but because Indians, in the main, were unwilling to give up their way of life to intermix. Consequently, by tying up natural resources to be of service to Americans, Natives were merely albatrosses to American economic and political growth and, thus, posed a threat to the spread of Jeffersonian republicanism. Jefferson's mature policy, therefore, was for allowance of those Indian nations, or more appositely, those willing members of a nation, to miscegenate with Americans and adopt American ways and the relatively rapid extirpation of all other Indian nations, ever being pushed westwardly. There was no room for pockets of Natives' settlements wedded to filiopiety.

It is all too facile to be hypercritical and condemnatory today of Thomas Jefferson. Ours is an intellectual climate in which we see the heroes of the Enlightenment as antiheroes, in which the great advances of scientists and inventors of the Enlightenment are seen as blights. We no longer talk seriously about human progress over time, though there are numerous unequivocal advances in the various sciences—e.g., medicine, astronomy, artificial

---

[1] Horsman writes that acquisition of Indians' lands is both necessary and sufficient for civilizing them: *viz.*, acquisition of their lands promotes their becoming civilized and their becoming civilized promotes acquisition of their lands. Reginald Horsman, "American Indian Policy in the Old Northwest, 1783–1812," *The William and Mary Quarterly*, Vol. 18, No. 1, 1961: 51.

[2] M. Andrew Holowchak, *Jefferson's Political Philosophy and the Metaphysics of Utopia* (London: Brill, 2017), and *"The disease of liberty": Jefferson, History, & Liberty, A Philosophical Study* (Wilmington, DE: Vernon Press, 2024).

intelligence, and biology—and they occur daily. Looking today at the big picture, as it were, most people recognize that the European settlers of the Americas did a great injustice to the Natives. That is facile to acknowledge, if only because we have the luxury of a distanced perspective. It certainly was not obvious to Jefferson that his Indian policy was injurious to Natives.

The big picture in Jefferson's day was radically different. To understand Jefferson's motives, we must enter his time, grasp his mindset and that of other American politicians, philosophers, natural scientists, and everyday Americans, and balance those things against the thoughts and interests of Native Americans, considered as separate tribes and in the aggregate. That is a considerable task and too large for my qualifications, and so I aim merely to offer conclusions in need of further critical analysis.

Whether Jefferson's policy was political or philosophical, it had as its aim the complete eradication of Indians' culture. And so, we must ask: Was Jefferson, in full cognizance of what he was doing to secure his empire for liberty, a willing agent of Native American genocide?

Jefferson's annual messages to the U.S. Congress and addresses/letters to Indians, even if sometimes ambivalent, show genuine concern for the wellbeing of Natives. Yet his, as I have already noted, is a qualified concern. He speaks of the rights entitled to free people (e.g., to own and sell property), and the treaties negotiated for Indians' lands concern them as free, equal, and fully capable of negotiating on their own behalf. Yet Jefferson's language in letters and addresses to them is typically paternalistic and understandably so. Natives are naturally the equals of all others in mind, morality, and taste, thinks Jefferson, but they have been retarded from intellectual, moral, and aesthetic maturation for many centuries by a manner of living, filiopietistic, that has forbidden maturation. In the stadial picture, they have been mired in the earliest stage of the civilizing process. Thus, it is not strange that Jefferson should write paternalistically to them. To his mind, they really are like children, waiting for some guiding hand to enable them to venture into adulthood.

That conceded it is impossible to believe that Jefferson thought Indians fully capable of reasoned negotiations with governmental agents—whether those of a state or those of the federal government. That is why he insisted on the need for the presence of an agent of the U.S. government for every valid transaction of land.

Jefferson ever enjoined Indians to civilize: to enclose plots of land, to take up plows and hoes, to raise farm animals. Yet husbandry was a lifestyle completely foreign to most Indians, and it was emasculating to the men and humiliating to the women, reduced to domestic chores such as weaving. The notion of fixed boundaries was also foreign and even reprehensible to them. The notion that a strictly (mathematically and not naturally) delineated tract of land belonged to one Indian nation was nothing ever entertained. Neither was the notion that within a particular nation, each "hunter/warrior" should have his own plot of land. In Indians' culture, goods were shared, not hoarded. There were no notions of the enclosure, of separating off something, and of thing t belonging exclusively to person P. In sum, prior to their interactions with Whites, there had been no reason for any Indian to entertain notions of rights such as life, liberty, and property, and no reason for any Indian to consider complicating living by having political systems with legislators and judges and taxation of land, given freely to Indians by the Great Spirit. Americans were introducing them to a highly complex manner of living in which the continual skirmishing of Indian tribes might seem as nothing when compared to the large, expensive, sanguinary, and protracted wars of the White Europeans and the continual worries that accompanied the privatization of goods. Americans were also introducing them to a religion that seemed disconnected from the activities of everyday life. None of those things ever occurred to Jefferson, or if any did, it did nothing to influence his Indian policy.

Thus, Jefferson never really placed himself in the position of the Natives to consider things from their perspective. That, of course, to those of us today who study the clash of two cultures so radically different from each other seems unpardonable. Yet, to grasp why he did not do so, we must consider things from Jefferson's perspective, to which I return at chapter's end.

Acknowledging their capabilities, Jefferson allowed for the gradual miscegenation of the two cultures and their integration into the society of Americans. Those Indian nations that refused merely awaited extermination.

And so, the Natives' options were integration or disintegration. Integration entailed not merely amalgamation but full acceptance of Americans' ways and, consequently, full acceptance of the inferiority of Natives' ways—hence, quick inadvertency and oblivion of a way of life centuries in the making. Disintegration entailed the death of all, or at least most, Native Americans through constant skirmishes with migrating Americans and through skirmishes and wars with other Aborigines upon being moved westward. There was also the possibility of a large war between the United States and the various nations of Natives, should Indians decide to amalgamate and fight one desperate war for survival. Jefferson certainly foresaw that some tribes would integrate, that other tribes, riven by disintegrative dissention, would dissolve, and that many other nations, resisting integration, would face slow extermination through warring with Americans or being moved and removed.

And so, there would soon be no place for Natives to be Natives in Jefferson's growing "empire for liberty." That is important to ask if Jefferson's Indian policy was genocidal.

Jefferson, it is well known, on a few occasions coupled "liberty" with "empire." The linkage has nothing to do with lust for power—titanolatry. He merely believed that humans were, by nature freedom loving. Thus, through the slow evolution of humans from barbaric hunters and gatherers to civilized husbandmen and tradespersons in small towns—the movement, progressive, inasmuch as humans' move from maximally inefficient to maximally efficient usage of land was a nature-guided unfolding of civic liberty.

After acquiring the Louisiana Territory in his first term as president, Jefferson writes to Benjamin Chambers (28 Dec. 1805) of the boons of that timely, felicitous acquisition.

> The addition of a country so extensive, so fertile, as Louisiana, to the great republican family of this hemisphere, while it substitutes, for our neighbors, brethren & children in the place of strangers, has secured the blessings of civil & religious freedom to millions yet unborn. by enlarging the empire of liberty, we multiply it's auxiliaries, & provide new sources of renovation, should it's principles at any time, degenerate; in those portions of our country which gave them birth. the securing for you the peace & friendship of the various Indian tribes is among the highly valued advantages of this acquisition.

The doubling of the country through purchase was, for Jefferson, of enormous consequence. Land for Jefferson meant possibilities. Americans of his day were not capitalists. They were defined, especially in the South, by the land that they owned. More than any other American of his day, Jefferson, who made a thorough study of the lands in and around Virginia in his *Notes on the State of Virginia*, could, with a *coup d'oeil* at a parcel of land suggest ways in which that land could best be put to human use.

Just after leaving the presidency, Jefferson writes to his successor, President James Madison (27 Apr. 1809), about acquiring the Florida lands and Cuba. Should Cuba come into U.S. hands, "I would immediately erect a column on the Southernmost limit of Cuba & inscribe on it a Ne plus ultra as to us in that direction. We should then have only to include the North in our confederacy, which would be, of course, in the first war, and we should have such an empire for liberty as she has never surveyed since the creation." There are 17 states at the time (Figure 12-1)—Vermont, Ohio, Kentucky, and Tennessee have been added to the original 13 states. Jefferson imagines here the acquisition of Cuba and Florida lands to the south and then the lands to the north, bounded by the eastern part of the Mississippi River, in possession of the U.S. since the war: what are now Michigan, Indiana, Illinois, Wisconsin, and the northeastern part of Minnesota. He concludes, "No constitution was ever before so well calculated as ours for extensive empire & self government."

Figure 12-1: U.S. Map, c. 1810

Jefferson—as I show in *"The disease of liberty": Thomas Jefferson, History, & Liberty*—not only believed inexorably that humans were rational but also that there was a movement to human history, essentially progressive. That movement was the slow but sure unfolding of liberty: humans civically engaged, peaceably inclined, and self-determined. The success of the American experiment—that a government could be large, well-ordered, and respectful of the rights of its citizens—would be a contagion for other nations to follow, and it would eventually (at least hopefully) lead to a global community of republican nations, engaged in respectful and mutually beneficial interactions and exchanges of goods.[3]

Victory over the British in the American Revolution forced Jefferson to confront the problem of ultramontane Indians—those beyond the Appalachian Mountains. Members of Aboriginal nations that wished to Americanize could do so and miscegenate with frontiersmen. All other members of nations would soon be "incentivized" to remove toward or beyond the Mississippi River. Acquisition of the Louisiana Territory in his first term as president decupled the problem. Jefferson then had to grapple with the Natives west of the Mississippi River.

Jefferson greatly understood infrastructure for economic stability and growth. The lands around the great rivers—the Ohio and the Mississippi Rivers and soon the Missouri River—needed to be settled by Americans to ensure ease of logistics concerning the transport of goods and safe passage of them up and down the rivers. As the 1806 letter to the Cherokees' chiefs intimates, Natives needed to be moved off the great rivers so that there would be no threat to American commerce on the rivers. That implies that the lands immediately west of the Mississippi River would be settled by Americans. Natives, I suspect, because of their tribal manner of living and because they were never fully at peace with each other and those around them, would ever pose a threat to Jefferson's great experiment of republican government over a large part or the whole of North America.

Moreover, there was the problem with unruly frontiersmen, who abused the federal government's incapacity to police the lands west of the Appalachian Mountains and saw their interest as law. As we have seen, the lawlessness of the American West—here including lands to the west and east of the Mississippi—could only be solved in the short term by heavy-handed federal policies that needed to be in place till parcels of those lands would become states and incorporated into the nation. Those policies were, in effect, bluffs. Enforcement was always impossible; those laws were dead letters. There were no "police" to enforce them. Moreover, even when American criminals were identified, they were seldom prosecuted. It was merely too costly to attempt prosecution, and the system in place was too tenuous to ensure justice.

---

[3] See M. Andrew Holowchak, *The Disease of Liberty,* chaps. 9 and 10.

The nodi of intransigent Indians and frontiersmen were exacerbated by political infighting. A singular instance was the Louisiana Purchase, about which many Federalists were not thrilled. There were furtive meetings at Hartford of Federalists from Massachusetts, New Hampshire, Connecticut, Rhode Island, and Vermont from December 15, 1814, to January 5, 1815, to discuss pressing political issues such as the dreadful War of 1812 and the possibility of secession. Pressing and relevant issues were removal of the three-fifths clause, the legality of the Louisiana Purchase, the Embargo of 1807, a requirement to have two-thirds of Congress approve declarations of war, restrictions of trade, and admission of new states. Three representatives from the secret meetings were subsequently sent to Washington to discuss their terms, but news of Andrew Jackson's stunning victory in the Battle of New Orleans preceded them, and thereby, the representatives lost whatever leverage they might have had and returned to Massachusetts.[4]

And so, the problems of rowdy Natives, unruly frontiersmen, and political infighting led to the worry apropos of failure of Jefferson's beloved political "experiment." That worry is center-stage in a letter to John Colvin (20 Sept. 1810). Jefferson asks whether circumstances do not sometimes require a prudent officer of a nation to go beyond the written laws and act rather than circumstances requiring him to act when the survival of a nation is at stake. An affirmative answer, which Jefferson gives, allows for temporary abeyance of key axioms of Jeffersonian republicanism, e.g., a weak executive and a strict adherence to written laws.

The letter to Colvin is an illustration of Jefferson's enormous political maturation, though it signals, too, much moral consequentialism. No code of laws can offer an inviolate blueprint for correct political action in all scenarios, as no code of laws anticipates all courses of events. Jefferson writes: "A strict observance of the written laws is doubtless *one* of the high duties of a good citizen, but it is not *the highest*. The laws of necessity, of self-preservation, of saving our country when in danger are of higher obligation. To lose our country by a scrupulous adherence to written law would be to lose the law itself, with life, liberty, property, and all those who are enjoying them with us, thus absurdly sacrificing the end to the means." Jefferson here acknowledges that there might be scenarios when the most anti-republican axioms are

---

[4] Kevin M. Gannon, "Escaping 'Mr. Jefferson's Plan of Destruction': New England Federalists and the Idea of a Northern Confederacy, 1803–1804," in *Journal of the Early Republic,* Vol. 21, No. 3, 2001: 413–433.

provisionally set into place, e.g., when the existence of a Jeffersonian republic is threatened by a nation ruled by a tyrant.

We are now in a position to ask this question: To what extent did American Indians fit into Jefferson's scheme of an empire of liberty?

There is no consensus among Jeffersonian scholars concerning the ingenuousness or disingenuousness of Jefferson's Native American policy. Almost all concede that Jefferson was, at least ostensibly, disposed favorably toward Indians. Some see his ostensible disposition as sincere; others, adopted it for reasons politic. I offer, for illustration, four views.

Jefferson's policy asserts Merrill Peterson, "had the appearance of deviousness, even hypocrisy: the great white father runs his red children into debt, kills off the game, acquires one tract of land after another, crowding the savages into smaller and smaller reserves, until they are compelled to take the white father's view of their own interests and turn to agriculture and the domestic arts." Yet Jefferson was not a hypocrite but merely a practicalist. He realized that Indians' future boded either annihilation or assimilation, and the latter was the only moral route.[5]

Bernard Sheehan is less harsh. Jefferson's actions, consistent with those of prior administrations, were based on genuine concern for American Indians' welfare. "From the earliest initiation of a national Indian policy, government authorities saw no contradiction in a policy designed to acquire the Indians' lands and at the same time to seek the natives' welfare." He saw the great Mississippi River as a natural border as formidable as the Atlantic Ocean to the East.[6]

Jefferson's Indian policy, says the first Thomas Jefferson Foundation scholar, Dumas Malone, was hypocritical, though perhaps only subconsciously so. As president, he had the obligation to "protect his own borders," and so he aimed to remove Natives from them "as soon as possible" and to replace them with

---

[5] Merrill D. Peterson, *Thomas Jefferson and the New Nation: A Biography* (London: Cambridge University Press, 1970), 774. Sayre writes of Jefferson's "fantasy of assimilation and incorporation." Jefferson was no fantast. He realized that full assimilation was impossible, but merely aimed for as much assimilation to which Natives were agreeable. Gordon M. Sayre, "Jefferson and Native Americans: Policy and Archive," in *The Cambridge Companion to Thomas Jefferson,* ed. Frank Shuffleton (Cambridge: Cambridge University Press, 2009), 70.

[6] Bernard W. Sheehan, "American Indians," in *Thomas Jefferson: A Reference Biography,* ed. Merrill D. Peterson (New York: Charles Scribners' Sons, 1986), 408.

less threatening American settlers. "Rationalizing his position in his own mind no doubt, he claimed that he was seeking to lead them into the path of peace and the blessings of agricultural society."[7] His policy was politic.

Anthony Wallace, we have seen, maintains that Jefferson's Indian policy was the result of an inveterate despotism as well as the despot's amaranthine fear that his dream of republicanizing the continent would be spoiled by the "savage murderers of innocent frontier families." Thus, Jefferson's policy was duplicitous. Yet Wallace qualifies that remark or whiffle-waffles. "If Jefferson was guilty of insincerity, duplicity, and hypocrisy in Indian affairs, it must be conceded that this shiftiness, like his political ruthlessness, was a weapon in his struggle to ensure the survival of the United States as a republic governed by Anglo-Saxon yeomen." Jefferson might have sincerely believed that his civilizing policy was in the best interest of Natives, but it also provided a "moral justification for land purchases"—"his primary interest."[8]

In 2000, there is Christian Keller published "Philanthropy Betrayed: Thomas Jefferson, the Louisiana Purchase, and the Origins of Federal Indian Removal Policy." Keller argues—and his thesis is a continuation of Sheehan's philanthropic thesis—that the notion of a need for westerly removal was Jefferson's, though not his original intention. "Close analysis of Jefferson's writings, both before and during his presidency, indicates that he always supported amalgamation of the tribes with white society, but that the route he believed best suited for this purpose changed direction." At some point—Keller is clear that there is no evidence of an exact time, though circumstances point to 1803 with the Louisiana Purchase—Jefferson adopted the notion that acculturation could not occur east of the Mississippi River, and so Natives must be removed westwardly, where acculturation could more continue in a less febrile manner. Jefferson's policy of integration failed because it was ethnocentrically white. "He was unable to reconcile his honorable ideal with cold reality."[9]

---

[7] Dumas Malone, *Jefferson the President, First Term* (Boston: Little, Brown & Company, 1970), 273.
[8] Anthony F.C. Wallace, *Jefferson and the Indians: The Tragic Fate of the First Americans* (Cambridge, MS: The Belknap Press, 1999), 17–20.
[9] Christian Keller, "Philanthropy Betrayed: Thomas Jefferson, the Louisiana Purchase, and the Origins of Federal Indian Removal Policy," in *American Philosophical Society*, Vol. 144, No. 1, 2000: 40–51.

Robert M. Owens, in a 2002 essay follows the lead of Wallace. Jefferson's policy of treating justly Native Americans was merely a political expedient. "Justice … always proved secondary to the desire for America's constantly expanding 'Empire for Liberty.'" He decided for the Indians what was in their best interest, and he "rationalized mightily." To him, sales of lands to Whites benefited Whites and Reds. Thus, "he showed little hesitation in squeezing tribal leaders until they ceded their territory."[10]

Paul Pierce, more recently too, comes down hard on Jefferson. His "western policy" encouraged the settlement of those territories by Americans while it encouraged Indians to "adapt to the realities of the modern world." He adds: "Here, then, was Jefferson's iron hand of imperialism wrapped in kid gloves. … Despite his interest in and appreciation of Indians and their cultures, when Jefferson looked West, he did not see the frontier filled with Indians but instead envisioned an opportunity to realize his dream of an agrarian, utopian society of independent Anglo-American farmers." All was founded on the myth of the venerable yeoman farmer, moving into the West to tame the land with modern agricultural techniques and get rid of the violence of early frontiersmen and Natives. For Pierce, the future was only white.[11]

Finally, there is David Bergeron's thesis. He maintains that one ought not to view the barbaric Indians as obstacles to be overcome in taming the continent—"this is … not a dichotomous issue"—but both as parts of "nature … imbued with possibilities of 'culture.'" Native Americans are a natural part of the American natural "landscape." So, too, is the land. Both Natives and their land are to be actualized through "their improvement by civilizing and settling them." The wild North American landscape needs to be tamed—deforested, irrigated, grubbed, etc.—and so too do the wild Native Americans. Bergeron ends: "For Thomas Jefferson … the Native American is respected less for what he is than for what he can become. His progress is unarguably good for him, but for the nation it is a necessity."[12]

---

[10] Robert M. Owens, "Jeffersonian Benevolence on the Ground: The Indian Land Cession Treaties of William Henry Harrison," in *Journal of the Early Republic*, Vol. 22, No. 3, 2002: 405.

[11] Jason E. Pierce, *Making the White Man's West: Whiteness and the Creation of the American West* (Denver: University of Colorado Press, 2016), 32–33.

[12] David Bergeron, "Thomas Jefferson and His Thinking about Native Americans: Understanding a Nature at the Basis of a Human Project," in *Revue française de science politique*, Vol. 67, No. 3, 2017, ii.

Figure 12-2: Indian Women Farming

There is likely not too much difference between the views of most authors. Wallace's criticisms are the sharpest, though not sustainable. States Richard White against Wallace, "If Jefferson's Indian policies were pretty much of a kind with, or more benign than, those that preceded or followed, then it is hard to say why his personal failings mattered." [13] The statement is spot on. Pierce's animadversions typify the focus on racialization of Jefferson's Western policy. Therein lies its chief defect. We cannot grasp the eighteenth-century intellectual climate by reducing it to racism. Keller blamed Jefferson for compromising his philanthropic ideals when reality proved unaccommodating. Here, one can counter-remonstrate: What else is a rational person supposed to do? Bergeron's thesis, however, tantalizes. He at least proffers a fresh, unique perspective. The American landscape, to be tamed, comes as a package: Land and Natives each must be improved. Cultivating the land entails civilizing Indians; civilizing the Indians entails cultivating the land.

I maintain that Jefferson was sincerely committed to the best interest of American Indians and, in general, had genuine affection for them and genuine sympathy for their plight. I add my qualification "in general" because during his day certain tribes—e.g., the Seminoles were especially hostile to Americans

---

[13] Richard White, "Dead Certainties," *New Republic*, Vol. 222, No. 4, 44.

during the Revolutionary War and thereafter[14]—were especially troublesome for interloping Americans. European settlement of North America was a reality; European American populational increase and migration to the West were realities. Consequently, the future of Natives—and this was consistently the federal government's policy—was extermination or miscegenation through full adoption of the ways of Whites. Both paths implied the disintegration of Native American culture. That was roughly the plan of Washington and Presidents Madison, Monroe, and Quincy Adams after Jefferson. What Jefferson underscored was the speedy acquisition of Indians' lands to keep away the ambitious British, French, and Spanish and the tacit push for Natives to intermix with Americans.

As we saw in the letter to Governor William Henry Harrison, Jefferson did acknowledge that Aborigines might not readily see that integration was their best option and only viable alternative, and so he wished that no mention of that to be made to them. Jefferson envisaged that acknowledgement of integration would have created large tension between Natives and the federal government. It would have shown that the U.S. government was committed not to the confinement of Indian culture to agricultural spaces but to extermination of Indian culture. Thus, dissimulation here was disingenuousness.

Many Natives saw what was inevitable. Indians, qua Indians, could be no part of Jefferson's empire of liberty, though Indians, qua individuals, could be. Their culture, filiopietistic, was backward-leaning, while Jeffersonian republicanism, progressive and scientific, was forward-leaning. And so, Jefferson was at least theoretically disposed to disallow numerous Indian nations on American lands, even if they pledged to pursue husbandry. That would be a pledge, to some degree, of integration but not full integration. Indian filiopiety had to be renounced. Otherwise, it would be, for Jefferson, an albatross to his great experiment of Jeffersonian republicanizing all or much of North America, and perhaps, in time, even South America. Consequently, some Natives certainly saw war with Whites, if not viable as a means of self-preservation, then a more manly way of facing extinction. That is graspable.

Thus, if Jefferson had to use, in the short term, duplicitous means to achieve integration, he was ready to do so. That was a maneuver that was agonizingly paternalistic and seemingly atypical of Jefferson, who, as a liberal, ever seemed

---

[14] John K. Mahon, *History of the Second Seminole War* (Gainesville, Florida: University of Florida Press, 1967), 19–25.

to champion individuals' right to self-determination. Yet, we must acknowledge here what we have often already acknowledged: Not all people had the same degree of self-determination. He saw Natives, though not naturally inferior to Whites in intelligence and moral and aesthetic sensitivity, as being culturally retarded and greatly in need of civilizing. Paternalism was warranted because paternalism was needed just as it is needed in the case of parents and their children. It had been part of Indian policy from the beginning because Indians, as savages and heathens, were not fully capable of seeing what was plainly in their best interest, or so thought Jefferson and most other American politicians.

When all things are considered, the plight of American Indians was a concern ancillary to Jefferson's fear about the failure of the confederation of states as a Jeffersonian republic as well as the individual states as Jeffersonian republics. Given Jefferson's obsession with seeing the contagion of liberty throughout his life—he was incontestably an Enlightenment utopist—his mature and unexpressed Indian policy could only have been willful integration of those Natives who wished to mix with Whites and continual westerly removal of those who did not and their eventual obsolescence. Consequently, while he cared much about the fate of Natives qua individuals, Natives' culture had to go.

That mature policy he entertained at least as early as 1793. In certain notes on a cabinet meeting of that year, Jefferson concedes that his Indian policy has always been preemptive. The passage is singular, and thus, I eschew paraphrase.

> I considered our right of preemption of the Indian lands, not as amounting to any dominion, or jurisdiction, or paramountship whatever, but merely in the nature of a remainder after the extinguishment of a present right, which gave us no present right whatever, but of preventing other nations from taking possession, and so defeating our expectancy; that the Indians had the full undivided and independent sovereignty as long as they choose to keep it, and that this might be forever; that as fast as we extend our rights by purchase from them, so fast we extend the limits of our society, and as soon as a new portion became encircled within our line, it became a fixed limit of our society.[15]

---

[15] Thomas Jefferson, "Notes on Cabinet Opinions" (26 Feb. 1793), *The Papers of Thomas Jefferson*, vol. 25, ed. John Catanzariti (Princeton: Princeton University Press, 1992), 271.

The passage reveals Jefferson's constant anxiety about the possibility of some breakdown in his plan for an empire for liberty—the encroachment of an acquisitive, predatory foreign power like Spain, England, or France.

Thus, Jefferson's mature Indian policy was to integrate or to disintegrate, and both options implied cultural disintegration. While integration was a sinisterly silent process, disintegration by continual removal to the West was obvious. From a bird's-eye or holistic view, the policy was disintegrative, sinisterly so. It entailed the dissolution of Natives' culture by breaking down cultural ties so that each individual Indian would be forced to decide at some point in his own best interest. Natives, in time, saw clearly the deceit of the interloping Americans and their political apologists. One female named Cooh-coo-cheeh, who housed a captive 12-year-old white boy, Oliver Spencer, explained to him the white man's expropriation of Indians' lands. Spencer recounts that episode when Cooh-coo-cheeh was speaking of "their rapid growth, their widely-spreading population, their increasing strength and power, their insatiable avarice, and their continued encroachments on the red men." He adds: "They [Whites] will not be satisfied until they have crowded the Indians to the extreme north, to perish on the great Ice lake, or to the far west. All [Natives] will at length be exterminated."[16] And so, we are in a position to ask again this intriguing question: Was Jefferson willingly espousing genocide?

In keeping with the Convention of the Prevention and Punishment of the Crime of Genocide (1948), "genocide" I define thus: "deliberate, hate-based actions aimed at killing or severely maltreating a large number of people of a particular ethnos (cultural group or nation) with the aim of annihilating that ethnos."[17] I note here that Jefferson's mature Indian policy, deliberate, offered no promise of the preservation of Indians' various *ethnoi*—I resist the tack of many scholars of seeing the many numerous tribes as one *ethnos*—and so, it is, following my definition, difficult not to indict Jefferson of genocide.

There is, however, a serious remonstrance to that indictment. It smacks of presentism. To understand that remonstrance, we must travel back to Jefferson's day and enter the portal of Jefferson's cavernous mind.

---

[16] Oliver M. Spencer, *Indian Captivity: A True Narrative of the Capture of Rev. O. M. Spencer by the Indians, in the Neighbourhood of Cincinnati* (New York: Carlton & Porter, 1835), 117.

[17] Convention of the Prevention and Punishment of the Crime of Genocide, https://legal.un.org/avl/pdf/ha/cppcg/cppcg_ph_e.pdf, accessed 15 Jan. 2024.

Jefferson was inescapably committed to intellectual, political, and moral human progress. That, in itself, is unremarkable, given the exciting intellectual climate of Enlightenment times. In that, he was no different from others such as Immanuel Kant, Marquis de Condorcet, and Louis-Sébastien Mercier.

There were numerous nomological disclosures in astronomy, physics, optics, and chemistry that led to the overthrow of Aristotle's telic cosmos, accepted roughly for 2,000 years by most intellectuals. Cognoscenti of Jefferson's day was—and this is not hyperbole—overwhelmed by the very many discoveries and advances of the sciences in Enlightenment times.[18] It is unfortunate that few scholars who study Jefferson have sufficient acquaintance with the intellectual, scientific climate of Jefferson's day. Without such acquaintance, no scholar can understand Jefferson.

The revolution in astronomy and physics began with Nicolaus Copernicus' (1473–1543) assertion of a sun-centered universe in his 1543 work *De revolutionibus orbium coelestium* (*On the Revolutions of the Celestial Orbs*). Tycho Brahe (1546–1601) studied the nighttime sky like no other prior to his day and left behind celestial observations of the sixteenth century that were astonishing—e.g., a 1572 nova without parallax—and that led to the discovery of three laws of planetary motion by pupil Johannes Kepler (1571–1630). Galileo Galilei (1564–1642, Figure 12-3), through observations of telescopes that he designed and constructed, noted that Jupiter had satellites revolving around it, thereby disproving Aristotle's dictum that all things revolved around the earth, that the moon was craterous, thereby challenging the notion that all bodies in the superlunary realm were perfect; that Venus, when seen through a telescope, exhibited a full set of phases, inconsistent with it orbiting the earth, though consistent with both it and the earth in the orb around it, orbiting the sun—thereby vindicating Copernicus. He also discovered, by rolling balls down inclined plains, that the rate of a body's fall was indifferent to its weight ($d \approx t^2$) *pace* Aristotle. At the end of the seventeenth century, Isaac Newton (1643–1727) synthesized the disclosures of predecessors in *Philosophiae Naturalis Principia Mathematica* (*Mathematical Principles of Natural Philosophy*, 1687). Newton discovered the Universal Law of Gravitation ($F \approx M_1 M_2 / d^2$). It posited that there was an attractive force, gravity, determined by the masses of any two bodies, considered as mass-points, and the distance between them. He then gave three laws of bodily motion that governed all bodies in the universe. The power of Newton's dynamical system was that it subsumed, thus explained, other

---

[18] Henry May, *The Enlightenment in America* (Cambridge: Oxford University Press, 1978).

disclosures, e.g., Kepler's laws and Galileo's Law of Falling Bodies and even Boyle's Law (below).

Figure 12-3: Galileo Galilei

There were discoveries in other sciences. In optics, Kepler and Newton were pioneers. Kepler, in *Astronomiae Pars Optica* (*The Optical Part of Astronomy*, 1604), explained vision via refraction within the eyes. He also studied pin-hole cameras, designed eyeglasses for defects of vision, and showed how both eyes were critically involved in depth perception. Newton's great contribution to optics was his prism experiment, which showed that white light entering a prism was separated into its constituent colors. In chemistry, there were, among others, Boyle and Lavoisier. Robert Boyle (1627–1691) discovered the Ideal Gas Law, which posited an inverse relationship between the pressure and volume of a gas in an enclosed space. He also advocated a mechanical philosophy, in which he maintained that all bodies comprised particles of one matter, though of different shapes and motions. Antoine Lavoisier (1743–1794) rightly explained combustion by oxidation, showed that respiration was an intake of oxygen, and proved that water was composed of hydrogen and oxygen.

There were also advances in biological taxonomy, mathematics, medicine, zoology, geology, and mineralogy, as well as countless inventions that aimed to ease the toil of human labor or lead to greater yield with similar labor (e.g., spinning jenny, carding the machine, and cotton gin), that could be put to immediate human usage (e.g., dictionary, thermometers, timepieces, eyeglasses, and the guillotine), that held the promise of future usage (e.g., steam engines, submarines, and balloons), or merely that led to greater human flourishing (e.g., vaccination, invention of piano, and machine for sheets of paper). There were, in addition, guns and cannons in war.

Figure 12-4: American Philosophical Society

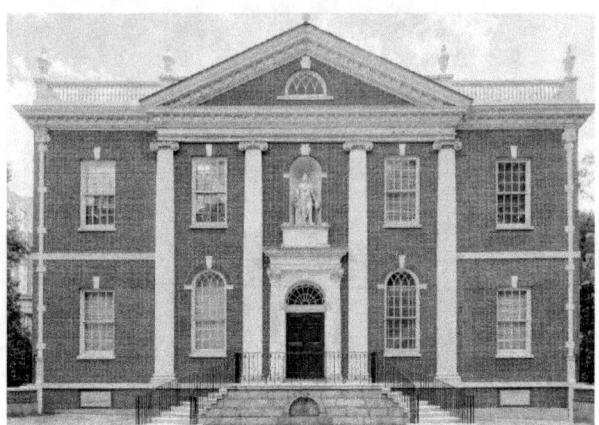

The abundant successes of the sciences of the time were perpetuated at scientific academies and societies—like the Royal Society of London (1662), Académie Royale des Sciences of Paris (1666) and American Philosophical Society of Philadelphia (1743, Figure 12-4), founded by Benjamin Franklin— and the growth of the number of societies was quick. The findings of such societies were published in journals such as *Philosophical Transactions of the Royal Society* and *Transactions of the American Philosophical Society,* as well as numerous smaller periodicals. New discoveries required new terminology, that is neology,[19] and so scientific encyclopedias and dictionaries were created. The overwhelming successes of those sciences were due to the freeing of human rationality—to the human embrace of liberty.

I give only a succinct and distressingly incomplete depiction of the numerous advances—discoveries and inventions—in the sciences of Jefferson's time. That depiction, however, is meant to show that the Enlightenment, to natural scientists and philosophers, was a time of almost boundless excitement and optimism. It was almost impossible for any intellectual who followed those advances not to get swept by the intellectual current, which promised

---

[19] For Jefferson on neology, see TJ to John Waldo, 16 Aug. 1813, and TJ to John Adams, 15 Aug. 1820.

increasingly greater understanding of the world and an ease of human living for all persons that had theretofore never been seen.

Thomas Jefferson, too, was indulgently and happily swept by that current. His investment in the Enlightenment was complete—perhaps greater than any other American of his day. Jeffersonian republicanism was a vain concept without knowledge. Jefferson's empire of liberty entailed the marriage of politics and science, and both flourished in the air of liberty. Jefferson writes to Joseph Willard (4 Mar. 1789) about the duty of the scions of the American Revolutionist to pursue the sciences in America: "We have spent the prime of our lives in procuring them the precious blessing of liberty. Let them spend theirs in shewing that it is the great parent of science and of virtue; and that a nation will be great in both always in proportion as it is free." Jefferson was not of disposition to allow any group of persons, any non-republican nation, or any race to interfere with his experiment.

In sum, Jefferson's political philosophy, Jeffersonian republicanism, was a commitment to government aligned inescapably with science, both requiring liberty for thriving. Advances in the various sciences were giving humans a heightened understanding of just how the universe worked as well as numerous inventions and disclosures that eased the burden of everyday life. Anything other than a wholesale investment in republican governing would be an obstacle both to its success and to its contagion for other nations. Jefferson, consequently, could not allow for the existence of numerous pockets of filiopietistic "nations" howsoever liberty-loving they might have been. Jefferson saw that he was proffering Natives not only a different but a much better manner of living. They could either integrate, in which case all aspects of Indian culture would soon evanescence, or disintegrate, in which case all aspects of Indian culture would soon evanescence.

I end by returning to the question of genocide. Jefferson's policy of integration or disintegration, essentially culturally disintegrative, seems neatly to fix Jefferson as a genocidalist, so long as we recognize the American Indian policy from Washington to Jefferson as genocidal. Nonetheless, there is one condition of my definition that disqualifies Jefferson: His policy was guided by above-board benevolence, not malevolence or malevolence discreetly packaged à la Wallace as benevolence. While it is easy today to say that Jefferson's benevolence was seriously misguided because he lacked the perspective that time gives critics, that is an assessment not so easily formed when we place ourselves in Jefferson's day and in Jefferson's shoes.

Chapter 13

American Indian Policy after Jefferson

"We the representatives…"

The three presidents after Jefferson—James Madison, James Monroe, and John Quincy Adams—roughly continued Jefferson's Indian policy, which was essentially Washington's, but with a large emphasis on the acquisition of Natives' lands and quiet enticements toward miscegenation. All recognized that removal to the West was inevitable, and extraordinary difficulties with civilizing Natives east of the Mississippi River—Indians eagerly embraced the vices of the superior American culture (e.g., inebriation), but not so eagerly the virtues (e.g., husbandry)—mandated their removal west of the Mississippi River. That removal was a stopgap—a means for those with the best of intentions to buy time to Christianize and civilize properly Natives.

James Monroe (1758–1831, Figure 13-1) recognized that Natives east of the Mississippi River needed to be removed to its west, but he was revolted by the notion of forcible removal. Thus, he aimed to supply inducements for Indians to move westward. He says in his 1824 State of the Union Address (Dec. 7) of the tribes within the limits of the American nation: "Many of the tribes have already made great progress in the arts of civilized life. This desirable result has been brought about by the humane and persevering policy of the Government, particularly by means of the appropriation for the civilization of the Indians. There have been established under the provisions of this act 32 schools, containing 916 scholars, who are well instructed in several branches of literature, and likewise in agriculture and the ordinary arts of life."

Old problems, unfortunately, have not perished. There are still large hostilities among the nations on the Upper Mississippi River, the Missouri River, and around the Upper Great Lakes due to intransigency vis-à-vis adopting the ways of the Whites, due to fighting with Americans, and due to intertribal warring. Monroe adds that there are several treaties circulating to address and mollify those hostilities, though it is not known what effect they will have. To facilitate willful westerly removal, Monroe proposed the radical move of an Indian government, modeled after the U.S. government, in the West to be gleaned by the purchase of lands of Western Indians and to be established by appropriation of 125 thousand dollars. The bill would pass through the Senate, but not through the house.[1]

Figure 13-1: James Monroe

That that proposal was likely more placebic than curative is shown by a singular incident, just after Madison's presidency, in which the policy of treating all Indian tribes as independent nations was put to the test. That test also exposed the hypocrisy of the federal government. On July 26, 1827, Georgia's Cherokee Nation, which was chiefly agricultural, drafted and adopted a constitution patterned after the U.S. Constitution. The Cherokee constitution was at the urging of Major Ridge (Pathkiller II, 1771–1839, Figure 13-2) and his son, John. The document, containing five articles, begins: "WE THE REPRESENTATIVES of the people of the CHEROKEE NATION in Convention assembled, in order to establish justice, ensure tranquility, promote our common welfare, and secure to ourselves and our posterity the blessings of liberty, acknowledging with humility and gratitude the goodness of the sovereign Ruler of the Universe, in offering as an opportunity so favorable to the design, and imploring his aid and direction in its accomplishment, do

---

[1] Francis Paul Prucha, *American Indian Policy in the Formative Years: The Indian Trade and Intercourse Acts 1790–1834* (Cambridge: Harvard University Press, 1962), 230.

ordain and establish this Constitution for the Government of the Cherokee Nation."[2]

In gist, the constitution declared that the Cherokees were of a status equal to that of any other nation on the globe—*viz.*, that negotiations with the U.S. government or with Georgia, in which they were situation, were to be done directly through delegates of the Cherokees and without assistance of intermediaries from the U.S. government or from Georgia.

Georgia, indignant over the notion of an *imperium in imperio,* challenged the Cherokees' right to frame a constitution. It declared that there never was an independent Cherokee "nation" in Georgia—that is, that the Cherokees were merely tenants of the state, which could remove them at its discretion at any time.[3]

Figure 13-2: Major Ridge

Georgia's outright dismissal of the Cherokee constitution and its reduction of the Cherokee nation to a tribe of unentitled and arrogant squatters posed a

---

[2] "Cherokee Constitution," *Cherokee Phoenix,* Vol., 1, No. 1, https://www.wcu.edu/library/DigitalCollections/CherokeePhoenix/Vol1/no01/constitution-of-the-cherokee-nation-page-1-column-2a-page-2-column-3a.html, accessed 9 June 2023.

[3] Acts of the General Assembly of the State of Georgia, 1827 (Milledgeville, 1827), 249–50.

serious problem for the federal government, because, since the days of Washington, it had treated all tribes as independent nations. President John Quincy Adams, beleaguered, addressed the U.S. Congress on December 2, 1828:

> At the establishment of the Federal Government, under the present Constitution of the United States, the principle was adopted of considering the Indian Tribes as foreign and independent powers; and also as proprietors of lands. They were moreover, considered as savages, whom it was our policy and our duty to use our influence in converting to Christianity, and in bringing them within the pale of civilization.
>
> In changing the system, it would seem as if a full contemplation of the consequences had not been taken. We have been far more successful in the acquisition of their lands than in imparting to them the principles, or inspiring them with the spirit of civilization. But in appropriating to ourselves their hunting grounds, we have brought upon ourselves the obligation of providing them with subsistence; and when we have had the rare good fortune of teaching them the arts of civilization, and the doctrines of Christianity, we have unexpectedly found them forming, in the midst of ourselves, communities claiming to be independent of ours, and rivals of sovereignty within the territories of the members of our Union. This state of things requires that a remedy should be provided.[4]

Adams' sentiments are telling. The U.S. government has typically treated Natives as independent powers with rightful ownership of their occupied lands. Yet it has also acknowledged the primitive nature of the Natives, badly in need of civilizing: American instruction and Christianizing. Some Natives, however, have taken the process of civilizing as an assertion of the right to an independent and equal existence. The scenario, says Adams, needs to be addressed, though he proffers no plan.

When the former Tennessean governor Andrew Jackson became president in 1829, the federal government returned, and unabashedly so, to the right-of-conquest policy, in effect prior to Washington's presidency. Jackson, before his

---

[4] "The Second Session of the Twentieth Congress commenced on Monday, December 1st. On the following day," *Cherokee Phoenix*, Vol. 1, No. 42, https://www.wcu.edu/library/DigitalCollections/CherokeePhoenix/Vol1/no42/the-second-session-of-the-twentieth-congress-commenced-on-monday-december-1st-on-the-following-day-page-2-column-3b1.html, accessed 9 June 2023.

presidency, had consistently maintained that Native Americans had no claim to sovereignty. Tribes were not separate nations. Indians had merely "a possessory right to the soil, for the purpose of hunting and not the right of domain." In consequence, the federal government was fully empowered and legally authorized to regulate all "the concerns of the Indians."[5]

Jackson was not hopelessly naïve or inflexibly biased—in today's language, incurably racist. He was merely fighting for Americans' interests and doing what he deemed to be in the best interest of American Natives.[6] From the Treaty of Paris that ended the Revolutionary War in 1783, through Jackson, England's sovereignty in North America had become America's. Indians enjoyed the "rights" to American soil and to live as they deemed fit only because of Americans' largesse. He was sure that governmental officials before him and most Americans of his day agreed. Prior presidents said many fine things about aiding the Indians in many fine acts and in many fine treaties, but they did nothing to show any Indian "right" of ownership of North American soil or independent existence on the continent. Jackson, who was not wont to dissimulate, was merely making explicit what had hitherto been implicit in the federal government's Indian policy.

The current policy, Jackson recognized, was not working. Moreover, it could not be enforced. Trading houses were established by prior presidents to win the trust of Indians provide them with implements for agriculture and other goods to ease their condition. Yet they were chiefly political instruments: They introduced Indians to items showily designed to demonstrate the superiority of white culture: iron cookware (instead of stone), iron (not stone) tomahawks, knives, needles, arrow points, files, scissors, combs, Whites' clothing as well as equipment for farming and bibelots and gimcracks, useless but showy.[7] Indian agent Thomas McKenney stated that Indians readily noted the superiority of Whites' goods—e.g., an iron tomahawk in preference to one of stone—and the effect was humiliation. Thus, their removal, at least, might allow them to civilize slowly and without constant reminders of their inferiority[8]—a hypothesis not so vacuous.

---

[5] Francis Paul Prucha, American Indian Policy in the Formative Years, 234–36.
[6] Daniel Feller, "Andrew Jackson: Domestic Affairs," UVA: Miller Center, https://millercenter.org/president/jackson/domestic-affairs, accessed 8 July 2023.
[7] Mary U. Rothrock, "Carolina Traders among the Overhill Cherokees, 1690–1760"in East Tennessee Historical Society's Publications, Vol. 1, 1929: 3–18.
[8] Thomas McKenney to James Barbour, 15 Nov. 1855.

Acquisition of and desire for Whites' goods permanently changed Natives' cultures. When Tenskwatawa ("One Whose Mouth Is Open"; 1775–1836; Figure 13-3), brother of Tecumseh and Shawnee prophet, denounced white Americans and remonstrated for a return to Indian filiopiety, he gained a following of thousands. He incited his followers to engage in fighting against a large American military force near his settlement at Prophetstown. The Indians faltered, however, and Tenskwatawa became uninfluential, and he was subsequently removed to Canada.[9] His insurrection, it is worthy of noting, was incited by the sort of preaching he had heard from white missionaries and it was fought with guns, not arrows and bows. Consequently, the uprising shows that it was not possible to return to the old ways.

Figure 13-3: Shawnee, the Prophet Tenskwatawa

Yet white traders also introduced Natives to alcohol and to guns, which white traders used as leverage in trade. Both "goods" changed irremediably Aborigines' culture. Once introduced to alcohol, Indians could never get their fill and tended to imbibe with the aim of complete insobriety. Indians also

---

[9] R. David Edmunds, *The Shawnee Prophet* (Lincoln: University of Nebraska Press, 1983).

quickly recognized the superiority of firearms, and their desire to have guns created a dependency on white traders and Indian agents for their upkeep.

To get their fill of booze, guns, and the numerous other goods Indians deemed needed, they were required to exchange furs. A good year of hunting, however, might lead to overhunting an area and a poor yield the following year. That might lead one tribe to hunt in the territory of another and hence to conflict.

In effect, Whites introduced and ensorcelled Natives, once frugal, with prodigality. They also imposed on them identity through individuality, not identity through tribal accomplishments—*viz.*, that one member of a tribe could gain a sense of identity through the courageous actions of another. The overall effect of Americanizing the Natives was abrading. Writes Alexis de Tocqueville, "Europeans, having scattered the Indian tribes into the wilderness, condemned them to a wandering, vagabond life, full of indescribable suffering." Their tribal identity was lost, their families were dispersed, their traditions were obscured, their habits were altered, their "needs" were increased, and their memories of the past were corrupted. The greatest harm was the loss of their sense of the past—erosion of Indians' filiopiety, around which their culture was centered. The result was an even greater degree of barbarity.[10] Quaker John Parrish visited the encampment of Senecan chief Farmer's Brother (c. 1730–1814) in the fall of some year unspecified and notes of happiness lost. It was an encampment of some 500 Senecans who were living in the woods and near a brook. There were some 80 commodious huts. Almost all the adults were busy. "The ease and cheerfulness of every countenance, and the delightfulness of the afternoon, which the inhabitants of the woods seemed to enjoy with a relish far superior to those who are pent up in crowded and populous cities, all combined to make this the most pleasant visit I have yet made to the Indians; and induced me to believe that before they became acquainted with the white people, and were infected with their vices, they must have been as happy a people as any in the world."[11] So, Indians' ruination was thereafter fated.

In effect, the Trade and Intercourse Acts and numerous treaties over the decades, so thought many, were mere window dressing to cover for the plan of the slow suffocation of Natives by breaking down tribal bonds. Andrew Jackson

---

[10] Alexis de Tocqueville, *Democracy in America*, ed. Isaac Kramnick (New York: Penguin, 2003), 373–74.

[11] J. Niles Hubbard, *Red Jacket and His People, 1750–1830* (New York: Burt Franklin, 1886), 156.

noted and execrated the hypocrisy, and he wished at least to be open with Indians vis-à-vis the real policy of which Americans had ever been in advocacy.

The Indian Removal Act of 1830, as we saw in Chapter 9, was put into effect during Jackson's tenure and followed through by his successor, Martin Van Buren. It forced some 60,000 Natives from roughly 20 tribes to remove west of the Mississippi River. Southern nations roughly settled into what is now Oklahoma; Northern nations, Kansas. Thousands died during removal.[12]

Much recently has been written on the marginalization and removal of Native Americans from their lands. John Bowes argues that Natives' removal from their lands of the Old Northwest was a concerted effort by state and federal governments as well as local citizens. The Indian Removal Act was not the catalyst but merely a symptom of the overall execration of Indians.[13] Jacob Lee proffers a thesis different from the conquest and removal view in a 2019 book on Colonial America and Native Americans. Using the Mississippi River and its tributaries both literally and metaphorically to situate his critical analysis, Lee shows how Native and Early Americans used rituals like calumet, marriage, and baptism to forge ties between the peoples.[14] In *Native Southerners*, Gregory Smithers examines the issue of Natives' attempts to preserve their cultures in the American South—from Texas to the Atlantic coast—in the wake of European encroachment. He focuses on Southern American Indians to the year 1840. Unlike Lee, Smithers' focus is the ties forged between Native factions that were needed for survival—how smaller tribes came together to form larger tribes.[15]

I end this book with the words of Red Jacket, on a visit to Hartford, Connecticut: "We stand a small island in the bosom of the great waters. We are encircled; we are encompassed. The evil spirit rides upon the blast, and the waters are disturbed. They rise, they press upon us, and the waves once settled

---

[12] Gary Clayton Anderson, "The Native Peoples of the American West," in *Western Historical Quarterly*, Vol. 47, No. 4, 2016: 407–33.

[13] John P Bowes, *Land Too Good for Indians Northern Indian Removal* (Norman: University of Oklahoma Press, 2016).

[14] Jacob E. Lee, *Masters of the Middle Waters: Indian Nations and Colonial Ambitions along the Mississippi* (Cambridge, MA: The Belknap Press of Harvard University Press, 2019).

[15] Gregory D. Smithers, *Native Southerners: Indigenous History from Origins to Removal* (Norman: University of Oklahoma Press, 2019).

over us, we disappear forever. Who then lives to mourn us? None. What marks our extermination? Nothing. We are mingled with the common elements."[16]

---

[16] Niles Hubbard, Red Jacket and His People, 208.

Appendix

Review of Wallace's Jefferson and the Indians

I came into possession of Wallace's book on November 1, 2010. Since then, I have thrice tried to read the book, but I could never get beyond the introduction, and that, for me, is unusual, even when it comes to books, especially books on Jefferson. In his introduction, Wallace—a Canadian-American anthropologist of some celebrity with a specialization in Native Americans—gives a depiction in a section titled "Jefferson's Character" that is unrecognizable to anyone who has rigorously studied Jefferson. Though a renowned specialist on Native Americans, Wallace adopts a selective approach to Jefferson's writings and makes scant use of secondary materials. Wallace's Jefferson is "a stiff, bookish country lawyer, the literary connoisseur with a flair for writing elegant prose" and well-schooled on "putting a philosophical gloss on the violently [sic] partisan, but not necessarily original, opinions he held on practically every subject."[1] One can readily recognize the uncritical uptake of the unflattering prose of Fawn Brodie's, Harold Levy's, Joe Ellis', and Robert Tucker and David Hendrickson's books, each of which he cites for his prefatory character assassination of Jefferson.

Wallace continues. Jefferson had a temperament that was "deeply controlling," yet he failed to recognize that, though he quickly recognized it in others. As proof, Wallace offers something written by Margaret Bayard Smith, a female contemporary of Jefferson. According to Smith, Jefferson once said, "How I wish that I had the power of a despot!" Wallace adds that that is a lust for power, scholars have noted, which Jefferson exercised all too freely. Wallace then goes on to elaborate on Jefferson's titanolatry.

Yet when we go to Smith's book, we find that the quote concerns Jefferson's large dismay about people cutting down "the fine trees scattered around the city-grounds [of Washington]." Smith continues: "The company at table stared at a declaration so opposed to his disposition and principles. 'Yes,' continued he, in reply to their inquiring looks, 'I wish I was a despot [note here that Wallace does not even get right the quote] that I might save the noble, the beautiful trees

---

[1] Anthony F.C. Wallace, *Jefferson and the Indians: The Tragic Fate of the First Americans* (Cambridge, MS: The Belknap Press, 1999), 14.

that are daily falling sacrifices to the cupidity of their owners, or the necessity of the poor.'"[2] Jefferson's titanolatry, it seems, is reducible to being a tree-hugger. So much for Jefferson's avowed lust for power!

In addition to his "desire to control" and "willingness to trample on civil liberty and use force to achieve national goals," there was Jefferson's "relentless moralism"—his amaranthine tendency to give his actions a moral slant. Yet his actions, says Wallace, were typically self-interested, not other-interested, though the self-interest Jefferson cunningly packaged habitually as benevolently intended virtuous actions.[3] If Jefferson could not be virtuous, he could at least look the part. And so, references to "the liberty of 'the people'" were instead veiled references—more appositely, projections—concerning his own fears of being persecuted by others. He longed ever for personal freedom, but as a false prophet, he projected and marketed that as political liberalism. Lusting after control, he feared being controlled by others. Thus, Jefferson "projected his private drama onto a national, indeed a global, scene, demanding liberty for the downtrodden everywhere, to the point of being prepared to force freedom on the unwilling."[4] Thus, his vision of a global "empire of liberty" was reducible to personal paranoia.

Jefferson "insisted that everyone he knew, and by extension *everyone*, be willing members of his happy family. He was both patriarch and queen bee, surrounded by workers and drones. It was he who decided what the happy family was and how its members should enjoy life, liberty, and the pursuit of happiness." Those who rejected his notion of a happy family "had to be coerced."[5] How Wallace gets from "everyone he knew" to "*everyone*" through means of "extension," whatever that might mean, goes unexplained. Yet it is clear that coercion must have played a large part in Jefferson's Indian policy, otherwise, Wallace would not spend so much energy in his preface in denigrating Jefferson.

Jefferson had a roseate "ideal society" that entailed liberty, equality, and a desert of rights, but all too frequently, the Indians were spoilers. They got in the way, and they needed to be removed, even exterminated. Jefferson sums up Wallace was guilty of insincerity, duplicity, and hypocrisy "in Indian affairs," but those were illustrations of his shiftiness and ruthlessness in guaranteeing

---

[2] Margaret Bayard Smith, *The First Forty Years of Washington Society* (New York: Charles Scribner's Sons, 1906), 11.
[3] Anthony F.C. Wallace, *Jefferson and the Indians*, 15.
[4] Anthony F.C. Wallace, *Jefferson and the Indians*, 15–16.
[5] Anthony F.C. Wallace, *Jefferson and the Indians*, 14–16.

that the United States would be "a republic governed by Anglo-Saxon yeomen." There was no place, it seems, for those who first occupied the land.[6]

Wallace's introduction makes it clear that his evaluation of Jefferson's character, which informs his assessments throughout the book, has been shaped by scholars from whom he draws—Brodie, Levy, Ellis, and Tucker and Hendrickson—none of whom can be said to have a strong love for Jefferson and all of whom have written just one book on Jefferson. There are astonishingly no references to the two great Jeffersonian scholars, Malone and Peterson—each of whom wrote much of Jefferson and Native Americans—anywhere in his book. That is unpardonable. There are no references to statements in Jefferson's own writings in support of Wallace's vitriolic assessment of Jefferson's character.

The nodi are these.

First, Wallace *begins* his analysis of Jefferson's views on Native Americans with an assessment of Jefferson's character, derived from four and only four rather slanted sources (five, if one counts his mistake on Smith's recollection). His assessment of Jefferson's character does not come after a study of Jefferson's views on and actions concerning Native Americans. His assessment of Jefferson's character does not come after a sweeping study of the most significant Jeffersonian scholars on Jefferson's character. That is the gist of Jefferson's objection to hasty theorizing in a letter to Charles Thomson (20 Sept. 1787). "The moment a person forms a theory, his imagination sees, in every object, only the traits which favor that theory." Wallace begins his book with condemnation of Jefferson and that throughout colors the book.

Second, if Jefferson's was such an irremediable paranoic and titanolatrist, one would expect to find ample examples of how Wallace's version of Jefferson's Indian policy, which I call the Subtle Muscularity Thesis on account of Wallace's introduction, radically differed from the policies of those presidents before him and immediately after him. Jefferson's gross psychological imbalance would have to have made some noteworthy difference in Jefferson's policy, otherwise it is vacuous. Wallace proffers no such illustrations throughout his book. What is the point of articulating a thesis that drives a book if nowhere in the book is the thesis defended?

However—and here is the elephantine rub—the book, minus the introduction, is anything but character-assassination. The main body of the book is a relatively tempered critical assessment of Jefferson's Indian policy and mostly without

---

[6] Anthony F.C. Wallace, *Jefferson and the Indians*, 19–20.

severe condemnation of the man behind the policy. I found myself, if only reluctantly because of my soured first impression, in agreement with the tenor of Wallace's argument, which, stripped of its conceits, is cogent and backed by a sufficiently good grasp of Jefferson's writings. It was as if the person who wrote the book was not the person who wrote the introduction.

In sum, the book, minus its introduction, is a valuable addition to the relatively scant literature on Jefferson's Indian policy. I recommend only that those persons aiming to read Wallace's book either skip the introduction or read it with my cautionary remarks in mind.

Index

A

Adair, James: 73, 81–83, 102
Adams, John: xi, xv, 53, 72, 96, 128, 128n40, 143, 177
Adams, John Quincy: 135, 137, 191, 199, 202
aesthetic sense: 84
American Philosophical: 51, 66, 196
Anderson, Terry: 139
Aristotle: 4, 194

B

Bacon, Nathaniel: 30
Barton, Benjamin Smith: 63, 65
Battle of Fallen Timbers: 158
Bayard, William: 54
Becker, Carl: xiii
Bergeron, David: 189
Black Hawk: 156
Blount, William: 125
Bouquet, Henri Louis: 32, 33, 39
Boyle, Robert: 195
Bowes, John: 206
Bowles, August: 125
Brackenridge, Henri Marie: 97–101
Brahe, Tyco: 194
Bryant, W.C.: 88
Buffon, Comte de: 8–9, 11–24, 73, 75, 81, 91

C

Campbell, David: 61, 62
Catherine the Great: 69
Chambers, Benjamin: 184
Chastellux, Marquis de: 16, 20
Cherokee Nation v. Georgia: 141
Cherokees: 125, 128, 141–42, 147, 167, 170, 171, 200–2
Chew, Elizabeth: 90
Chickahominies: 20
Chickasaws: 61, 134, 167
Choctaws: 169–70
Cicero: 84
Claiborne, William: 118
Clark, William: 90
Colvin, John: 186
Copernicus, Nicholas: 194
Creeks: 50–51, 167
Cresap: 85
Croghan, George: 32, 39
Crowfoot: 109–10

D

Dearborn, Henry: 126, 127, 146
Delawares: 165
Demosthenes: 84
Dodge, John: 34–35, 39
Duane, James: 156
Ducoigne, Jean Baptiste: 90n28
Dunbar, William: 61
Dunmore, Lord: 86
Du Ponceau, Peter: 65

F

Farmer's Brother: 205
Five Nations: 26
Fletcher, Robert: 136, 137–38
Franklin, Benjamin: 23–24, 196

G

Galileo: 194
Gilmer, George: 134
Goldsmith, Oliver: 7–8
Greenberg, Joseph: 70

H

Hamilton, Henry: 80, 81
Handsome Lake: 167–68
Harmar, Josiah: 117
Harrison, William Henry: 174–77
Hawkins, Benjamin: 49–51, 52, 54,
    61, 118, 125, 126, 146, 150, 152,
    162, 174
Hellenbrand, Harold: 42n4, 90
Hierocles: 79
Hill, Peter: 139
Horsman, Reginald: 161, 180n1
Hubbard, J. Niles: 163
Hutchins, Thomas: 32, 33

I

Indian Removal Act: 206

J

Jackson, Andrew: 52, 141, 142, 186,
    202, 203
Jefferson, George: 64
Jefferson, Martha: 77
Jefferson, Peter: xiv
Jefferson, Thomas:
    ambivalence to Indians: xi, xv,
        176
    on Blacks: 148n9
    and collection of Indian
        artifacts: 89–91
    empire for liberty: xv, 179–98
    Fifth Annual Message: 167
    First Annual Message of:
        on mammoth: 13, 163
    Fourth Annual Message: 164–65
    on miscegenation of Indians:
        xvi, 148, 150–51
    and neoterism: 53–54
    and preemption of Indians'
        lands: 147–48, 192
    and rationality of Indians: 181
    Second Annual Message: 163
    Second Inaugural Address: 166
    stadialism of: 3
    Third Annual Message: 164
    and three types of society: 42
Johnson v. McIntosh: 117, 138, 157
Johnson, William: 32, 112, 138
Jones, David: 102

K

Kaskaskias: 165
Keller, Christian: 188, 190
Kennedy, Roger: 105
Kepler, Johannes: 194, 195
Knox, Henry: xiv, 119–20, 128, 136,
    147, 162

L

Lafayette, Marquis de: 21n28

Index 215

Lafitau, François: 72–73
Lakotas: 136
Lavoisier, Antoine: 195
Law, Thomas: 84
Lee, Jacob: 206
Lewis and Clark Expedition: xii, 65
Lewis, Meriwether: xii–xiii, 53, 63, 64, 65, 66, 172
Little Turtle: xii
Linn, William: 60
Linnaeus, Carl: 5–7
Locke, John: 131–32
Logan: 84–86
Louisiana Purchase: 186, 188
Ludlow, William: 3

M

Madison, James: 42, 54, 55n6, 59, 134, 143, 152, 183, 191, 199, 200
Major Ridge: see Pathkiller
Malone, Dumas: 187
Manahoacs: 25–26, 27, 93
Mandans: 173
Marshall, John: 118, 137–39, 141, 147, 156
Massawomecs: 29
Mattaponis: 29–30
McKenney, Thomas: 146
McLeod, W.C.: 47
Meigs, Return: 118, 134, 146
Milligan, Joseph: 53
Missouri Baptist Association: 122
Monacans: 25, 26–28, 93
Monroe, James: 191, 199–200
Mooney, James: 30
moral-sense/moral-sentiment theory: 77
Morris, Robert: 154

Morris, Thomas: 88, 154
Morse, Jedidiah: 151n11

N

Native Americans:
　aesthetic sensibility of: 84–92
　and American education: 149n10
　American policy toward: 113–29
　and Asians: 67–70
　barrows of: 93–104
　British policy toward: 110–13
　courage of: 17, 32, 79
　drudgery of females: 11, 19, 79–80
　and family: 17
　and farming: xii
　filiopiety of: 153, 166
　genocide of: 193–97
　intelligence of: 20
　on land: 135–36
　languages of: 53–73
　laws of: 41–52
　morality of: xi, 47–48, 75–83
　number of children of: 19
　origins of: 53–74
　and private property: 168n7
　and religion: 155–56
　and sexual potency: 76
　and torture: 81–82
　tribes of: 25–40
　and witchcraft: 48–49
Newton, Isaac: 194
Northwest Ordinance: 116, 122
Notes on Virginia: 25–26, 47, 75, 76, 91, 93–97, 101, 102, 105, 184
Nottoways: 31

O

Ogden, David: 155
Ogden, Thomas: 155
Old Tassel: 154
Outassete: xi
Owens, Robert: 189

P

Pamunkeys: 29, 30–31
Panis: 64
Parish, John: 205
Parsons, General: 103
Pathkiller: 200, 201
Peck, John: 136, 137–38
Peterson, Merrill: 187
Phillips, William: 80, 81
Piankeshaws: 165
Pierce, Paul: 189, 190
Powhatans: 25, 27, 30, 43–47, 93
Prucha, Francis Paul: 127, 157

R

Randolph, Peyton; 78
Randolph, Thomas Jefferson: 78
Raynal, Abbé: 73
Red Jacket: 86–87, 155, 206
Red Stick War: 52
Refinesque, Constantine Samuel: 66
Rittenhouse, David: 24
Ross, John: 141
Roundtree, Helen: 43n5
Royal Society of London: 196
Rutledge, Edward: 70–71

S

Sayre, Gordon:15n13, 187n5
Schuyler, Philip: 156
Senecas: 48, 205
Seven Years War: 110
Sevier, John: 134
Sheehan, Bernard: xiii–xiv, 146–47, 153, 187
Shephard, William: 154
Sibley, John: 63, 69
Small, William: 78
Smith, Benjamin Barton: 67
Smith, Daniel: 61
Smith, John: 42–43
Smith, Margaret Bayard: 209
Smithers, Gregory: 206
Spencer, Oliver: 18, 80, 168n7, 193
Stiles, Ezra: 68, 103, 105
Stuart, John: 113

T

Tecumseh: 158
Tenskwatawa: 204
Thomson, Charles: 163n4
Trade and Intercourse Acts: 122, 127, 205
Treaty of Greenville: 158
Treaty of Holston: 125
Tuscarorans: 26

U

Uquanchogs: 55–60, 61
Usner, Daniel: 128n40

V

Vatel Emmerich: 132–33

Volney, Comte de: 8

W

Waldo, John: 53
Wallace, Anthony: xiii, xiv, 67, 105. 146–47, 159, 188, 190, 209–12
Washington, George: xii, xiii, 21n28, 23, 101, 119, 121, 123, 127, 191
Weaver, John: 139
Whitcomb, Samuel: 151n12

Willard, Joseph: 197
Winthrop, John: 134
Wirt, William: 141
Wolves: 173
Worcester v. Georgia: 142
Wythe, George: 78

Y

Yazoo Land Act: 136

www.ingramcontent.com/pod-product-compliance
Lightning Source LLC
Chambersburg PA
CBHW072108010526
44111CB00037B/2047